Philip Jodidio

Serpentine Gallery Pavilions

TASCHEN

CONTENTS

CREDIT

All photographs, plans, and drawings by the respective
architects or Arup unless otherwise noted. The photographers/
copyright owners (The Serpentine Gallery is abbreviated „SG"):
Photo Ludwig Abache © SG VII.08 bottom / © Iwan Baan
VII.02–04, 07–08 top, 09, 16 top, 18–22 top; VIII.08–09, 10, 16–18 top,
19; IX.02–03, 07–15, 16–17, 23; X.02–04, 07–13, 20–23 / photo
Thierry Bal © SG 18 right, 20 / photo Helène Binet © SG I.02–09 /
© Mark Blower 14–18 left, 19 right / photo Simon Brown &&&
Creative Ltd © SG 12 right / © Richard Bryant/Arcaid IV.04, 11, 12–
13, 15; VI.07, 10, 11, 17 / photo Deborah Bullen © SG VIII.21 bottom /
photo Alison Clarke © SG IX.16 / © Peter Cook/VIEW III.04; IV.07 /
photo Louise Coysh © SG VI.16 / © Allan Crow/VIEW II.11 / ©
Richard Davies 10 / © Sylvain Deleu II.04, 10, 18–19; III.08, 09, 10–11,
14–15, 16–23; IV.02–03, 08–09, 16–19, 22–23; VI.02–04, 08–09, 14–15,
20–21 / photo Alastair Fyfe © SG VIII.05 / © Leonardo Finotti
VII.12–13 and back cover / photo Michael Frantzis © SG IV.20–21 /
© Dennis Gilbert/VIEW III.07 / © Hugo Glendinning 09 right / ©
Nick Guttridge/VIEW II.20, 21; III.02–03, 13; VI.23 / © Luke Hayes/
VIEW I.10–17, 19; VIII.02–03, 11, 22–23; X.14, 16–19 / © G Jackson/
Arcaid IX.18 top / photo Dafydd Jones © SG I.18 / © Raf Makda/
VIEW 02 / © James Newton/VIEW cover / photo John Offenbach ©
SG VII.16–17; IX.04, XI.02–03, 07, 10–11, 20–21 / © Mikael Olsson
VIII.04 / photo Declan O'Neill © SG 12 left, 13; VII.22 bottom / ©
Paul Raftery/VIEW 06–07 / © John MacLean/VIEW IV.14 / ©
Christian Richters/VIEW X.15 / photo Mark Robinson © SG IV.10;
VII.05 / © Nick Rochowski/VIEW IX.19, 20–22 / © Steve Roden/
Paul Panhuysen VI.22 / © Philippe Ruault 22; XI.04, 08–09, 12–19,
22–23 / © Georgina Slocombe IX.18, bottom, 20 / © Morley von
Sternberg/Arcaid VII.07–09 / © Edmund Sumner/VIEW 04; II.12;
VI.20–21; VII.10, 14, 15, 23 / © Stephen White 09 left, 11; II.02–03, 14–
17, 22, 23; III.06, 12, 16 left / © James Winspear/VIEW VI.12–13

IMPRINT

To stay informed about upcoming TASCHEN titles,
please request our magazine at www.taschen.com/
magazine or write to TASCHEN, Hohenzollernring 53,
D-50672 Cologne, Germany; contact@taschen.com;
Fax: +49–221–254919. We will be happy to send you a
free copy of our magazine, which is filled with
information about all of our books.

© 2011 TASCHEN GmbH
Hohenzollernring 53, D–50672 Köln, Germany
www.taschen.com

Editorial coordination: Florian Kobler, Cologne
Design: Sense/Net Art Direction,
Andy Disl and Birgit Eichwede, Cologne. www.sense-net.net
Production: Ute Wachendorf, Cologne
English translation: Kristina Brigitta Köper, Berlin
French translation: Jacques Bosser, Montesquiou

Printed in Spain
ISBN 978-3-8365-2613-5

Interview with JULIA PEYTON-JONES and HANS ULRICH OBRIST

Prior to the first of the Serpentine Summer Pavilions in 2000, you had a number of exhibitions or works that dealt with the relationships between art and architecture. What were some of those?

Julia Peyton-Jones The earliest example since I've been with the Gallery would be Dan Graham, who installed a piece on the Serpentine Gallery lawn in 1992. Graham's glass pavilion accompanied a group exhibition entitled *Like Nothing Else in Tennessee* taking place in the galleries. This work really began to incorporate pavilions into our artistic program. The next example of a structural intervention was by Richard Wilson (*Jamming Gears*, 15 August–15 September 1996), who we invited to do the last exhibition before we closed the Serpentine Gallery for renovation by John Miller + Partners.[1] It played with the concept of the gallery as a building site and incorporated much of the equipment that would later be used in the construction, including forklift trucks, building-site huts, and a large rectangular pit. Using industrial machines, he was able to drill, bore, expose, and cut to whatever degree he wanted. During the renovation, we initiated a project called *Inside-Out*, for which we commissioned five artists to make site-specific work on our lawn while the gallery was closed. Tadashi Kawamata, for example, took doorways, windows, and various other architectural elements from the building before it was renovated and then built a freestanding structure that was like a skeleton that mirrored the architecture of the Serpentine (*Relocation*, 1997). Anya Gallaccio's project, *Keep Off The Grass*, 1997, involved planting a garden while the renovation was taking place, creating something vibrant and alive to echo the adjacent building's rejuvenation. Rasheed Araeen made a cubic sculpture on the lawn whose form was predicated on a system of triangles and trapezoids. This colorful structure in many ways foreshadowed Toyo Ito's Pavilion of 2002 (*Algorithm*), which was similarly based on formal mathematics. Richard Deacon and Bill Culbert were also commissioned as part of *Inside-Out*—all of these projects together seeded the

Noch vor dem ersten Serpentine-Sommerpavillon im Jahr 2000 gab es eine Reihe von Ausstellungen und Arbeiten, die sich mit der Wechselbeziehung von Kunst und Architektur befassten. Welche waren das zum Beispiel?

Julia Peyton-Jones Das früheste Beispiel in meiner Zeit hier an der Galerie ist Dan Graham, der 1992 eine Arbeit auf dem Rasen der Serpentine Gallery installierte. Grahams Glaspavillon begleitete *Like Nothing Else in Tennessee,* eine Gruppenausstellung, die damals in den Räumen der Galerie zu sehen war. Damit wurde im Grunde erstmals ein Pavillon in unser künstlerisches Programm eingebunden. Das nächste Beispiel für eine bauliche Intervention stammt von Richard Wilson (*Jamming Gears*, 15. August bis 15. September 1996), den wir eingeladen hatten, die letzte Ausstellung vor der Sanierung der Galerie durch John Miller + Partners[1] zu gestalten. Wilson spielte mit der Vorstellung der Galerie als Baustelle und arbeitete mit Geräten wie Gabelstaplern, Baucontainern oder einer großen rechteckigen Grube. Mithilfe der Maschinen durfte er bohren, fräsen, freilegen und schneiden so viel er wollte. Während der Sanierung initiierten wir das Projekt *Inside-Out*, für das wir fünf Künstler baten, ortsspezifische Arbeiten auf dem Rasen zu realisieren, während die Galerie geschlossen war. Tadashi Kawamata beispielsweise entfernte vor der Sanierung Türrahmen, Fenster und verschiedene andere architektonische Elemente aus dem Gebäude, mit denen er eine frei stehende Konstruktion baute, die wie ein Skelett wirkte – ein Spiegelbild der Serpentine Gallery (*Relocation, 1997*). Für Anya Gallaccios Projekt, *Keep Off The Grass,* 1997, wurde ein Garten angelegt; so entstand etwas Dynamisches, Lebendiges und gleichsam ein Echo der Renovierung der Galerie. Rasheed Araeen schuf eine kubische Skulptur auf dem Rasen, die auf einem System von Dreiecken und Trapezen basierte. Diese farbenfrohe Konstruktion war in vielerlei Hinsicht ein Vorgeschmack auf Toyo Itos Pavillon von 2002 (*Algorithm*), der in ähnlicher Weise auf mathematischen Formeln fußte. Im Rahmen von *Inside-Out* beauftragten wir auch Richard Deacon und

Avant de construire le premier des pavillons d'été de la Serpentine en 2000, vous aviez déjà organisé plusieurs expositions sur les relations entre l'art et l'architecture. Pouvez-vous en donner quelques exemples?

Julia Peyton-Jones Chronologiquement, le premier exemple est sans doute celui de Dan Graham qui avait installé une pièce sur la pelouse de la Serpentine Gallery en 1992. Ce pavillon en verre accompagnait une exposition de groupe intitulée « Like Nothing Else in Tennessee ». Cette œuvre introduisait ainsi le concept de pavillon dans notre programme artistique. Le second exemple d'intervention structurelle fut signé Richard Wilson (*Jamming Gears*, 15 août–15 septembre 1996), avant la fermeture de la Serpentine pour sa rénovation par John Miller and Partners (1996–98)[1].
Il a joué avec le concept de la galerie en tant que bâtiment et intégré certains éléments qui allaient être utilisés dans le chantier, comme des chariots élévateurs, des cabanes préfabriquées et une grande fosse rectangulaire. Grâce à des outils industriels, il a pu percer, transpercer, exposer et découper à volonté.
Pendant les travaux, nous avons initié un projet intitulé « Inside-Out », pour lequel nous avons demandé à cinq artistes de réaliser des œuvres spécifiques installées sur notre pelouse pendant la fermeture de la galerie. Tadashi Kawamata s'est emparé de portes, de fenêtres et de divers éléments architecturaux du bâtiment pour en faire une construction autoporteuse, une sorte de squelette qui renvoyait à l'architecture de la Serpentine (*Relocation*, 1997). Le projet d'Anya Gallaccio, (*Keep Off the Grass*, 1997) consistait en la plantation d'un jardin pendant la durée du chantier pour créer un élément vivant en écho au rajeunissement du bâtiment. Rasheed Araeen avait réalisé une sculpture cubique dont la forme était déterminée par un système de triangles et de trapèzes. Cette structure très colorée annonçait à de multiples égards le pavillon de Toyo Ito en 2002 (*Algorythm*) qui reposerait de façon similaire sur des

1 - Dan Graham, *Two-Way Mirror and Hedge Labyrinth*, 1989. Zinc, sprayed steel, two-way mirror, clear glass, and blue cypress trees. Installation view of *Like Nothing Else in Tennessee*, 17 March–26 April 1992.

Dan Graham, *Two-Way Mirror and Hedge Labyrinth*, 1989. Zink, gespritzter Stahl, Einwegspiegel, Klarglas und blaue Zypressen. Installationsansicht von *Like Nothing Else in Tennessee*, 17. März–26. April 1992.

Dan Graham, *Two-Way Mirror and Hedge Labyrinth* (Miroir sans tain et labyrinthe de haie), 1989. Zinc, acier galvanisé, miroir sans tain, verre clair et cyprès bleus. Vue de l'installation de « Like Nothing Else in Tennessee » (Comme rien d'autre au Tennessee), 17 mars–26 avril 1992.

JULIA PEYTON-JONES
is Director, Serpentine Gallery, and Co-Director, Exhibitions and Programmes.

HANS ULRICH OBRIST
is Co-Director, Exhibitions and Programmes and Director, International Projects.

1

2

idea of expanding our programming out onto the lawn, the park, and beyond.

The renovation was our first experience of really working with architects per se, which is in some ways very different from working with artists. To coincide with the reopening, we needed to create extra space and we invited Seth Stein, the British architect, to make a canopy for the significant number of people who came to the opening. He devised something very effective despite having no budget and very little time. It stayed up for three days. Then, for the 1999 Summer Party, the designer Ron Arad also did a kind of canopy, which was made of ping-pong balls. He also installed a ping-pong table. It was a fantastic structure. We had tremendous fun working with artists, architects, and designers. It dawned on me that commissioning architecture in this way was truly exciting and it absolutely had to be part of the future of the Serpentine Gallery.

This way of working became an integral part of your method.
JP-J The ethos of speed and temporality has always been part of the program. We had often put together exhibitions that were up for one weekend. Nonetheless, they were fully curated shows that explored the history of the Serpentine by showing the works of artists who had previously exhibited here. The purpose of that was to show visitors who might not have known our work exactly what we were about. If it is one night, that is fine, and if it is one year, that is good too. For a visitor that might only visit our gallery once, we work to make their experience significant.

Were there other early exhibitions that dealt in a substantive way with architecture?
JP-J Another significant artist who completely embraced the building was Doug Aitken (*New Ocean*, 12 October–25 November 2001). He explored the Serpentine from the basement of the building to the weathervane on the roof and completely reoriented how visitors entered the Serpentine. The entrance was through a small door in the lobby that led to the

Bill Culbert. Insgesamt waren diese Projekte der Ursprung unserer Idee, das Programm auf die Rasenfläche und den Park auszudehnen.

Die Sanierung war unsere erste Erfahrung einer direkten Kooperation mit Architekten, was in vieler Hinsicht völlig anders ist als eine Zusammenarbeit mit Künstlern. Zur Wiedereröffnung brauchten wir zusätzlich Platz und baten den britischen Architekten Seth Stein, einen Anbau zu entwerfen, quasi als Festzelt für die vielen Menschen, die zur Eröffnung erwartet wurden. Er entwickelte eine sehr wirkungsvolle Lösung, obwohl er kein Budget und sehr wenig Zeit hatte. Dann entwarf Ron Arad für die Sommerparty 1999 eine Art Markise aus Tischtennisbällen – eine fantastische Konstruktion. Mir wurde dabei immer deutlicher, wie faszinierend es war, Architektur auf diese Weise in Auftrag zu geben und dass dieses Vorgehen in der weiteren Zukunft der Galerie unbedingt eine Rolle spielen sollte.

Diese Art zu arbeiten wurde zum integralen Bestandteil Ihrer Strategie, richtig?
JP-J Das Ethos von Geschwindigkeit und zeitlicher Beschränkung war schon immer Teil des Programms. Wir konzipierten oft Ausstellungen, die nur ein Wochenende lang zu sehen waren. Trotzdem waren es umfassend kuratierte Ausstellungen, die sich mit der Geschichte der Serpentine auseinandersetzten, indem sie das Werk von Künstlern präsentierten, die hier früher ausgestellt hatten. Wir wollten den Besuchern, die unsere Arbeit vielleicht nicht kannten, zeigen, was wir zu leisten imstande waren. Ist es für einen Abend, dann ist das in Ordnung, ist es für ein Jahr, dann ist das auch in Ordnung. Wir arbeiten daran, den Besuch unserer Galerie zu etwas Besonderem zu machen, selbst für Besucher, die nur ein einziges Mal kommen.

Gab es andere frühe Ausstellungen, die sich substanziell mit Architektur auseinandersetzten?
JP-J Doug Aitken war ein weiterer bedeutender Künstler, der das gesamte Gebäude mit einbezog

recherches mathématiques formelles. Richard Deacon et Bill Culbert participèrent également à « Inside-Out ». Ensemble, tous ces projets réunis avaient en germe l'idée d'étendre notre programmation à la pelouse, au parc et même au-delà.

La rénovation fut notre première expérience de travail concret avec des architectes, ce qui était en soi très différent de la collaboration avec des artistes. Pour célébrer la réouverture, nous avions besoin d'espace supplémentaire et avons invité l'architecte britannique Seth Stein à concevoir un auvent permettant d'accueillir la foule. Il trouva une solution très efficace malgré la faiblesse du budget et le manque de temps. Elle dura trois jours. Puis, pour notre réception de l'été 1999, le designer Ron Arad a fabriqué une sorte d'auvent en balles de ping-pong et installé une table pour ce jeu. C'était une construction fantas-Lorsque Doug tique. J'ai réalisé que commander des œuvres architecturales était une tâche passionnante qui devait absolument être présente dans les futurs projets de la Serpentine Gallery.

Cette façon de travailler est devenue partie intégrante de votre méthode...
JP-J Les principes de vitesse et de temporalité ont toujours fait partie de notre programme. Nous avons souvent organisé des réceptions pour notre protectrice, la princesse de Galles, et monté des expositions qui ne duraient que le temps d'un week-end. Elles étaient néanmoins préparées avec soin et exploraient l'histoire de la Serpentine en montrant les œuvres d'artistes qui y avaient exposé. Le but était de montrer à des invités qui ne connaissaient peut-être pas notre travail, ce que nous pouvions faire exactement. Que ces manifestations durent une nuit ou un an, c'est tout aussi bien. Si un visiteur ne doit visiter notre galerie qu'une seule fois, nous voulons que cette expérience lui apporte quelque chose.

Avez-vous organisé dans le passé des expositions qui abordaient l'architecture de manière substantielle ?

3

4

usually off-limits basement, our workshop, and store, where newly commissioned video works were shown. The exit from this space was through an existing trapdoor that led into the exhibition galleries. *New Ocean* was the best example of handing over the building to an artist. When Aitken did his show, Daniel Libeskind's Pavilion out on the lawn had just been taken down.

The first time you called on an architect to design a pavilion outside the actual Serpentine building was with Zaha Hadid in 2000. How did that come about?
JP-J In 1997, our patron, the Princess of Wales, accepted an invitation to come to a gala dinner to celebrate the renovation. We wanted to build something that resolutely reflected our exhibition program but cost no more than a readymade tent. We commissioned Zaha Hadid because we knew that she would design something that was resolutely about the future of architecture and mirrored what the Serpentine stood for. Tragically, Princess Diana died (31 August 1997) before the renovation was completed, and the dinner was delayed.[2]

But you were not really free to do whatever you wanted, were you?
JP-J To commission a pavilion in the park is a fantastic opportunity, but as we are in a Royal Park, there are considerable limitations. Before 2000, any work sited on our lawn had to be erected and dismantled in the space of a month, significantly narrowing the possibilities of realizing ambitious projects. The secretary of state for Culture, Media, and Sport at the time was a visionary man called Chris Smith. He was a friend of the arts and when he saw the Zaha Hadid Pavilion he said: "I love this." So I said, "Would you let it stay?" And he said, "Absolutely." He interceded with The Royal Parks and set a precedent for approval to be given for semipermanent structures to be built on the Serpentine Gallery lawn. With the assistance of the now-renowned chef Allegra McEvedy, we set up what was basically a field

(*New Ocean*, 12. Oktober–25. November 2001). Er befasste sich vom Keller bis zur Wetterfahne mit dem ganzen Gebäude und ordnete die Zugangswege der Besucher neu. Der Eingang führte nun durch eine kleine Tür in der Lobby hinunter in den sonst nicht zugänglichen Keller, unsere Werkstatt und das Lager, wo neu in Auftrag gegebene Videoarbeiten gezeigt wurden. Verlassen konnte man diesen Raum durch eine vorhandene Falltür, die zu den Ausstellungsräumen führte. *New Ocean* war das beste Beispiel dafür, was passiert, wenn man einem Künstler das gesamte Gebäude überlässt. Als Aitken diese Ausstellung realisierte, war Daniel Libeskinds Pavillon draußen auf dem Rasen gerade abgebaut worden.

Das erste Mal, dass Sie einen Architekten damit beauftragten, einen Pavillon außerhalb der Galerieräume zu entwerfen, war im Jahr 2000 mit Zaha Hadid. Wie kam es dazu?
JP-J 1997 hatte unsere Schirmherrin, die Prinzessin von Wales, zugesagt, an einem Galadiner anlässlich der erfolgreichen Sanierung teilzunehmen. Wir wollten etwas bauen, das konsequent unser Ausstellungsprogramm widerspiegelt, aber trotzdem nicht mehr kostete als ein Festzelt von der Stange. Wir beauftragten Zaha Hadid, weil wir wussten, dass sie etwas entwerfen würde, das in architektonischer Weise absolut zukunftsweisend wäre und reflektierte, wofür die Serpentine steht. Tragischerweise starb Prinzessin Diana [am 31. August 1997] noch vor Abschluss der Sanierungsarbeiten und das Diner musste verschoben werden.[2]

Trotzdem hatten Sie nicht wirklich freie Hand, alles zu tun, was Sie wollten, oder?
JP-J Einen Pavillon für den Park in Auftrag zu geben, ist eine fantastische Chance, aber da wir uns in einem königlichen Park befinden, gibt es erhebliche Einschränkungen. Vor 2000 musste jede Konstruktion auf unserem Rasen innerhalb eines Monats errichtet und wieder abgebaut werden. Das schränkte die Möglichkeiten für ehrgeizige Projekte erheblich ein. Der damalige Staatsminister für Kultur, Medien und

JP-J Un autre artiste important à s'emparer du bâtiment tout entier fut Doug Aitken (*New Ocean*, 12 octobre–25 novembre 2001). Il l'explora de la cave à la girouette et réorienta entièrement la façon dont les visiteurs pénétraient dans la galerie. L'entrée se faisait maintenant par une petite porte dans le hall d'accueil qui conduisait aux sous-sols – habituellement interdits aux visiteurs –, à notre atelier, à nos réserves où étaient présentées de nouvelles vidéos spécialement commandées pour l'occasion. La sortie se faisait par une porte dérobée qui donnait sur les galeries d'exposition. *New Ocean* fut le meilleur exemple de notre façon de confier le bâtiment à un artiste et l'expérience fut extrêmement réussie. Lorsque Doug réalisa cette intervention, le pavillon de Daniel Libeskind venait juste d'être démonté.

Lorsque vous avez fait appel pour la première fois à un architecte pour concevoir un pavillon devant l'édifice de la Serpentine, vous vous êtes adressée à Zaha Hadid. Comment cette démarche vous est-elle venue?
JP-J En 1997, nous avions invité la princesse de Galles à un dîner de gala pour célébrer notre rénovation. Nous voulions quelque chose qui reflète résolument notre programme d'expositions, mais ne coûte pas plus cher qu'une tente du commerce. Nous avons fait appel à Zaha Hadid parce que nous savions qu'elle créerait quelque chose qui parlerait vraiment du futur de l'architecture et refléterait le positionnement de la Serpentine. Malheureusement, la disparition tragique de la princesse Diana le 31 août 1997, avant l'achèvement du chantier, fit que le dîner fut reporté[2].

Étiez-vous réellement libre de faire ce que vous souhaitiez?
JP-J. Faire construire un pavillon dans un parc est une opportunité fantastique, mais un parc royal est soumis à des contraintes considérables. Avant 2000, toute œuvre sur notre pelouse devait être érigée et démantelée en l'espace d'un mois, ce qui réduisait drastiquement la possibilité de tout projet ambitieux.

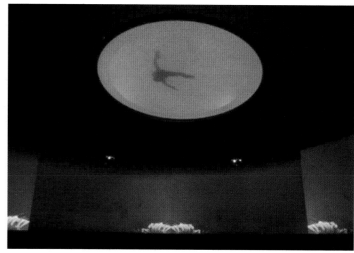

5 - Doug Aitken, *New Ocean*, 2001.
Installation view, 12 October–25 November
2001.

Doug Aitken, *New Ocean*, 2001.
Installationsansicht, 12. Oktober–25.
November 2001.

Doug Aitken, *New Ocean* (Nouvel océan*),*
2001. Vue de l'installation, 12 octobre–25
novembre 2001.

kitchen and created the first outdoor café at the Serpentine Gallery. And the Pavilion series had begun.

There is usually a division between art and architecture that keeps institutions like the Serpentine from calling so overtly on an architect for a temporary structure.
JP-J Yes, but it's a fictitious division. For the Serpentine, we use the same principles and work in the same way to commission artists and to commission architects. The creative process is what's important. It is a proposal that comes out of discussions and is a response to a site. Commissioning works is really something that's quite natural in the life of an arts organization. Once you embrace the idea of commissioning artists, it follows that you can commission designers or architects. The fear of actual construction—though Zaha's Pavilion was not terrifically challenging on that front—had been addressed in the renovation of the building. Working with her was a counterpoint to the experience of working on the renovation which really was hard-core construction. Building a summer pavilion was lighter as a process.

In a way you were calling on the long history of temporary pavilions designed by well-known architects, were you not?
Hans Ulrich Obrist Many essential inventions of architecture come from temporary pavilions or exhibitions. If one looks at Mies van der Rohe's Barcelona Pavilion (1929), Alvar Aalto's Finnish Pavilion for the World Exhibition in Paris (1937), Le Corbusier and Iannis Xenakis' Philips Pavilion at the World Fair in Brussels (1958), or Buckminster Fuller's Geodesic Dome for the American National Exhibition in Moscow (1959), for example, one can see them as part of the unwritten history of 20th-century architecture. Since they are not lasting structures, they are somehow not seen as part of the canon. In this lighter form, which is not meant to stand forever, experiments can happen. What is unusual with the Serpentine Pavilions is that the series has been sustained. If it had stopped after Zaha Hadid or Daniel Libeskind,

Sport, Chris Smith, war ein Kunstfreund und Visionär. Als er den Pavillon von Zaha Hadid sah, meinte er: „Das gefällt mir." Also fragte ich: „Würden Sie uns gestatten, ihn stehen zu lassen?" und er erwiderte: „Absolut." Er intervenierte bei der königlichen Parkverwaltung und schuf damit einen Präzedenzfall für die Genehmigung semipermanenter Bauten auf dem Rasen der Serpentine Gallery. Mit Unterstützung der inzwischen sehr bekannten Köchin Allegra McEvedy bauten wir so etwas wie eine Feldküche und realisierten das erste Freiluftcafé an der Serpentine Gallery. Es war die Geburtsstunde unseres Pavillon-Programms.

Gibt es nicht normalerweise eine Trennung zwischen Kunst und Architektur, die Institutionen wie die Serpentine daran hindert, so direkt einen Architekten für die Gestaltung eines temporären Baus zu engagieren?
JP-J Ja, aber diese Trennung ist eine Fiktion. An der Serpentine arbeiten wir nach denselben Prinzipien, ob wir nun Künstler oder Architekten beauftragen. Der kreative Prozess ist das Entscheidende. Das Konzept entwickelt sich aus Gesprächen und ist eine Reaktion auf den Standort. Arbeiten in Auftrag zu geben, ist eigentlich im Alltag einer Kunstinstitution ganz selbstverständlich. Mit der Angst vor der eigentlichen Bautätigkeit – auch wenn Zahas Pavillon in dieser Hinsicht keine größere Herausforderung war – hatten wir uns schon bei der Sanierung des Gebäudes auseinandergesetzt. Mit Hadid zu arbeiten, war ein Kontrapunkt zu unseren Erfahrungen mit der Sanierung, die tatsächlich „Hardcore"-Bauarbeiten mit sich gebracht hatte. Einen Sommerpavillon zu bauen, war ein leichterer Prozess.

In gewisser Weise nehmen Sie Bezug auf die lange Geschichte temporärer Pavillons, die von berühmten Architekten entworfen wurden, sehe ich das richtig?
Hans Ulrich Obrist Viele wesentliche Erfindungen in der Architektur sind das Resultat temporärer Pavillons oder Ausstellungen. Schaut man sich bei-

Chris Smith, le secrétaire d'État à la Culture, les Médias et le Sport de cette époque était un visionnaire. Ami des arts, il assista à notre dîner de gala et lorsqu'il vit le pavillon de Zaha Hadid, m'assura combien il l'appréciait. À ma demande de le laisser en place un certain temps, il répondit : « Absolument. » Il intervint auprès de l'administration des Parcs royaux et créa un précédent pour l'approbation de structures semi-permanentes sur la pelouse de la Serpentine. Avec l'assistance d'Allegra McEvedy, chef devenu depuis très connu, nous avons monté une cuisine de campagne et créé le premier café en plein air de la Serpentine Gallery. Telle fut la genèse du programme des Pavillons.

N'existe-t-il pas habituellement de barrière entre l'art et l'architecture qui empêche des institutions comme la vôtre de faire appel aussi directement à un architecte pour édifier une structure temporaire ?
JP-J Si, mais c'est une division fictive. Nous appliquons les mêmes principes et travaillons de la même façon lorsque nous passons des commandes à des artistes ou à des architectes. C'est le processus créatif qui compte. C'est un projet qui naît de discussions et répond à la spécificité du site. Commanditer des œuvres est quelque chose d'assez naturel dans la vie d'un organisme qui se consacre à l'art. Une fois que vous avez passé une commande à un artiste, vous pouvez le faire auprès de designers ou d'architectes. Nous avions déjà dû faire face aux affres d'un grand chantier lors de notre rénovation et le projet de Zaha Hadid n'était pas vraiment un défi à cet égard. Travailler avec elle fut le contrepoint de notre expérience de la rénovation qui était vraiment un projet « lourd ». Construire un pavillon d'été était un processus plus léger.

D'une certaine façon, vous vous appuyez sur la longue histoire de pavillons temporaires dessinés par des architectes célèbres ?
Hans Ulrich Obrist De nombreuses inventions essentielles de l'architecture viennent de pavillons

6   7

it would have been one of these sparks of which there are many examples. What is so incredible is that it did not stop.

You describe this as a natural process, and yet you have reached a result that nobody else has found—associating a contemporary art institution with regular ephemeral architectural commissions.
JP-J One of the reasons is that it wasn't a portentous decision to do something. It was an organic process that developed naturally in terms of form and content over time. If we'd really planned to do something every year with the greatest architects who had not at the time of our invitation built in the UK, it might have failed. But because it was so modest in its conception and so playful in its reality, the program took root. It was a natural evolution from the earlier projects we had been involved with. One should also remember that the Serpentine isn't very large. If we'd been working in a larger building, we might have had less reason to look to the adjoining lawn for space.

Why did you impose the requirement that the architect should not have built in the UK before being commissioned for the Serpentine Pavilion?
JP-J Because it is about exhibiting architecture, just as we are a space for exhibiting art. When I became director of the Serpentine Gallery in 1991, there were many architects who had built internationally but hadn't been commissioned in the UK. This was a source of wonder. The British public might have read about the buildings of Frank Gehry, but they hadn't seen one here. Would you have to find the price of an airfare to experience what a Gehry structure is like? Our answer was: "No, come and see it here." Hans Ulrich and I began to work together in the 1990s when I invited him to curate the group exhibition *Take Me (I'm Yours)* at the Serpentine Gallery. This was our first collaboration prior to Hans Ulrich joining the Serpentine Gallery as co-director of Exhibitions

spielsweise Mies van der Rohes Barcelona-Pavillon (1929), Alvar Aaltos finnischen Pavillon für die Weltausstellung in Paris (1937), Le Corbusiers und Iannis Xenakis' Philips-Pavillon auf der Weltausstellung in Brüssel (1958) oder Buckminster Fullers geodätische Kuppel für die amerikanische Nationalausstellung in Moskau (1959) an, dann kann man diese Bauten als Teil der ungeschriebenen Architekturgeschichte des 20. Jahrhunderts verstehen. Weil sie nicht dauerhaft waren, gelten sie irgendwie nicht als Teil des architektonischen Kanons. Dabei ermöglicht diese leichtere, temporäre Form Experimente. Das Ungewöhnliche an den Serpentine-Pavillons ist, dass es die Serie noch immer gibt. Wäre sie nach Zaha Hadid oder Daniel Libeskind zu einem Ende gekommen, wäre sie nichts als einer der Funken gewesen, für die es so viele Beispiele gibt. Was so unglaublich ist, ist dass sie eben nicht abgerissen ist.

Sie beschreiben das Ganze als einen natürlichen Prozess. Trotzdem haben Sie etwas erreicht, was niemand sonst geschafft hat, eine Institution für zeitgenössische Kunst mit regelmäßigen Aufträgen für temporäre Architekturprojekte in Verbindung zu bringen.
JP-J Einer der Gründe dafür ist, dass es keine ominöse Entscheidung war, etwas zu tun. Es war etwas Organisches, das sich formal und inhaltlich ganz selbstverständlich im Lauf der Zeit entwickelt hat. Wenn wir tatsächlich geplant hätten, jedes Jahr gemeinsam mit den größten Architekten, die zum Zeitpunkt unserer Einladung noch nicht in Großbritannien gebaut hatten, etwas zu realisieren, wäre es vielleicht gescheitert. Doch weil das Konzept so bescheiden und die Umsetzung so spielerisch war, konnte das Programm irgendwie Wurzeln schlagen. Es war eine natürliche Weiterentwicklung früherer Projekte, an denen wir gearbeitet hatten. Man sollte auch nicht vergessen, dass die Serpentine nicht besonders geräumig ist. Hätten wir für unsere Arbeit ein größeres Gebäude zur Verfügung gehabt, hätte es vielleicht weniger Anlass gegeben, den angrenzenden Rasen als Standort in Betracht zu ziehen.

temporaires ou d'expositions. Si l'on considère le pavillon finlandais d'Alvar Aalto pour l'Exposition universelle de New York en 1939, le pavillon Philips de Le Corbusier et Iannis Xenakis (Exposition universelle de Bruxelles, 1958), ou le dôme géodésique de Buckminster Fuller pour l'Exposition nationale américaine à Moscou (1959), on peut vraiment y voir un chapitre non encore écrit de l'architecture du XXᵉ siècle. Ces constructions qui ne durent pas ne font pas partie des canons. Mais des expérimentations peuvent être menées sous cette forme plus légère, qui n'est pas supposée durer pour l'éternité. Ce qui est inhabituel dans les pavillons de la Serpentine, c'est que la série se soit développée, poursuivie. Si elle s'était arrêtée après Zaha Hadid ou Daniel Libeskind, elle n'aurait été qu'un de ces feux de paille de créativité dont on trouve tant d'exemples. Ce qui est incroyable, c'est que les choses n'en soient pas restées là.

Vous décrivez cette histoire comme un processus naturel et, cependant, vous avez atteint à un résultat que personne d'autre n'avait envisagé : associer une institution d'art contemporain à des commandes régulières d'architecture éphémère.
JP-J Une des raisons est que nous n'avons pas pris la décision solennelle de faire quelque chose. Cela a été un processus organique qui s'est développé naturellement avec le temps, aussi bien en termes de forme que de contenu. Si nous avions prévu de faire quelque chose chaque année avec les quelques plus grands architectes qui n'avaient pas encore construit au Royaume-Uni, cela n'aurait peut-être pas marché. C'est parce que ce projet était très modeste dans sa conception et si ludique dans sa réalité, qu'il a réussi à prendre racine. C'était une évolution naturelle d'autres projets dans lesquels nous nous étions impliqués. Si nous avions travaillé dans un bâtiment plus grand, peut-être n'aurions-nous pas eu besoin de lorgner vers la pelouse pour gagner de la place.

6 - *Serpentine Gallery 24-Hour Interview Marathon*, 28–29 July 2006. This event took place in the pavilion designed by Rem Koolhaas and Cecil Balmond with Arup.

Serpentine Gallery 24-Hour Interview Marathon, 28.–29. Juli 2006. Die Veranstaltung fand im Pavillon von Rem Koolhaas und Cecil Balmond statt (Zusammenarbeit mit Arup).

Serpentine Gallery 24-Hour Interview Marathon (Serpentine Gallery, Interview marathon de 24 heures), 28–29 juillet 2006. Cette manifestation s'est déroulée dans le pavillon conçu par Rem Koolhaas et Cecil Balmond, avec la collaboration d'Arup.

7 - Hans Ulrich Obrist, Co-Director, and Julia Peyton-Jones, Director, Serpentine Gallery, London. *Serpentine Gallery 24-Hour Interview Marathon*, 28–29 July 2006.

Hans Ulrich Obrist, Kodirektor, und Julia Peyton-Jones, Direktorin, Serpentine Gallery, London. *Serpentine Gallery 24-Hour Interview Marathon*, 28.–29. Juli 2006.

Hans Ulrich Obrist, codirecteur, et Julia Peyton-Jones, directrice, Serpentine Gallery, Londres. *Serpentine Gallery 24-Hour Interview Marathon*, 28–29 juillet 2006.

8   9

8 - Rem Koolhaas and Jeff Koons. *Post-Marathon*, 13–14 October, 2006. This event took place in the pavilion designed by Rem Koolhaas and Cecil Balmond with Arup.

Rem Koolhaas und Jeff Koons. *Post-Marathon*, 13.–14. Oktober 2006. Die Veranstaltung fand im Pavillon von Rem Koolhaas und Cecil Balmond statt (Zusammenarbeit mit Arup).

Rem Koolhaas et Jeff Koons. *Post-Marathon*, 13–14 octobre 2006. Cette manifestation s'est déroulée dans le pavillon conçu par Rem Koolhaas et Cecil Balmond, en collaboration avec Arup.

9 - Damien Hirst seen during the *Serpentine Gallery 24-Hour Interview Marathon*, 28–29 July 2006.

Damien Hirst während des *Serpentine Gallery 24-Hour Interview Marathon*, 28.–29. Juli 2006.

Damien Hirst pendant le *Serpentine Gallery 24-Hour Interview Marathon*, 28–29 juillet 2006.

and Programs and director of International Projects in 2006. One evening in 2005, I attended his screening of a Peter Smithson film at the Courtauld Institute. This sparked an intense conversation on the issue of architecture in Britain and what we viewed to be a general resistance within the public to engage with its contemporary forms. It is still possible to find people in the Serpentine Pavilions who say that in general they do not like contemporary architecture. But then you say, "Hang on, what do you think you are standing in?" That is a wonderful moment, where there is a change of perception.

HUO Both Julia and I felt that there is often a resistance to engage with contemporary architecture. One example is Ludwig Mies van der Rohe's unrealized project for London. Lord Palumbo, chair of the Pritzker Architecture Prize jury and chairman of the Board of Trustees of the Serpentine Gallery, tried to realize Mies's structure near St. Paul's Cathedral in 1984 but, unfortunately, it never came to pass. My initial discussions with Julia were fueled by the fact that our own backgrounds had led us to have very different experiences of working with architects. Whereas Julia had collaborated with architects to build the annual Serpentine Pavilions, I had worked closely with architects on exhibition design for shows such as *Cities on the Move*, which I curated with Hou Hanru and for which we worked with architects including Yung Ho Chang, Rem Koolhaas and Ole Scheeren, and Shigeru Ban. And at the Arc en Rêve center for architecture in Bordeaux, I had worked with Rem Koolhaas, Stefano Boeri, Sanford Kwinter, and Alex MacLean on the *Mutations* project, and together we commissioned Jean Nouvel to design the exhibition for Bordeaux and, when the show traveled to Tokyo, we invited SANAA to design the installation.

JP-J Commissioning a structure to be built is a different process and requires a specific form of collaboration. We were both curious to see what pooling our knowledge would bring to this process. My formula for our collaboration is 1+1 = 11.
What is interesting is that, although the Pavilion series has evolved over 10 years, the guidelines for

Warum haben Sie es zum Kriterium gemacht, dass ein Architekt, wenn er den Auftrag für den Pavillon bekommt, noch nicht in Großbritannien gebaut haben sollte?

JP-J Weil es darum geht, Architektur auszustellen, genauso wie wir ein Raum sind, der Kunst präsentiert. Als ich 1991 Direktorin der Serpentine Gallery wurde, gab es viele Architekten, die weltweit gebaut hatten, aber noch keine Aufträge in Großbritannien erhalten hatten. Das erstaunte uns sehr. Musste man tatsächlich Geld für ein Ticket nach Kalifornien ausgeben, um ein Gebäude von Frank Gehry persönlich zu sehen? Unsere Antwort lautete: „Nein, kommt hierher und seht es Euch an." Hans Ulrich und ich begannen unsere Zusammenarbeit in den 1990er-Jahren, als ich ihn einlud, die Gruppenausstellung *Take Me (I'm Yours)* an der Serpentine Gallery zu kuratieren. 2006 kam er als Kodirektor und Leiter für Ausstellungen, Programme und internationale Projekte an die Serpentine.
2005 besuchte ich die Vorführung eines Films von Peter Smithson am Courtauld Institute. Dieser Besuch führte zu einer intensiven Debatte über Architektur in Großbritannien und den in unseren Augen allgemein herrschenden Widerstand in der Öffentlichkeit, sich auf zeitgenössische Architektur einzulassen. Noch heute kann man Menschen in den Serpentine-Pavillons begegnen, die sagen, dass sie zeitgenössische Architektur generell nicht mögen. Und dann sagt man: „Moment mal, was glauben Sie denn, worin Sie gerade stehen?" Das ist ein wunderbarer Moment, wenn sich die Wahrnehmung verändert.

HUO Julia und ich hatten beide das Gefühl, dass es oft Widerstände gibt, sich mit zeitgenössischer Architektur auseinanderzusetzen. Ein Beispiel ist Ludwig Mies van der Rohes nicht realisiertes Projekt für London. Lord Palumbo, Vorsitzender der Jury des Pritzker-Preises und des Kuratoriums der Serpentine, unternahm 1984 den Versuch, den Mies'schen Entwurf nahe der Londoner St. Paul's Cathedral realisieren zu lassen. Leider wurde dies nie bewilligt. Anfangs wurden die Diskussionen zwischen Julia und mir dadurch verstärkt, dass wir unterschiedliche Er-

Pourquoi avez-vous imposé que l'architecte choisi n'ait encore jamais construit au Royaume-Uni pour recevoir commande d'un pavillon ?

JP-J Parce qu'il s'agit d'exposer l'architecture exactement comme nous le faisons avec l'art. Lorsque je suis devenue directrice de la Serpentine Gallery en 1991, beaucoup d'architectes qui avaient construit dans le monde entier n'avaient encore rien fait en Grande-Bretagne. C'était vraiment surprenant ! Le public britannique avait peut-être lu quelque chose sur Frank Gehry, mais n'en avait rien vu. Fallait-il prendre un billet d'avion pour la Californie pour découvrir ce qu'était vraiment une œuvre de Gehry ? Notre réponse était : « Non, venez chez nous. » Hans Ulrich et moi-même avons commencé à collaborer dans les années 1990 avec l'exposition « Take Me (I'm Yours) » à la Serpentine. Ce fut notre première collaboration avant qu'il ne rejoigne la galerie comme codirecteur des expositions et des programmes et directeur des projets internationaux en 2006. Un soir de 2005, j'ai assisté à la projection d'un film de Peter Smithson au Courtauld Institute. Il déclencha une conversation intense sur les enjeux de l'architecture en Grande-Bretagne et ce que nous considérions comme une résistance générale du public envers les formes contemporaines. Vous pouvez encore trouver aujourd'hui des gens qui visitent un pavillon de la Serpentine et disent qu'en principe, ils n'aiment pas l'architecture contemporaine. On a envie de leur dire « Mais regardez bien, dans quoi pensez-vous donc vous trouver ? » C'est un merveilleux moment d'assister à un changement de perception.

HUO Julia et moi sentions une résistance fréquente à l'acceptation de l'architecture contemporaine. Un exemple en est le projet non réalisé de Ludwig Mies van der Rohe pour Londres. Lord Palumbo, président du jury du prix Pritzker d'architecture et président du conseil d'administration de la Serpentine Gallery, avait essayé de faire réaliser le projet de Mies près de la cathédrale Saint-Paul en 1984, mais sans succès. Mes discussions initiales avec Julia se nourrissaient du fait que nous avions eu des expériences de

10

11

the structures were there in quite a natural way right from the beginning. As soon as Chris Smith said, "Yes, the Zaha Hadid Pavilion can stay up," then the question was: "Do we do it again?" The next architect we invited was Daniel Libeskind, who at the time had recently completed the Jewish Museum in Berlin. Daniel had to work to a very tight schedule, and, on top of that, there was no dedicated budget to fund the construction. In a way, the financial and time restrictions form an important conceptual component of each Pavilion. The fact that these structures, designed by world-renowned architects, are realized without any budget and without the luxury of time is a remarkable challenge. It makes a statement about what's possible with contemporary architecture.

How do you make your choices?
JP-J The process of selecting the architects is led by the Gallery's core curatorial thinking. The discussions with the architects and their team are direct, and every aspect of the project is transparent, making for an extremely engaging and enjoyable experience. We don't set up a competition, as would usually be the case with architectural projects, because the decision is a curatorial one.

With the exception of Oscar Niemeyer, you have had an avant-garde bent to your choices. Nor have you chosen other older masters who have not built in the UK.
JP-J One criterion is that we are looking for architects who have made a significant contribution to the field through the uniqueness of their architectural language. Another condition is that they haven't built in this country. Our Pavilion has to be the passion of the principal architect and it becomes a close personal dialogue with them. This was certainly the case with Niemeyer. Oscar Niemeyer is a titan of 20th-century architecture whose work was no longer foremost in people's minds. It is still shocking to us that Niemeyer has never built in the UK.

fahrungen in der Kooperation mit Architekten gemacht hatten. Während Julia beim Bau der jährlichen Serpentine-Pavillons mit Architekten zu tun hatte, hatte ich eng mit Architekten zusammengearbeitet, um die Ausstellungsarchitektur für Schauen wie *Cities on the Move* zu realisieren, die ich mit Hou Hanru kuratiert hatte. Dafür kooperierten wir mit Architekten wie Yung Ho Chang, Rem Koolhaas, Ole Scheeren und Shigeru Ban. Am Architekturzentrum Arc en Rêve in Bordeaux hatte ich mit Rem Koolhaas, Stefano Boeri, Sanford Kwinter und Alex MacLean am *Mutations*-Projekt gearbeitet. Gemeinsam hatten wir Jean Nouvel mit der Ausstellungsarchitektur in Bordeaux beauftragt. Als die Schau nach Tokio weiterzog, baten wir SANAA, die Installation zu entwerfen.
JP-J Ein Bauwerk in Auftrag zu geben, ist ein vollkommen anderer Prozess und erfordert eine spezifische Form von Kooperation. Meine persönliche Formel für unsere Zusammenarbeit lautet 1 + 1 = 11. Interessant ist, ist dass sich die Vorgaben für die Bauten von Anfang an recht natürlich ergeben haben, obwohl sich die Pavillon-Reihe in über zehn Jahren weiterentwickelt hat. Sobald Chris Smith gesagt hatte: „Ja, der Zaha-Hadid-Pavillon kann stehenbleiben", kam die Frage auf: „Machen wir das wieder?" Der nächste Architekt, den wir einluden, war Daniel Libeskind, der damals gerade das Jüdische Museum in Berlin realisiert hatte. Daniel musste unter enormem Zeitdruck arbeiten; hinzu kam, dass es kein separates Budget für den Bau gab. In gewisser Weise sind die finanziellen und zeitlichen Einschränkungen ein entscheidender konzeptueller Bestandteil jedes Pavillons. Diese Herausforderungen zeigen, was in der zeitgenössischen Architektur machbar ist.

Wie treffen Sie Ihre Auswahl?
Der Prozess der Architektenauswahl wird vom kuratorischen Grundprinzip der Galerie bestimmt. Jeder Aspekt des Projekts ist transparent, wodurch das Ganze zu einer außerordentlich angenehmen Erfahrung wird. Wir schreiben keinen Wettbewerb aus, wie das bei architektonischen Projekten üblich ist, weil die Entscheidung eine kuratorische ist.

collaboration très différentes avec des architectes. Alors qu'elle avait collaboré avec des architectes pour la construction des pavillons d'été, j'avais travaillé de très près avec des architectes à la conception d'expositions comme « Cities on the Move » dont j'avais été le commissaire avec Hou Hanru et pour laquelle nous avions collaboré avec des gens comme Yung Ho Chang, Rem Koolhaas, Ole Scheren ou Shigeru Ban. Au Centre d'architecture Arc en rêve de Bordeaux, j'avais collaboré avec Koolhaas, Stefano Boeri, Sanford Kwinter et Alex MacLean sur le projet « Mutations » et, ensemble, nous avions demandé à Jean Nouvel d'en concevoir l'exposition pour Bordeaux et à SANAA pour Tokyo.
JP-J Commander la construction d'un bâtiment est un processus différent qui demande une forme spécifique de collaboration. Nous étions tous deux curieux de voir ce que la réunion de nos connaissances apporterait à ce processus. Pour ce type de collaboration, ma formule est 1+1=11. Il est intéressant de noter que même si la série des pavillons a évolué en dix ans, des règles de conception se sont imposées de façon assez naturelle dès le départ. Dès que Chris Smith a déclaré : « Oui, le pavillon de Zaha Hadid a le droit d'exister », la question suivante était : « Allons-nous pouvoir le refaire ? » Le second architecte invité fut Daniel Libeskind qui dut travailler selon un calendrier très serré et sans budget dédié. D'une certaine façon, les problèmes de temps et de financement sont un des composants conceptuels forts de la genèse de chacun de ces pavillons. Le fait que ces structures conçues par des architectes de réputation internationale soient réalisées sans guère de budget, sans le luxe qu'apporte le temps est un remarquable défi. C'est aussi un aspect de ce qui est possible en architecture contemporaine.

Comment choisissez-vous les architectes ?
JP-J Le processus de sélection des architectes est lié à la philosophie curatoriale de la galerie. Les discussions avec les architectes et leurs équipes sont directes et chaque aspect du projet est transparent,

10 - Saul Williams, *Serpentine Gallery Poetry Marathon*, 17–18 October 2009, in the pavilion designed by Kazuyo Sejima + Ryue Nishizawa/SANAA.

Saul Williams, *Serpentine Gallery Poetry Marathon*, 17.–18. Oktober 2009 im Pavillon von Kazuyo Sejima + Ryue Nishizawa/SANAA.

Saul Williams, *Serpentine Gallery Poetry Marathon* (Marathon de poésie de la Serpentine Gallery), 17–18 octobre 2009, dans le pavillon conçu par Kazuyo Sejima + Ryue Nishizawa/SANAA.

11 - The Ginger Light, *Serpentine Gallery Poetry Marathon*, 17–18 October, 2009, in the Pavilion designed by Kazuyo Sejima + Ryue Nishizawa/SANAA.

The Ginger Light, Serpentine Gallery Poetry Marathon, 17.–18. Oktober 2009 im Pavillon von Kazuyo Sejima + Ryue Nishizawa/SANAA.

The Ginger Light (La lumière gingembre), *Serpentine Gallery Poetry Marathon*, 17–18 octobre 2009, dans le pavillon conçu par Kazuyo Sejima + Ryue Nishizawa/SANAA.

12   13

12 - Jacques Roubaud, *Serpentine Gallery Poetry Marathon*, 17–18 October 2009.

Jacques Roubaud, *Serpentine Gallery Poetry Marathon*, 17.–18. Oktober 2009.

Jacques Roubaud, *Serpentine Gallery Poetry Marathon*, 17–18 octobre 2009.

13 - Julia Peyton-Jones, director, Serpentine Gallery, and co-director, Exhibitions and Programs, *Serpentine Gallery Poetry Marathon*, 17–18 October 2009.

Julia Peyton-Jones, Direktorin der Serpentine Gallery und Kodirektorin für Ausstellungen und Programme, *Serpentine Gallery Poetry Marathon*, 17.–18. Oktober 2009.

Julia Peyton-Jones, directrice de la Serpentine Gallery et codirectrice des expositions et des programmes, *Serpentine Gallery Poetry Marathon*, 17–18 octobre 2009.

Why has Arup been associated with all the Pavilions?
JP-J When we commissioned Libeskind, Arup was working with him on the V&A Spiral. Libeskind wanted to work with Cecil Balmond and since then Cecil and his team at Arup have been integral to the project. Everybody who is involved with it becomes part of a closely knit group.

Why is it that since Ron Arad designed a canopy for you, you have not called on designers as opposed to architects?
JP-J. We recently invited the German designer Konstantin Grcic to curate a show of design in the Gallery (*Design Real*, 26 November 2009–7 February 2010). The Pavilions are principally about commissioning architects, and there is still some work to be done in showing the work of significant architects in the UK.

You don't see architecture as being closer to art than design?
JP-J That does not come into our thinking. We are an institution that is about the presentation of contemporary culture.

Were you never tempted to associate works of art with the Pavilions? Georg Kolbe's *Alba* figured in the Barcelona Pavilion by Mies van der Rohe after all.
HUO In 2006, there was a site-specific frieze by Thomas Demand in the Pavilion and an exhibition of his work inside the Serpentine Gallery, but we have otherwise intentionally avoided placing art objects inside the Pavilions. Our approach is very much an integrated program, within which we can build many bridges between disciplines.
JP-J There is a kind of social sculpture that takes its rightful place in the Pavilions: the program really embraces how people use the Pavilion and reorder the space and even the furniture to make it their own. The SANAA Pavilion drew an astonishing number of visitors; it was the third best attended de-

Mit Ausnahme von Oscar Niemeyer hatten Sie bisher eine Avantgarde zu Gast, die Ihren Neigungen entspricht. Abgesehen davon haben Sie keine Altmeister eingeladen.
Ein Kriterium ist, dass wir nach Architekten suchen, die durch ihre unverwechselbare architektonische Sprache einen entscheidenden Beitrag auf ihrem Gebiet geleistet haben. Eine weitere Bedingung ist, dass sie noch nicht in diesem Land gebaut haben. Unser Pavillon muss für den Chefarchitekten ein leidenschaftliches Anliegen sein und wird zu einem persönlichen Dialog mit ihm. Bei Niemeyer war das der Fall. Oscar Niemeyer ist ein Titan der Architektur des 20. Jahrhunderts. Es schockiert uns noch immer, dass er nie in Großbritannien gebaut hat.

Warum ist Arup bei allen Pavillons dabei?
JP-J Als wir Libeskind beauftragten, kooperierte Arup gerade mit ihm an der *Spiral*, dem Erweiterungsbau des Victoria & Albert Museum. Und Libeskind wollte mit Cecil Balmond arbeiten. Seither ist Cecil mit seinem Team bei Arup integraler Bestandteil des Projekts. Jeder der Beteiligten wird zum Mitglied einer eingeschworenen Gemeinschaft.

Wie kommt es, dass Sie sich nicht an Designer, sondern an Architekten gewendet haben, obwohl Ron Arad doch schon eine Markise für Sie entworfen hatte?
JP-J Vor Kurzem haben wir den deutschen Designer Konstantin Grcic eingeladen, eine Designausstellung in der Galerie zu kuratieren (*Design Real*, 26. November 2009–7. Februar 2010). Bei den Pavillons geht es in erster Linie darum, Architekten zu beauftragen, und nach wie vor gibt es einiges zu tun, wenn es darum geht, das Werk großer Architekten in Großbritannien zu präsentieren.

Sie glauben nicht, dass Architektur enger mit der Kunst verwandt ist als Design?
JP-J Dieser Aspekt spielt keine Rolle in unserem Denken. Wir sind eine Institution, der es um die Präsentation zeitgenössischer Kultur geht.

ce qui en fait une expérience extrêmement plaisante et captivante. Nous ne mettons pas sur pied un concours, comme c'est généralement le cas en architecture. Les conservateurs décident.

À l'exception d'Oscar Niemeyer, vos choix semblent cependant orientés vers l'avant-garde. Vous n'avez pas choisi d'autres grandes figures historiques qui n'avaient pas encore construit au Royaume-Uni.
JP-J Un de nos critères est la recherche d'architectes qui apportent une contribution significative par le caractère exclusif de leur langage architectural. Une autre condition est qu'ils n'aient pas encore construit dans ce pays. Notre pavillon doit être un objet de passion pour son auteur tandis que se crée avec lui un dialogue personnel étroit. Ce fut certainement le cas avec Niemeyer. Oscar Niemeyer est un titan de l'architecture du XXᵉ siècle, mais dont l'œuvre n'était plus guère présente dans l'esprit des gens. Pour nous, il reste choquant qu'il n'ait jamais rien construit au Royaume-Uni.

Pourquoi Arup a-t-il été associé à la création de tous les pavillons?
JP-J L'agence Arup travaillait déjà avec Daniel Libeskind sur la « spirale » du Victoria and Albert Museum. Libeskind nous a dit qu'il voulait collaborer avec Cecil Balmond et, depuis, Cecil et son équipe de chez Arup font partie intégrante des projets. Tous ceux qui s'y impliquent forment un petit groupe très lié.

Puisque Ron Arad avait dessiné pour vous un auvent, pourquoi n'avez-vous pas fait appel à des designers par opposition, en quelque sorte, aux architectes?
JP-J Nous avons récemment invité le designer allemand Konstantin Grcic à être le commissaire d'une exposition sur le design (*Design Real*, 26 novembre 2009–7 février 2010). Mais l'idée des pavillons est de passer une commande à un architecte. Et il y a encore beaucoup de travail à faire pour montrer ici ce que font les grands architectes.

14

sign "exhibition" worldwide (according to *The Art Newspaper*). Since 2001, the events program, *Park Nights*, has been a central part of the Pavilion series. *Park Nights*, which incorporates public talks, performances, music, and events, attracts up to 250 000 visitors each summer. And when Hans Ulrich joined the Serpentine Gallery team in 2006, he conceived of an annual event for the Pavilions that would bring together an extraordinary group of artists, poets, musicians, architects, and scientists for a weekend of intense conversation and exchange: the Marathon. The marathon format was something he had previously explored in Stuttgart in 2005. These Marathons are a focal point in our calendar. The Pavilion is a public space, there are no barriers. The public can simply walk in and take possession of the building.

You really would not want a fixed work of art within a pavilion, aside perhaps from the Thomas Demand that Hans Ulrich refers to?
JP-J I would struggle with the idea of an architect creating a container for fixed objects. It is not about creating a venue for another kind of exhibition. The new "wing" that we create every year is the exhibition itself. One of the most important things we bring to the table is an unparalleled freedom for architects. The brief is very simple: all we ask is that the pavilion might be an example of their architectural "language."

In 2005 the Summer Pavilion was the result of a collaboration between the Portuguese architects Álvaro Siza and Eduardo Souto de Moura. Did they propose to work together?
JP-J No, we suggested that they work together since they had collaborated for the Portuguese Pavilion at the 1998 Lisbon World's Fair. In this context, you certainly cannot create a forced marriage. There is too little time for people to get to know each other. The Pavilion takes six months from conception to completion.

Waren Sie je versucht, Kunstwerke mit den Pavillons zu verknüpfen? Schließlich war ja auch Georg Kolbes *Alba* im Barcelona-Pavillon von Mies van der Rohe zu sehen.
HUO 2006 gab es einen ortsspezifischen Fries von Thomas Demand im Pavillon und parallel dazu eine Ausstellung seiner Arbeiten in der Serpentine Gallery. Abgesehen davon haben wir es bewusst vermieden, Kunstobjekte in den Sommerpavillons zu platzieren. Unser Ansatz ist programmatisch betont übergreifend. Auf diese Weise können wir viele Brücken zwischen den Disziplinen bauen.
JP-J Es ist eine Art Soziale Plastik, die ihren rechtmäßigen Platz in den Pavillons beansprucht: Das Bauprogramm berücksichtigt, wie Menschen den Pavillon nutzen, den Raum neu ordnen und sogar das Mobiliar einsetzen, um ihn sich zu eigen zu machen. Der Pavillon von SANAA zog eine erstaunliche Anzahl von Besuchern an; er war die drittmeist besuchte „Designausstellung" weltweit (laut *The Art Newspaper*). Seit 2001 ist das Veranstaltungsprogramm *Park Nights* zentraler Bestandteil unserer Pavillon-Reihe. Die *Park Nights*, die öffentliche Vorträge, Performances, Konzerte und andere Veranstaltungen umfassen, ziehen jeden Sommer bis zu 250 000 Besucher an. Als Hans Ulrich sich 2006 dem Team anschloss, konzipierte er den *Marathon*, eine jährliche Veranstaltung für den Pavillon, die eine außergewöhnliche Gruppe von Künstlern, Dichtern, Musikern, Architekten und Wissenschaftlern für ein Wochenende voll intensiver Gespräche und des Austauschs zusammenbringt. Schon 2005 hatte er in Stuttgart Erfahrungen mit dem *Marathon*-Format gemacht. Diese *Marathons* sind ein Schwerpunkt in unserem Kalender. Der Pavillon ist ein öffentlicher Raum, jeder kann eintreten und das Gebäude in Besitz nehmen.

Sie würden tatsächlich kein physisches Kunstwerk in einem Pavillon wollen, abgesehen vielleicht von der Thomas-Demand-Arbeit, die Hans Ulrich erwähnt hat?
JP-J Es geht hier nicht darum, einen Ort für eine weitere Art von Ausstellung zu schaffen. Der neue

Pensez-vous que l'architecture est plus proche de l'art que du design ?
JP-J Cette question ne fait pas partie de notre réflexion. Nous sommes une institution dont la mission est de faire connaître la culture contemporaine.

N'avez-vous jamais été tentée d'associer des œuvres d'art à l'expérience des pavillons ? Après tout, on voit bien l'*Alba* de Georg Kolbe dans le pavillon de Barcelone de Mies van der Rohe...
HUO En 2006, on a pu voir une frise spécifiquement créée par Thomas Demand pour le pavillon de l'année et une exposition de son travail dans la galerie, mais en dehors de cet exemple nous avons volontairement évité de présenter des objets artistiques à l'intérieur des pavillons d'été. Notre approche est celle d'un programme intégré, qui nous permet de lancer de nombreuses passerelles entre les disciplines.
JP-J Il existe cependant une sorte de « sculpture sociale » qui trouve à juste titre sa place dans les pavillons. Le programme couvre concrètement la manière dont les gens utiliseront le pavillon, réorganiseront l'espace et même le mobilier pour se l'approprier. Celui de SANAA a attiré un nombre de visiteurs étonnant. Ce fut la troisième « exposition » dans le monde pour le nombre de visiteurs selon *The Art Newspaper*. Depuis 2001, le programme de manifestations *Park Nights* (Nuits du Parc) est pour nous un élément programmatique essentiel. Il regroupe des débats publics, des performances, de la musique et des événements, et attire jusqu'à 250 000 personnes chaque été. Lorsqu'Hans Ulrich a rejoint l'équipe de la Serpentine en 2006, il a conçu une manifestation annuelle pour les pavillons, qui a réuni un groupe extraordinaire d'artistes, de poètes, de musiciens, d'architectes et de scientifiques à l'occasion d'un intense week-end de conversations et d'échanges :
le « Marathon ». Il avait déjà exploré ce format à Stuttgart en 2005. Les « Marathons » sont un moment essentiel de notre calendrier. Le pavillon est un lieu public, sans barrières. Le public peut tout simplement y entrer et en prendre possession.

15 - Gilbert & George, *Serpentine Gallery Manifesto Marathon*, 18–19 October 2008, in the Frank Gehry Pavilion.

Gilbert & George, *Serpentine Gallery Manifesto Marathon*, 18.–19. Oktober 2008 im Pavillon von Frank Gehry.

Gilbert & George, *Serpentine Gallery Manifesto Marathon*, 18–19 octobre 2008, dans le pavillon de Frank Gehry.

You had another team in 2006 with Rem Koolhaas and Cecil Balmond. How did that occur?
JP-J In 2006, there was a mutual agreement to share the credit between Cecil and Rem. They've worked together for decades. It was Rem Koolhaas who proposed the coauthorship.
HUO The Koolhaas–Balmond Pavilion was the venue for the first of our nonstop conversations or Marathons. During this 24-hour event, Rem Koolhaas and I interviewed 72 leading cultural figures based in London, mapping the city through conversations with the protagonists who inhabit it. Similarly, the Experiment Marathon in 2007 (conceived with Olafur Eliasson) mapped the interface between art and science, while the 2008 Manifesto Marathon charted artist's relationship to politics, polemics, and poetics, a theme that was further explored in the Poetry Marathon of 2009 as well as this year's Map Marathon. The Marathons are all about going beyond the fear of pooling knowledge. I see it as a sketch for a transdisciplinary school.

To what extent would you say that there is a real collaboration between you and the architects; is there a real dialogue? Do the designs tend to evolve very much from the initial concept to the finished result?
JP-J Absolutely. There's 100 percent collaboration between the members of the team. Some of the designs are close to the way they were initially conceived. This was the case with Oscar Niemeyer or Álvaro Siza's first drawings, for example. There is always a very real feeling of working together to make the Pavilion.
HUO The principal architect is always very directly involved. It is very intense—short but intense. These commissions adopt Cedric Price's view that architecture should be more than hardware; it should also be about content.

„Flügel", den wir jedes Jahr entstehen lassen, ist selbst Ausstellung. Wir bieten den Architekten eine beispiellose Freiheit. Alles, worum wir die Architekten bitten, ist den Pavillon in ihrer typischen architektonischen „Handschrift" zu gestalten.

Der Sommerpavillon 2005 war das Ergebnis einer Zusammenarbeit zwischen den portugiesischen Architekten Álvaro Siza und Eduardo Souto de Moura. Hatten die beiden vorgeschlagen, zusammenzuarbeiten?
JP-J Nein, wir hatten die Zusammenarbeit angeregt, weil die beiden schon 1998 den portugiesischen Pavillon für die Weltausstellung in Lissabon gemeinsam entworfen hatten. In einem Kontext wie diesem kann man definitiv keine Zwangsheirat anordnen. Die Zeit ist zu kurz, als dass die Beteiligten sich kennenlernen könnten. Es sind sechs Monate vom Entwurf bis zur Fertigstellung des Pavillons.

2006 hatten sie mit Rem Koolhaas und Cecil Balmond ein weiteres Team. Wie kam es dazu?
JP-J 2006 gab es das beiderseitige Einverständnis, Cecil und Rem gemeinsam als Urheber zu nennen. Sie arbeiten seit Jahren zusammen. Es war übrigens Rem Koolhaas, der die Koautorenschaft vorschlug.
HUO Der Pavillon von Koolhaas und Balmond war der Schauplatz unserer ersten Nonstop-Gesprächsrunden, den *Marathons*. Während dieser 24-stündigen Veranstaltung interviewten Rem Koolhaas und ich 72 führende kulturelle Persönlichkeiten aus London und kartierten die Stadt anhand der Protagonisten, die hier leben. 2007 zeichnete der (mit Olafur Eliasson entwickelte) *Experiment Marathon* auf ähnliche Weise die Schnittstelle zwischen Kunst und Naturwissenschaft nach, während es beim *Manifesto Marathon* von 2008 um das Verhältnis des Künstlers zu Politik, Polemik und Poetik ging. Dieses Thema wurde sowohl im *Poetry Marathon* (2009) vertieft als auch im diesjährigen *Map Marathon*. Bei den *Marathons* geht es in erster Linie darum, die Angst zu überwinden, Wissen zu teilen. Ich verstehe sie als Entwurf für eine transdisziplinäre Schule.

Vous ne voulez donc pas d'œuvre d'art à l'intérieur du pavillon, en dehors peut-être de la pièce de Thomas Demand à laquelle Hans Ulrich faisait allusion?
JP-J Je me battrai contre l'idée d'un architecte voulant créer un conteneur pour objets statiques. Notre propos n'est pas de créer un lieu pour un autre type d'exposition. La nouvelle « aile » que nous créons chaque année est en soi une exposition. L'une des choses que nous proposons aux architectes, c'est une liberté sans équivalent. Tout ce que nous demandons est que le pavillon soit représentatif de leur « signature » architecturale.

Le pavillon de 2005 était le fruit de la collaboration entre Alvaro Siza et Edouardo Souto de Moura. Vous ont-ils proposé de travailler ensemble?
JP-J Non, nous avons suggéré qu'ils le fassent, ce qui avait déjà été le cas pour le Pavillon portugais de l'Exposition universelle de Lisbonne en 1998. Dans ce contexte, vous ne pouvez pas pousser à un mariage forcé. Les délais sont trop courts pour que les gens aient le temps de se connaître. Six mois se déroulent de la conception à la réalisation.

Vous avez également dirigé un autre travail d'équipe en 2006 avec Rem Koolhaas et Cecil Balmond. Comment cela s'est-il déroulé?
JP-J En 2006, le crédit a été partagé entre Cecil et Rem par accord mutuel. Ils travaillaient ensemble depuis des décennies. C'est Rem Koolhaas qui a proposé cette signature commune.
HUO Le pavillon Koolhaas-Balmond a été le lieu de la première de nos conversations non-stop ou « Marathons ». Au cours de cet événement qui a duré 24 heures, Rem Koolhaas et moi avons interrogé 72 grands noms de la culture basés à Londres, dressant une cartographie de la ville à travers ces conversations avec les protagonistes qui l'habitent. De même, « Experiment Marathon » en 2007 (conçu avec Olafur Eliasson) retraçait l'interface entre l'art et la science tandis que le « Manifesto Marathon » de 2008

16   17

You have worked with some notably difficult personalities. Can you truly say that there have not been conflicts in the process of realizing the Summer Pavilions?

JP-J There are many reasons why the Pavilion process can be challenging—the pressure of time, for example. One of the qualities of the project is the sense of a team coming together to resolve the issues. If this sense of teamwork did not exist, the commission would not have lasted for 10 years. The principal architect has to have a passion for doing it. We ask them to go the extra mile and then another 100 on top of that. It is our job to make it possible for them. We try to smooth the way as much as we can. Everybody is focused on getting the job done.

You resist the idea of having artists and architects work together on these projects, and yet in 2007 you had an artist, Olafur Eliasson, teamed with an architect, Kjetil Thorsen. Did you not contradict yourselves in that instance?

HUO A number of artists, like Eliasson, have a double practice as artists and architects, and some employ architects in their studios. Eliasson's work often takes architectural form. Beside Thorsen, he has worked with a number of architects including Tadao Ando on Takeo Obayashi's house, the so-called Jewel Box. More recently, Eliasson has been commissioned to design the façade of Harpa, Reykjavik's new concert hall and conference center.

But Eliasson is honestly better known as an artist, and he collaborated with an architect on the 2007 Pavilion.

JP-J Olafur Eliasson has a team of 10 or more people devoted to his architectural projects. In the case of the collaboration with Thorsen, he was wearing his architectural hat and using the architectural unit in his office.

In welchem Maße gibt es einen echten Dialog bzw. eine echte Zusammenarbeit zwischen Ihnen und den Architekten? Verändern sich die Entwürfe stark vom anfänglichen Konzept bis hin zum fertigen Ergebnis?

JP-J Es gibt eine 100-prozentige Kooperation zwischen den einzelnen Teammitgliedern. Manche der ursprünglichen Entwürfe werden fast genau so ausgeführt, wie sie anfangs konzipiert wurden. Das war so bei Oscar Niemeyer oder Álvaro Siza. In allen Fällen gibt es eine enge Zusammenarbeit, mit dem Ziel, den Pavillon entstehen zu lassen.

HUO Der verantwortliche Architekt ist immer sehr direkt beteiligt. Es ist sehr intensiv – kurz, aber intensiv. Diese Auftragsarbeiten folgen Cedric Price's Auffassung, dass Architektur mehr sein sollte als Hardware; es sollte eben auch um Inhalte gehen.

Sie haben mit einigen bekanntermaßen schwierigen Persönlichkeiten kooperiert. Gab es bei der Realisierung der Sommerpavillons wirklich keine Konflikte?

JP-J Es gibt viele Gründe, warum der Prozess eine große Herausforderung sein kann – etwa wegen des Zeitdrucks. Eine der Qualitäten des Projekts ist das Gefühl, ein Team zu haben, das gemeinsam Probleme löst. Wenn dieser Teamgeist nicht funktionieren würde, hätte sich das Programm nicht zehn Jahre lang bewährt. Der leitende Architekt muss leidenschaftlich dazu entschlossen sein. Wir bitten die Architekten, noch einen Schritt weiterzugehen, und dann noch einmal 100 dazu. Es ist unsere Aufgabe, ihnen das zu ermöglichen. Jeder konzentriert sich darauf, die Aufgabe zu bewältigen.

Sie verzichten bewusst darauf, Künstler und Architekten bei diesen Projekten kooperieren zu lassen und doch hatten Sie 2007 ein Team aus einem Künstler, Olafur Eliasson, und einem Architekten, Kjetil Thorsen.

HUO Eine Reihe von Künstlern, etwa Eliasson, sind als Künstler und Architekten tätig und manche beschäftigen Architekten in ihren Studios. Eliassons

dressait l'état des relations des artistes avec la politique, la polémique et la poésie, thème approfondi dans le « Poetic Marathon » de 2009 et le « Map Marathon » de 2010, qui traitent tous de la nécessité d'aller au-delà des réticences à mettre en commun nos connaissances. J'y vois une esquisse d'école transdisciplinaire.

Dans quelle mesure pouvez-vous dire qu'existe une vraie collaboration entre vous et les architectes, un vrai dialogue ? Les projets évoluent-ils beaucoup entre le concept initial et le résultat final ?

JP-J Absolument. La collaboration entre les membres de l'équipe se fait à 100 %. Certains des projets initiaux sont exécutés comme ils ont été conçus. Ce fut le cas avec les premiers dessins d'Alvaro Siza. Nous avons toujours le sentiment bien réel de travailler ensemble.

HUO L'architecte principal est toujours très directement impliqué. C'est très intense. Bref mais intense. Ces commissions illustrent le point de vue de Cedric Price selon lequel l'architecture devrait être davantage que de la technique ; elle devrait aussi traiter le contenu.

Vous avez travaillé avec des personnalités notoirement difficiles. Pouvez-vous vraiment dire qu'il n'y a jamais eu de conflits dans la réalisation des pavillons ?

JP-J De nombreuses raisons peuvent rendre le processus de réalisation délicat, la pression des délais par exemple. L'une des caractéristiques de ce projet est un sens de l'équipe, qui se constitue peu à peu pour tenter de répondre aux défis posés. Si nous ne travaillions pas ainsi, l'expérience n'aurait pas duré dix ans. L'architecte en charge du projet doit se passionner pour cette aventure. Nous lui demandons beaucoup et encore davantage. Notre travail est de rendre les choses possibles. Nous essayons de lui paver la voie. Tout le monde se concentre sur le succès du projet.

16 - Claude Parent, *Serpentine Gallery Manifesto Marathon*, 18–19 October 2008, in the Frank Gehry Pavilion.

Claude Parent, *Serpentine Gallery Manifesto Marathon*, 18.–19. Oktober 2008 im Pavillon von Frank Gehry.

Claude Parent, *Serpentine Gallery Manifesto Marathon*, 18–19 octobre 2008, dans le pavillon de Frank Gehry.

17 - *Park Nights*: Thomas Adès and Frank Gehry, Serpentine Gallery Pavilion 2008.

Park Nights: Thomas Adès und Frank Gehry, Serpentine Gallery Pavilion 2008.

Park Nights : Thomas Adès et Frank Gehry, pavillon de la Serpentine Gallery 2008.

18   19

18 - Marina Abramović, *Serpentine Gallery Manifesto Marathon*, 18–19 October 2008.

Marina Abramović, *Serpentine Gallery Manifesto Marathon*, 18.–19. Oktober 2008.

Marina Abramović, *Serpentine Gallery Manifesto Marathon*, 18–19 octobre 2008.

19 - *Park Nights*: Emily Wardill, Serpentine Gallery Pavilion 2008, designed by Frank Gehry.

Park Nights: Emily Wardill, Serpentine Gallery Pavilion 2008 von Frank Gehry.

Park Nights : Emily Wardill, dans le Pavillon 2008 conçu par Frank Gehry.

Did he approach you in this instance?
JP-J We invited Eliasson and Thorsen to work as a team. Every year it is the same—we select the designer of the Pavilion in exactly the same way as we select the artists for the exhibition program. After Siza and Souto de Moura we had Eliasson and Thorsen, which is a different kind of collaboration. We also had the collaboration between Koolhaas and Balmond, so there was a series of collaborations for a time, a sort of mini-theme that we explored and that we may return to.

The 2007 Summer Pavilion appears to have been different from the others in a number of respects.
HUO The Eliasson–Thorsen Pavilion had internal complexity. Eliasson linked this with the idea of the folly, which Cedric Price defined as a distortion of space and time. There's also the tradition of the grotto in the 18th-century English garden. This linked with the 2006 program, when we had Thomas Demand's work *Grotto* in the gallery. Lately, architecture had become obsessed with exteriors and the Eliasson–Thorsen Pavilion was a chance to contemplate the interior complexity of a structure.

In the same year as the Eliasson–Thorsen collaboration, there was also the brief presence of an umbrella-like structure designed by Zaha Hadid...
HUO *Lilas* was a temporary installation that took inspiration from complex natural geometries such as flower petals. It was erected in a relatively short period of time and one could imagine structures such as *Lilas* popping up in every city across the world.

In 2007, you had an artist who wants to be an architect (Eliasson) and the following year, an architect who wants to be an artist (Gehry). Was it not a sculpture that Frank Gehry created for you in 2008?
JP-J It seemed to me to strongly relate to the house he designed for himself in Santa Monica in the late

Arbeit nimmt häufig architektonische Formen an. Abgesehen von Thorsen hat er mit verschiedenen Architekten zusammengearbeitet, darunter mit Tadao Ando am Haus für Takeo Obayashi, der *Jewel Box*. In jüngerer Zeit erhielt Eliasson den Auftrag, die Fassade des neuen Konzerthauses und Konferenzzentrums Harpa in Reykjavik zu gestalten.

Eliasson ist jedoch bekannter als Künstler und er arbeitete für den Pavillon 2007 mit einem Architekten zusammen.
JP-J Olafur Eliasson hat ein Team von zehn oder mehr Mitarbeitern, die sich ganz seinen Architekturprojekten widmen. Bei der Kooperation mit Thorsen entschied er sich für die Rolle des Architekten und nutzte die Architekturabteilung seines Studios.

Hat er Sie in diesem Fall angesprochen?
JP-J Wir haben Eliasson und Thorsen eingeladen, als Team zu arbeiten. Wir wählen die Architekten des Pavillons auf genau dieselbe Weise aus, wie wir Künstler für das Ausstellungsprogramm auswählen. Nach Siza und Souto de Moura hatten wir Eliasson und Kjetil Thorsen, was eine andere Art von Kooperation war. Außerdem gab es die Zusammenarbeit von Koolhaas und Balmond, es war also eine Reihe von Kooperationen, eine Art Minithema, das wir ausgelotet haben und zu dem wir vielleicht irgendwann zurückkehren werden.

Der Sommerpavillon von 2007 scheint in vielerlei Hinsicht anders als die anderen gewesen zu sein.
HUO Der Pavillon von Eliasson und Thorsen war von einer verinnerlichten Komplexität. Eliasson stellte den Bezug zur „Folly" her, die Cedric Price als Verzerrung von Raum und Zeit definiert hat. Darüber hinaus gibt es im englischen Gartenbau des 18. Jahrhunderts die Tradition der Grotte. Dies wiederum schlägt den Bogen zum Programm 2006, als wir Thomas Demands Arbeit *Grotto* in der Galerie hatten. In jüngster Zeit ist Architektur zunehmend auf das Äußere fixiert und so war der Eliasson-Thorsen-Pavillon eine Gele-

Vous résistez à l'idée de faire travailler ensemble des architectes et des artistes sur ces projets mais pourtant, en 2007, un artiste, Olafur Eliasson, a fait équipe avec un architecte, Kjetii Thorsen. N'est-ce pas là une contradiction ?
HUO Un certain nombre d'artistes, comme Eliasson, ont une double pratique d'architecte et d'artiste, et certains emploient des architectes dans leur atelier. Les travaux d'Eliasson prennent souvent une forme architecturale. Par ailleurs, Thorsen a travaillé avec d'autres architectes dont Tadao Ando sur la maison de Takeo Obayashi, la « Jewel Box » (Boîte à bijoux). Plus récemment, Eliasson s'est également vu confier la conception de la façade d'HARPA, le nouveau centre de concerts et de conférences de Reykjavik.

Mais Eliasson est quand même plus connu comme artiste, et il a collaboré avec un architecte pour le pavillon de 2007.
JP-J Olafur Eliasson dispose d'une équipe d'au moins dix collaborateurs qui se consacrent à ses seuls projets architecturaux. Dans le cadre de cette collaboration avec Thorsen, il portait sa casquette d'architecte et faisait appel à l'équipe d'architecture de son studio.

Est-ce lui qui vous a approchés ?
JP-J Nous avons invité Eliasson et Thorsen à travailler en équipe. Chaque année nous faisons de même : nous sélectionnons le concepteur du pavillon exactement de la même manière que nous choisissons des artistes pour les expositions de la galerie. Après Alvaro Siza et Eduardo Souto de Moura, nous avons donc eu Olafur Eliasson et Kjetil Thorsen, ce qui est un type de collaboration différent. Nous avons également bénéficié de la collaboration de Koolhaas et Balmond, ce fut donc une brève succession de pavillons en collaboration, une sorte de mini-thème que nous avons exploré et auquel nous reviendrons peut-être.

Le pavillon de 2007 semble néanmoins différent à un certain nombre d'égards...

20

21

1970s and the new house he was designing for himself at the time he worked on the Pavilion. He was 100 percent involved in the project. The structure was a kind of arch and a performance space. The acoustics were very good. Part of his concept was that Thomas Adès should play in that space. It was the most extraordinary evening. What was interesting was the relationship between the scale of the Gehry Pavilion and that of the Serpentine Gallery building, and the way Gehry framed the gallery from the road. It was a performative space, and that's an element that has been significant for all of the Pavilions.

In some sense you are integrating the Pavilions into a wider conception of art as performance, are you not?
HUO It depends not only on the architecture but on how the structure is played with by us and by the public. The park in the summer has a very democratic sensibility to it. For Gehry in 2008, integrating time and sound into the Pavilion was essential. In the future, we might consider asking a composer to do a soundtrack, or to create a soundscape for the structure.

The Pavilions are often sold after their time in Kensington Gardens, are they not?
JP-J Selling the Pavilions is an important part of our policy and allows us to cover up to 40 percent of the budget. They're conceived in this way for legacy reasons as well. The Toyo Ito Pavilion, for example, was installed at Battersea Power Station . The Ito, the Frank Gehry, and the Jean Nouvel Pavilions have been relocated to the South of France. These Pavilions, and all the others, have a long life.
The 2009 and 2010 Pavilions seem to be quite opposite in their conception. The 2009 structure, by SANAA, was almost ethereal and made a clear connection between the park and the Serpentine Gallery. The Jean Nouvel structure in 2010, on the contrary, seems to have an almost separate existence.

genheit, sich auf das komplexe Innenleben eines Gebäudes zu besinnen.

Im selben Jahr wie die Kooperation von Eliasson und Thorsen gab es außerdem ein kurzes Zwischenspiel mit einer schirmartigen Konstruktion von Zaha Hadid ...
HUO *Lilas* war eine temporäre Installation, die sich von komplexen natürlichen Geometrien, wie etwa Blütenblättern, inspirieren ließ. Sie wurde in relativ kurzer Zeit errichtet und es ist durchaus vorstellbar, dass Konstruktionen wie *Lilas* weltweit in jeder nur denkbaren Stadt auftauchen.

2007 hatten Sie einen Künstler, der Architekt sein will (Eliasson), und im folgenden Jahr einen Architekten, der Künstler sein will (Gehry). War es nicht im Grunde eine Skulptur, die Frank Gehry 2008 für Sie realisierte?
JP-J In meinen Augen gab es auffällige Bezüge zu dem Wohnhaus, das er in den späten 1970er-Jahren für sich in Santa Monica gebaut hatte und zu seinem neuen Haus, das er gerade entwarf, als er am Pavillon arbeitete. Das Ganze war eher eine Art Torbogen und eine Bühne. Die Akustik war sehr gut. Ein Aspekt des Konzepts war der geplante Auftritt von Thomas Adès. Es wurde ein ganz außergewöhnlicher Abend. Interessant waren die Beziehung zwischen der Größe von Gehrys Pavillon und dem Serpentine-Gebäude sowie die Art und Weise, wie Gehry die Galerie von der Straße her rahmte. Es war ein performativer Ort, ein Aspekt, der für alle Pavillons prägend war.

In gewisser Weise sind die Pavillons für Sie Teil eines erweiterten Begriffs von Kunst als Performance, richtig?
HUO Das hängt nicht nur von der Architektur ab, sondern auch davon, wie der Bau von uns und der Öffentlichkeit oder dem Publikum bespielt wird. Im Sommer hat der Park etwas sehr Demokratisches. Für Gehry war es 2008 von entscheidender Bedeutung, Zeit und Klang in den Pavillon zu integrieren. In Zukunft werden wir vielleicht einen Komponisten be-

HUO Le pavillon Eliasson-Thorsen possédait une réelle complexité interne. Eliasson a lié cet aspect à l'idée de folie, ce que Cedric Price a défini comme une distorsion de l'espace et du temps. On y trouve aussi la tradition de la grotte dans les jardins anglais du XVIIIe siècle, ce qui était en lien avec notre programme de 2006, lorsque Thomas Demand exposa une œuvre intitulée *Grotto* dans la galerie. Récemment, l'architecture s'est focalisée sur l'aspect extérieur et le pavillon Eliasson-Thorsen a été l'occasion de contempler la complexité intérieure d'une structure.

L'année du pavillon Eliassson-Thorsen fut aussi celle de la brève présence d'une structure en parapluie signée Zaha Hadid...
HUO *Lilas* était une installation temporaire qui tirait son inspiration de géométries naturelles complexes tels les pétales de fleurs. Elle fut érigée en un laps de temps relativement court et l'on pourrait imaginer que des structures de ce type s'implantent un peu partout, dans n'importe quelle ville du monde.

En 2007, vous receviez donc un artiste qui veut être un architecte (Eliasson) et l'année suivante, un architecte qui veut être un artiste (Gehry). Frank Gehry n'a-t-il pas d'ailleurs créé pour vous une sculpture en 2008 ?
JP-J Ce projet m'a paru très lié à celui de la maison qu'il s'était construite à Santa Monica à la fin des années 1970 ainsi qu'à une autre, toujours pour lui, sur laquelle il travaillait au même moment que le pavillon. Il s'est impliqué à 100 % dans ce projet. C'était une sorte d'arche, de lieu pour performances. L'acoustique était très bonne. Une partie du concept était que Thomas Adès devait y jouer. Ce fut une soirée extraordinaire. Il était intéressant de voir le rapport d'échelle entre le pavillon de Gehry et le bâtiment de la Serpentine, et la façon dont il encadrait celui-ci à partir de la route. C'était un espace pour performances, un élément très important pour tous nos pavillons.

22 - Christian Boltanski, *Les archives du coeur (The Heart Archive)*. Installation view, 10 July–8 August 2010.

Christian Boltanski, *Les archives du coeur (Archiv des Herzens)*. Installationsansicht, 10. Juli–8. August 2010.

Christian Boltanski, *Les archives du cœur*. Vue de l'installation, 10 juillet–8 août 2010.

JP-J What Jean Nouvel did was to look at the Serpentine building in three parts. He took it as the model for his design. That mirroring is his interpretation of the Serpentine. It is a matter of volumes in the Pavilion that relate to the volumes of the Serpentine building but this relationship may not be obvious for the casual visitor. Jean Nouvel focused on the park. Yet there are elements of the design that lead the visitor to the Serpentine. The tilted, sweeping wall was a beacon within the park that drew people to the Serpentine.

The SANAA Pavilion resembled a reflective cloud or a floating pool of water, sitting atop a series of delicate columns. The undulating aluminum roof moved in and out of existing trees, giving the building an ethereal quality. Nouvel's Pavilion was rendered in a vivid red that made it visually dominant in the landscape and, you could say, achieved an opposite effect to the SANAA Pavilion. Nouvel's structure is remarkably flexible, however, and it opened out onto the park and the activities that happen there. There were spaces for outdoor enjoyment: table-tennis tables, draughts, chess, Frisbees, and kites. Its emphasis on play drew a link with Cedric Price's unrealized Fun Palace, an interdisciplinary space conceived of as a "laboratory of fun."

Might not one say in a sense that the Jean Nouvel Pavilion rejected the Serpentine rather than embracing it as did SANAA?

JP-J We do ask the architects to consider the existing building. When you work with artists you're not prescriptive. We've chosen, in the same way, to give the architects a brief that's open rather than restrictive. There is a mention of the building but it is very light. If they obscure the Serpentine, we might test them on their reasons for this, but in the end, it's their design. The Serpentine Pavilions are the fruit of an unparalleled freedom, which is a very unique situation.

HUO Jean Nouvel made us look at the context—the green grass, which he refers to with his choice of red. These Pavilions are in a very open situation: they can

auftragen, einen Soundtrack für den Bau zu schreiben oder eine Klanginstallation zu realisieren.

Werden die Pavillons nach ihrem Einsatz in Kensington Gardens nicht oft verkauft?
JP-J Der Verkauf der Pavillons ist ein entscheidender Aspekt unseres Konzepts und erlaubt uns, bis zu 40 Prozent des Budgets zu bestreiten. Aber auch im Sinne des kulturellen Erbes werden die Pavillons auf diese Weise geplant. Der Pavillon von Toyo Ito etwa wurde am Kraftwerk Battersea wieder aufgestellt un dann wie die von Frank Gehry und Jean Nouvel nach Südfrankreich umgesiedelt. Diese Pavillons haben, ebenso wie alle anderen, eine lange Lebensdauer.

Die Pavillons von 2009 und 2010 sind konzeptionell fast gegensätzlich. Der Bau von SANAA 2009 war geradezu flüchtig und stellte eine klare Verbindung zwischen Park und Serpentine Gallery her. Im Gegensatz dazu scheint der Bau von Jean Nouvel 2010 eine fast unabhängige Existenz zu führen.
JP-J Jean Nouvel hat das Gebäude der Serpentine als in drei Teile gegliedert aufgefasst. Das war das Grundmodell für seinen Entwurf. Es ist eine Frage der Volumina des Pavillons, die Bezug auf die Volumina der Serpentine nehmen, auch wenn diese Wechselbeziehung für den flüchtigen Betrachter vielleicht nicht unmittelbar zu erkennen ist. Jean Nouvel konzentrierte sich auf den Park. Dennoch gab es Elemente im Entwurf, die den Besucher zur Serpentine hinführten wie zum Beispiel die schiefe, ausgreifende Wand, die wie ein Leuchtfeuer im Park wirkte. Der Pavillon von SANAA hingegen erschien als eine spiegelnde Wolke oder ein fließendes Wasserbecken, das auf einer Reihe filigraner Stützen ruhte. Das gewellte Aluminiumdach schwang sich zwischen den Bäumen hindurch und verlieh der Konstruktion etwas Ätherisches. Nouvels Pavillon war leuchtend Rot, was ihn zum dominanten Element innerhalb der Landschaft werden ließ. Er hatte, so könnte man sagen, den entgegengesetzten Effekt des SANAA-Pavillons. Trotzdem war Nouvels Bau erstaunlich flexibel,

En un sens, vous intégrez les pavillons dans une conception plus large de l'art en tant que performance...
HUO Cela dépend non seulement de l'architecture mais aussi de la façon dont nous et le public jouons avec elle. En été, le parc se découvre une sensibilité très démocratique. Pour Frank Gehry en 2008, intégrer le temps et le son dans son pavillon était essentiel. Dans le futur, nous aimerions qu'un compositeur nous propose une bande son ou un paysage sonore.

Les pavillons sont souvent vendus après leur brève existence dans les jardins de Kensington, n'est-ce-pas?
JP-J La vente des pavillons fait partie de notre politique et nous permet de couvrir jusqu'à 40 % du budget. Ils sont conçus pour être déplacés, ne serait-ce que pour des raisons juridiques. Le pavillon de Toyo Ito, par exemple, a été remonté pour un temps près de la Battersea Power Station et après, comme ceux de Frank Gehry et de Jean Nouvel réinstallé dans le sud de la France. Ces pavillons, et tous les autres, ont en fait une longue durée de vie.

Les pavillons de 2009 et 2010 semblent assez opposés dans leur conception. Celui de 2009, par SANAA, était presque éthéré et faisait un lien aisé entre le parc et la Serpentine Gallery. Celui de Jean Nouvel en 2010, au contraire, semble mener une existence séparée.
JP-J Ce qu'a fait Jean Nouvel est de considérer le bâtiment de la Serpentine comme composé de trois parties. Il en a fait le modèle de son projet. Ce reflet est donc son interprétation de la Serpentine. Les volumes du pavillon sont en relation avec ceux du bâtiment de la Serpentine, mais dans une relation qui n'est peut-être pas évidente pour le visiteur non informé. Jean Nouvel s'est concentré sur le parc, mais on trouve néanmoins des éléments qui conduisent le visiteur vers la Serpentine. Le grand mur incliné, par exemple, joue un rôle de signal dans le parc, mais il attire les gens vers la Serpentine.

23   24

be approached from the park, from the road, or even seen from above. The SANAA Pavilion made a single continuity of the park and the gallery. Each year it's different, but each of these architects has succeeded in creating a destination, where most of the year there is only a modest lawn.

What can you say about your future plans for the Pavilions?

JP-J The urgency to exhibit contemporary architecture will remain. Soundscapes are a possibility for future Pavilions, as are more collaborations. But it is always led by the people we work with. The solution is likely to be more in the hands of the architects we commission than our own. It certainly doesn't feel as though the Pavilions have completed their run. There are still many opportunities to present great structures by architects at the Serpentine. We have invited Peter Zumthor to design the Pavilion for 2011 and, from our early meetings, his thinking indicates that his Pavilion will develop the series in further new and interesting ways.

The Summer Pavilions have clearly allowed you to broaden the horizon of the Serpentine.

JP-J There is something about the plurality of programs that we undertake in the summer; we blossom like the park does. In 2010, we had Jean Nouvel's Pavilion on the lawn, Christian Boltanski's project *Les archives du coeur* [The Heart Archive] installed at the entrance to the gallery, and inside the building, a solo show by Wolfgang Tillmans. Then there were the *Park Nights* events and an educational program that included a series of Family Sundays where children were invited to join artists and designers to creatively respond to the architecture of the Pavilion. Out in the park, we worked with The Royal Parks to realize *Turning the World Upside Down*, a major exhibition of sculptures by Anish Kapoor. For an institution of our size, that's quite remarkable. Following on from this, The Royal Parks has awarded a license to the Serpentine Gallery to establish a new

öffnete sich zum Park und den Aktivitäten, die sich dort abspielen. Es gab Tischtennisplatten, Dame und Schach, Frisbees und Drachen. Diese Betonung des Spielerischen ist eine Verbindung zu Cedric Price' nicht realisiertem *Fun Palace,* einem interdisziplinärem Raum, der als „Spaßlabor" konzipiert wurde.

Könnte man sagen, dass Jean Nouvel sich eher von der Serpentine distanzierte, als sich wie SANAA auf sie einzulassen?

JP-J Wir bitten die Architekten sehr wohl darum, den bestehenden Bau zu berücksichtigen. Wenn man mit Künstlern arbeitet, macht man keine Vorschriften. Deshalb haben wir uns auch entschieden, den Architekten eine Auftragsbeschreibung zu geben, die eher offen als restriktiv ist. Das Gebäude wird zwar erwähnt, doch ist dieser Hinweis eher zurückhaltend. Verunklaren die Architekten die Serpentine, sprechen wir sie vielleicht auf ihre Gründe an, aber letztendlich ist es ihr Entwurf. Die Serpentine-Pavillons sind das Ergebnis einer beispiellosen Freiheit, was eine ganz einzigartige Situation ist.

HUO Jean Nouvel lenkte unseren Blick auf den Kontext – auf das grüne Gras, auf das er mit seiner Wahl der Farbe Rot Bezug nimmt. Die Pavillons liegen in einem sehr offenen Umfeld, man kann sich ihnen vom Park her nähern, von der Straße her, sie sogar von oben sehen. Der Pavillon von SANAA verband den Park und die Galerie zu einem einzigen Kontinuum. Jedes Jahr ist es anders, doch allen Architekten ist es gelungen, dort einen Anziehungspunkt zu schaffen, wo sonst nur eine bescheidene Rasenfläche ist.

Was können Sie über Ihre zukünftigen Pläne für die Sommerpavillons sagen?

JP-J Die Dringlichkeit, zeitgenössische Architektur auszustellen, bleibt bestehen. Klanginstallationen sind eine Option für künftige Pavillons, ebenso wie weitere Kooperationen. Doch letztendlich wird das alles von den Personen angestoßen, mit denen wir arbeiten. Die Lösung liegt eher in den Händen der Architekten, die wir beauftragen. Es gibt nach wie vor viele Möglichkeiten, großartige Bauten von Architek-

Le pavillon de SANAA faisait penser à un nuage réfléchissant ou à une flaque d'eau en suspension, reposant sur une succession de colonnes délicates. Cette toiture ondulante en aluminium s'étirait entre les arbres existants, conférant au pavillon un aspect éthéré. Celui de Nouvel était traité dans un rouge vif qui assurait sa domination visuelle dans le paysage, aboutissant à un effet opposé à celui de SANAA. Le projet Nouvel était néanmoins remarquablement souple et s'ouvrait sur le parc et les activités prévues. On y trouvait des endroits pour s'amuser en plein air comme des tables de ping pong, de jeux de dames, d'échecs, des frisbees, des cerfs-volant. Cet accent mis sur le jeu rappelait le Fun Palace non réalisé de Cedric Price, un espace interdisciplinaire qui aurait été un « laboratoire du jeu ».

Ne pourrait-on dire en un sens que le pavillon de Jean Nouvel rejetait la Serpentine Gallery plutôt qu'il ne l'intégrait comme l'avait fait SANAA ?

JP-J Nous demandons aux architectes de prendre en compte le bâtiment existant. Lorsque vous travaillez avec des artistes, vous ne pouvez être trop prescriptif. Nous mentionnons la présence du bâtiment, mais de façon sommaire. De même, nous avons choisi de donner aux architectes un brief plus ouvert que restrictif. S'ils masquent la Serpentine, nous pouvons leur en demander les raisons, mais au final c'est leur projet. Les pavillons de la Serpentine sont le fruit d'une liberté sans équivalent, ce qui est une situation unique.

HUO Jean Nouvel nous faisait voir le contexte – l'herbe verte – à laquelle il se référait par le choix de la couleur rouge. Les pavillons se trouvent dans une situation très ouverte, on peut les approcher du parc, de la route, et même du ciel. Le pavillon SANAA créait une continuité entre la galerie et le parc. À chaque fois, l'approche est différente, mais chacun des architectes a réussi à créer un lieu où l'on a envie d'aller, là où ne s'étend le reste de l'année qu'une modeste pelouse.

Que pouvez-vous dire de vos futurs projets pour ces pavillons d'été ?

gallery in the Magazine building in Kensington Gardens, which will be called the Serpentine Sackler Gallery. It's an exciting opportunity to bring this unique listed building back into public use. In light of the history of the Pavilions, choosing which architect to work with on the renovation of the Magazine building was relatively easy. Zaha Hadid will carry out the restoration of the building and design an adjoining pavilion to be used as a social space and restaurant. It is wonderfully exciting to be undertaking this renovation with the architect of our first Pavilion and it seems fitting to bring the Serpentine's engagement with architecture full circle in this way.

ten an der Serpentine zu präsentieren. Wir haben Peter Zumthor eingeladen, den Pavillon für 2011 zu entwerfen. Schon bei unseren ersten Treffen mit ihm zeigten seine Ideen, dass sein Pavillon die Reihe auf neue und interessante Weise fortschreiben wird.

Die Sommerpavillons haben Ihnen ganz offensichtlich erlaubt, den Horizont der Serpentine zu erweitern.

JP-J Die Vielfalt der Programme, die wir im Sommer veranstalten, ist etwas Besonderes – wir blühen auf, genau wie der Park. 2010 hatten wir Jean Nouvels Pavillon auf dem Rasen, Christian Boltanskis Projekt *Les Archives du Coeur (Die Archive des Herzens)* am Eingang zur Galerie und im Gebäude selbst eine Einzelausstellung von Wolfgang Tillmans. Dann waren da noch die Veranstaltungen der *Park Nights* und ein Bildungsprogramm, zu dem auch Familiensonntage gehörten, an denen Kinder eingeladen waren, gemeinsam mit Künstlern und Designern kreativ auf die Architektur des Pavillons zu reagieren. Draußen im Park hatten wir in Zusammenarbeit mit der königlichen Parkverwaltung *Turning the World Upside Down* realisiert, eine große Ausstellung mit Skulpturen von Anish Kapoor. Für eine Institution unserer Größe ist das bemerkenswert. Danach hat die Parkverwaltung der Serpentine Gallery die Eröffnung einer neuen Galerie im Magazin von Kensington Gardens erlaubt: die Serpentine Sackler Gallery. Es ist eine großartige Gelegenheit, dieses einzigartige denkmalgeschützte Gebäude der Öffentlichkeit wieder zugänglich zu machen. Mit Blick auf die Geschichte der Pavillons war es einfach, einen Architekten auszuwählen, der die Sanierung des Magazins übernehmen würde. Die Restaurierung des Gebäudes und der Entwurf eines Pavillonanbaus, der als Treffpunkt und Restaurant genutzt werden soll, liegt in den Händen von Zaha Hadid. Es ist wunderbar aufregend, diese Sanierung mit derselben Architektin in Angriff zu nehmen, die unseren ersten Pavillon entworfen hat. Es scheint nur passend, dass sich der Kreis angesichts des Engagements der Serpentine Gallery für die Architektur auf diese Weise wieder schließt.

JP-J L'urgence d'exposer l'architecture contemporaine demeurera. Les paysages sonores sont un des thèmes possibles pour de futurs pavillons, de même que les collaborations. La solution est probablement davantage entre les mains des architectes qu'entre les nôtres. Nous n'avons certainement pas l'impression que l'expérience de ces pavillons soit en fin de course. Il existe encore tant de possibilités de présenter de grands projets de grands architectes ! Nous avons invité Peter Zumthor à concevoir le Pavillon 2011 et, si j'en crois nos premières réunions, sa réflexion va dans des directions nouvelles et intéressantes.

Les pavillons d'été vous ont certainement permis d'élargir les horizons de la Serpentine...

JP-J La pluralité des programmes que nous proposons chaque été est en effet intéressante. Comme le parc, chaque été nous refleurissons. En 2010, nous avons eu le pavillon de Jean Nouvel sur la pelouse, le projet de Christian Boltanski *Les Archives du cœur*, à l'entrée de la galerie et, à l'intérieur, une exposition personnelle de Wolfgang Tillmans. Puis se sont déroulées les *Park Nights* et un programme éducatif comprenant une série de dimanches familiaux où l'on invitait les enfants à rencontrer des artistes et des designers pour réagir avec créativité à l'architecture du pavillon. Plus loin dans le parc, nous avons collaboré avec The Royal Parks pour réaliser « Turning the World Upside Down », une grande exposition de sculptures d'Anish Kapoor. Pour une institution de notre taille, c'est assez remarquable. À partir de cette expérience, The Royal Parks nous ont accordé l'autorisation de créer une nouvelle galerie dans le bâtiment « The Magazine » situé dans les Kensington Gardens qui s'appellera la Serpentine Stackler Gallery. C'est une opportunité passionnante de rendre ce bâtiment classé à une utilisation publique. Zaha Hadid sera chargée de la restauration des lieux et concevra un pavillon adjacent pour un restaurant et un lieu de réception. Nous nous réjouissons d'entreprendre cette rénovation avec l'architecte de notre premier pavillon, en une sorte de retour aux sources de l'engagement de la Serpentine en faveur de l'architecture.

Postscript

Following this interview, the Serpentine Gallery confirmed that Pritzker Prize–winning architect Peter Zumthor had been invited to design the Serpentine Gallery Pavilion in 2011. Also in 2010, the Serpentine Gallery commissioned Zaha Hadid to undertake the renovations of its new public gallery, the Serpentine Sackler Gallery, which will be housed in the Magazine building in Kensington Gardens. Plans include an adjoining pavilion to be used as a social space and restaurant, creating a permanent architectural landmark in the heart of London. Commissioning new work will be at the heart of the Serpentine Sackler Gallery's programs, including an annual large-scale light installation inside the building and an outdoor playscape for children, encouraging families and adults of all ages to explore explore art through creative play. The Serpentine Sackler Gallery is due to open in time for the London 2012 Olympic and Paralympic Games.

Postskriptum

Nach diesem Interview bestätigte die Serpentine Gallery, man habe den Pritzker-Preisträger Peter Zumthor eingeladen, den Serpentine-Pavillon für 2011 zu entwerfen. Außerdem beauftragte die Galerie Zaha Hadid mit der Sanierung der neuen Räumlichkeiten für die Serpentine Sackler Gallery. Die Planungen sehen unter anderem einen Nebenpavillon vor, der für gesellschaftliche Events und als Restaurant genutzt werden soll. Im Mittelpunkt der neuen Serpentine Sackler Gallery werden Auftragswerke stehen, darunter jährlich stattfindende Lichtinstallationen in den Galerieräumen sowie Spiellandschaften im Außenraum, in denen Familien mit Kindern und Erwachsene jeden Alters die Kunst durch spielerische Kreativität entdecken können. Die Eröffnung der Serpentine Sackler Gallery ist rechtzeitig zu den Olympischen und den Paralympischen Spielen 2012 in London geplant.

Postcriptum

À la suite de cet entretien, la Serpentine Gallery a confirmé que l'architecte Peter Zumthor, prix Pritzker 2009, avait été invité à concevoir le Pavillon 2011 de la Serpentine. La Serpentine Gallery a par ailleurs demandé à Zaha Hadid de rénover sa nouvelle galerie, la Serpentine Sackler Gallery, occupant le bâtiment appelé The Magazine dans les jardins de Kensington. Ses plans comprennent un pavillon adjacent qui servira d'espace de réception et de restaurant, nouveau monument architectural permanent au cœur de Londres. La commande d'œuvres nouvelles sera au centre des programmes de la Serpentine Sackler Gallery, qui prévoient entre autres une installation lumineuse annuelle de grandes dimensions à l'intérieur du bâtiment et un « paysage de jeux » à l'extérieur, destiné aux enfants. Les familles et les adultes de tous âges pourront ainsi découvrir et explorer l'art de manière créative. La Serpentine Sackler Gallery devrait ouvrir ses portes pour les Jeux olympiques et paralympiques qui se dérouleront à Londres en 2012.

[1] John Miller had also been responsible for the renovation of the Whitechapel Art Gallery (1985), and the 20th-Century Galleries, National Portrait Gallery (1994), both in London, UK.
[2] In the grounds of the Gallery is a permanent work by artist and poet Ian Hamilton Finlay, dedicated to the Serpentine's former patron Diana, Princess of Wales. The work comprises eight benches, a tree-plaque, and a carved stone circle at the Gallery's entrance.

[1] John Miller zeichnete außerdem verantwortlich für die Renovierung der Whitechapel Art Gallery (1985) und die Galerien des 20. Jahrhunderts in der National Portrait Gallery (1994), beide in London, Großbritannien.
[2] Auf dem Gelände der Galerie befindet sich eine fest installierte Arbeit des Künstlers und Dichters Ian Hamilton Finlay für Diana, Prinzessin von Wales, die ehemalige Schirmherrin der Serpentine Gallery. Die Arbeit besteht aus acht Bänken, einer Baumplakette und einem gemeißelten Steinkreis am Eingang der Galerie.

[1] John Miller a également été chargé de la rénovation de la Whitechapel Art Gallery (1985) et des 20th-Century Galleries de la National Portrait Gallery, toutes deux à Londres.
[2] On trouve non loin de la galerie une œuvre de l'artiste et poète Ian Hamilton Finlay, dédiée à Diana, princesse de Galles. L'œuvre se compose de huit bancs, une plaque sur un arbre et un cercle de pierres sculptées à l'entrée de la galerie.

ZAHA HADID

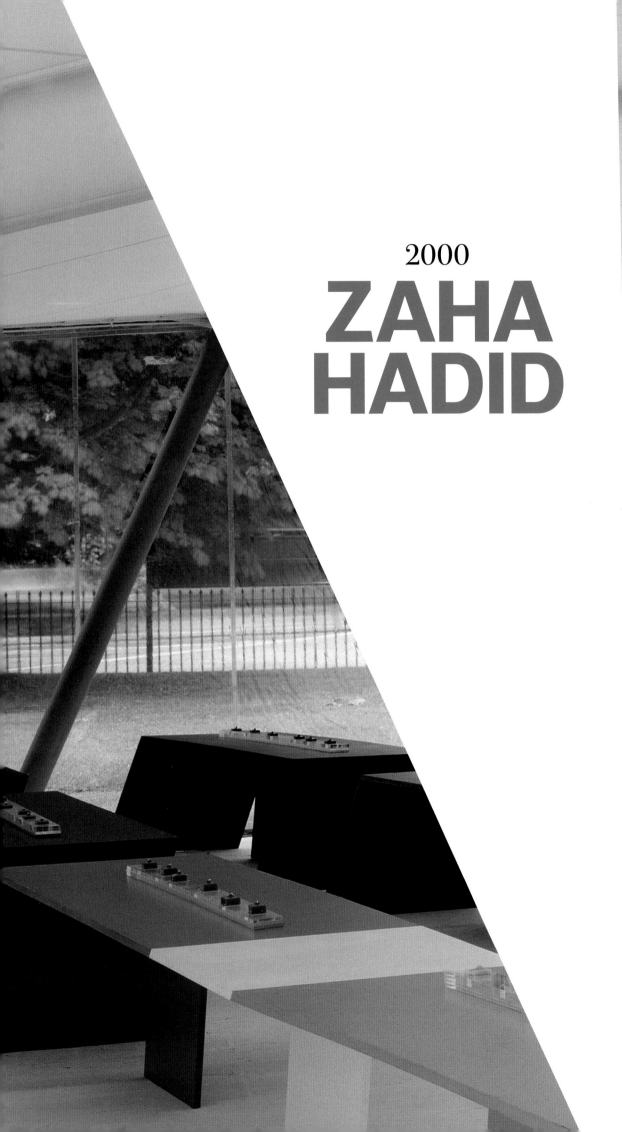

2000

ZAHA
HADID

The first of the Serpentine Summer Pavilions set the trend. Zaha Hadid had surely created a substantial reputation for her work, but had not yet built in the UK. She was a trustee of the Serpentine as well, so it was quite natural to ask her to create a "temporary sculptural structure" for the Gallery's 30th Anniversary Gala Dinner on 20 June 2000. Even today, the descriptions of the event held in the Gallery say that the structure was only meant to stand until June 22 and to open to the public during the single afternoon of June 22. In fact, it stayed open all summer, setting the duration and nature of pavilions to come. Further, the press release of the Serpentine suggested that this was not the first, but the third temporary architectural event they had sponsored, since Ron Arad and Seth Stein had already created ephemeral works on site. Measuring 600 square meters in floor area, the pavilion with its triangulated roof and steel structure was planar and angular. Lighting set between two layers of roof fabric and the black-and-white furniture designed by the architect contributed to its dynamic and unusual appearance. Since the Serpentine had been making use of more traditional marquee structures at a time when *Vanity Fair* sponsored the gallery, it was incumbent on Zaha Hadid to "reinvent the accepted idea of a tent or marquee." Although she subsequently returned to a space nearby with her 2007 installation *Lilas*, the Baghdad-born architect showed the rapidity of her design capacities with her first pavilion. Despite a budget that provided the means for merely the design of an improved tent, Hadid made a considerable impression in London. The idea of a summer event space, created in a very short span of time and intended to last only three months, was very much the product of Zaha Hadid's first success at the Serpentine in June 2000.

Der erste Serpentine-Sommerpavillon war richtungsweisend. Zaha Hadid hatte sich fraglos einen Ruf für ihr Werk erworben, jedoch immer noch nicht in Großbritannien gebaut. Außerdem war sie Mitglied im Verwaltungsrat der Serpentine Gallery, sodass es nahe lag, sie zu bitten, eine „temporäre, skulpturale Konstruktion" für das Galadiner zum 30. Jahrestag der Galerie am 20. Juni 2000 zu entwerfen. Der Bau sollte eigentlich nur bis zum 22. Juni stehen. Letztendlich blieb er den ganzen Sommer über geöffnet und definierte damit Dauer und Art der später folgenden Pavillons. Darüber hinaus hieß es in der Presseerklärung der Serpentine, dies sei nicht das erste, sondern vielmehr das dritte Architekturevent der Galerie, denn schon Ron Arad und Seth Stein hatten hier temporäre Arbeiten realisiert. Der Pavillon mit seiner Grundfläche von 600 m², seinem aus Dreiecksformen konzipierten Dach und seiner Stahlkonstruktion war flächig und kantig zugleich. Seine Dynamik und ungewöhnliche Erscheinung gewann zusätzlich durch die Beleuchtung, die zwischen den zwei Schichten des textilen Dachs integriert war, sowie durch das schwarzweiße Mobiliar. Weil die Serpentine eher traditionelle Markisen genutzt hatte, als noch *Vanity Fair* die Galerie sponserte, war es Zaha Hadids Aufgabe, „konventionelle Vorstellungen von einem Zelt bzw. einer Markise neu zu definieren". Trotz eines Budgets, das im Grunde nur die Gestaltung eines besseren Festzelts erlaubt hätte, hinterließ Zaha Hadid mit ihrem Pavillon in London einen beachtlichen Eindruck. Das Konzept eines Veranstaltungsorts für den Sommer, der in kürzester Zeit geplant und nur drei Monate lang genutzt wird, ist maßgeblich jenem ersten Erfolg zu verdanken, den Zaha Hadid an der Serpentine Gallery im Jahr 2000 verbuchen konnte.

Ce premier pavillon d'été de la Serpentine allait lancer le mouvement. Si Zaha Hadid jouissait déjà d'une réputation établie, elle n'avait encore jamais construit au Royaume-Uni. Comme elle faisait partie du conseil d'administration de la Serpentine Gallery, il parut naturel de lui demander de concevoir « une structure sculpturale temporaire » pour le dîner de gala du 30ᵉ anniversaire de la galerie qui devait se dérouler le 20 juin 2000. Encore aujourd'hui, les descriptifs de cet événement indiquent que cette structure n'était prévue que pour durer jusqu'au 22 juin. En fait, elle est restée ouverte tout l'été, ce qui annonçait ce que serait la fonction et la durée d'existence des pavillons à venir. Par ailleurs, le communiqué de presse de la Serpentine précisait que ce n'était pas le premier mais le troisième événement architectural temporaire initié par la galerie, puisque Ron Arad et Seth Stein avaient déjà monté des œuvres éphémères sur le même site. De 600 mètres carrés au sol, ce pavillon à ossature en acier et toit triangulé était de forme planaire et anguleuse. Le système d'éclairage disposé entre les deux épaisseurs de toile de la couverture ainsi que le mobilier noir et blanc conçu par l'architecte contribuaient à lui donner un aspect dynamique surprenant. La Serpentine avait déjà mis en place des tentes plus traditionnelles lorsque le magazine *Vanity Fair* était son sponsor, mais il revenait à Zaha Hadid de « réinventer l'idée reçue de tente ou de marquise ». Elle avait montré sa réactivité conceptuelle et fait une impression considérable à Londres, alors que son budget était à peine celui d'une marquise améliorée. L'idée d'un espace événementiel estival, créé en un court laps de temps et destiné à ne durer que trois mois, doit sans doute beaucoup à ce premier succès de Zaha Hadid sur la pelouse de la Serpentine en juin 2000.

The light, folded forms of the structure, with its roof coming down to touch the lawn of the Serpentine, was the first of the Summer Pavilions.

Leichte, gefaltete Formen mit einem Dach, das bis auf den Rasen der Serpentine heruntergezogen war, prägten den ersten Sommerpavillon.

Premier des pavillons de la Serpentine, dans l'ordre chronologique, cette structure signée Zaha Hadid se composait de plans pliés. Sa « toiture » descendait jusqu'à la pelouse.

2000 **ZAHA HADID**

Zaha Hadid Architects
Studio 9
10 Bowling Green Lane
London EC1R OBQ
UK

Tel: +44 20 72 53 51 47
Fax: +44 20 72 51 83 22
E-mail: press@zaha-hadid.com
Web: www.zaha-hadid.com

Zaha Hadid studied architecture at the Architectural Association (AA) in London beginning in 1972 and was awarded the Diploma Prize in 1977. She then became a partner of Rem Koolhaas at OMA and taught at the AA. She has also taught at Harvard, the University of Chicago, in Hamburg, and at Columbia University in New York. She completed the Vitra Fire Station (Weil am Rhein, Germany, 1990–94), and exhibition designs such as that for *The Great Utopia* (Solomon R. Guggenheim Museum, New York, USA, 1992). More recently, Zaha Hadid entered a phase of active construction with such projects as the Lois & Richard Rosenthal Center for Contemporary Art (Cincinnati, Ohio, USA, 1999–2003), which was, surprisingly, the first art museum to be designed by a woman in the United States. She followed up with the Phaeno Science Center (Wolfsburg, Germany, 2001–05); the Central Building of the new BMW Assembly Plant in Leipzig (Germany, 2005); Ordrupgaard Museum Extension (Copenhagen, Denmark, 2001–05); the Mobile Art, Chanel Contemporary Art Container (various locations, 2007–); and the MAXXI, the National Museum of 21st Century Arts (Rome, Italy, 1998–2009). Her most recent projects include the Guangzhou Opera House (Guangzhou, China, 2006–10); the Sheik Zayed Bridge (Abu Dhabi, UAE, 2005–12); and the Aquatics Center for the 2012 Olympic Games in London (UK). In 2004, Zaha Hadid became the first woman to win the coveted Pritzker Prize.

Zaha Hadid studierte ab 1972 an der Architectural Association (AA) in London und erhielt 1977 den Diploma Prize. Anschließend wurde sie Partnerin von Rem Koolhaas bei OMA und unterrichtete an der AA. Darüber hinaus lehrte sie in Harvard, an der Universität von Chicago, in Hamburg sowie an der Columbia University in New York. Sie realisierte unter anderem eine Feuerwache für Vitra (Weil am Rhein, Deutschland, 1990–94) und Ausstellungsarchitekturen wie *The Great Utopia* (Solomon R. Guggenheim Museum, New York, 1992). In jüngerer Zeit begann für Hadid eine Phase des aktiven Bauens, etwa mit dem Lois & Richard Rosenthal Center for Contemporary Art (Cincinnati, Ohio, 1999–2003), erstaunlicherweise das erste Kunstmuseum in den USA, das von einer Frau entworfen wurde. Weiterhin folgten das Phaeno Wissenschaftszentrum (Wolfsburg, 2001–05), das Zentralgebäude des neuen BMW-Werks in Leipzig (2005), der Anbau für das Museum Ordrupgaard (Kopenhagen, 2001–05), der Mobile Art Chanel Contemporary Art Container (verschiedene Standorte, seit 2007) sowie das MAXXI Nationalmuseum für Kunst des 21. Jahrhunderts (Rom, 1998–2009). Ihre jüngsten Projekte sind unter anderem das Opernhaus in Guangzhou (China, 2006–10) sowie die Scheich-Zajed-Brücke (Abu Dhabi, VAE, 2005–12) und das Aquatics Center für die Olympischen Spiele 2012 in London. 2004 erhielt Zaha Hadid als erste Frau den begehrten Pritzker-Preis.

Zaha Hadid a fait ses études à l'Architectural Association (AA) de Londres de 1972 à 1977, date à laquelle elle a reçu le prix du Diplôme. Elle est ensuite devenue partenaire de Rem Koolhaas/OMA et a enseigné à l'AA ainsi qu'à l'université Harvard, à l'université de Chicago, à Hambourg et à l'université Columbia à New York. En 2004, elle a été la première femme à remporter le prix Pritzker. Parmi ses réalisations: un poste d'incendie pour Vitra (Weil am Rhein, Allemagne, 1990–94), et des mises en espace d'expositions comme « The Great Utopia » au Solomon R. Guggenheim Museum (New York, 1992). Plus récemment, elle est entrée dans une phase active autour d'importants chantiers dont le Lois & Richard Rosenthal Center for Contemporary Art (Cincinnati, Ohio, 1999–2003) qui, étonnamment, a été le premier musée construit par une femme aux États-Unis. Ont suivi le Centre des sciences Phaeno (Wolfsburg, Allemagne, 2001–05); le bâtiment central de la nouvelle usine BMW de Leipzig (2005); l'extension du musée Ordrupgaard (Copenhague, 2001–05); le pavillon Mobile Art, Chanel Contemporary Art Container (divers lieux, 2007–); le Musée national des arts du XXIᵉ siècle (MAXXI, Rome, 1998–2009). Parmi ses projets récents figurent l'Opéra de Guangzhou (Chine, 2006–10); le pont Cheikh Zayed (Abou Dhabi, EAU, 2005–12) et l'Aquatics Center prévu pour les Jeux olympiques de Londres 2012.

"Briefly brilliant..."
THE GUARDIAN

The interior, with furniture also designed by Zaha Hadid, was directly related to the airy forms of the roof of the pavilion.

Der Innenraum mit seinem ebenfalls von Zaha Hadid gestalteten Mobiliar hat eine unmittelbare Verwandtschaft zum Dach des Pavillons.

Le mobilier intérieur avait été dessiné par Zaha Hadid, dans l'esprit des formes aériennes de la toiture du pavillon.

2007 **ZAHA HADID**

Lilas, a tensile fabric installation, was accompanied by lighting guided up to the fabric surfaces along very thin seams radiating "about the parasols…like the veining of flowers."

Lilas, eine textile Spannkonstruktion, wurde durch Licht ergänzt, das den Textilflächen entlang filigraner Nähte folgte, die strahlenförmig „wie die Adern einer Blüte … über die Schirme" liefen.

Lilas, installation en tissu extensible, était mise en valeur par un éclairage suivant les plans et les fines coutures du tissu irradiant « sur les parasols… comme les veinures d'un pétale de fleur ».

Erected for the Serpentine Gallery's Summer Party, this installation consisted of essentially three identical fabric structure parasols. Freestanding on a 310-square-meter platform and accessible from all sides, the 5.5-meter-high structures were arrayed around a central point. As Hadid explained, "Each parasol develops sculpturally from a small articulated base to a large cantilevered diamond shape. Taking inspiration from complex natural geometries such as flower petals and leaves, the three parasols overlap to create the pavilion's main conceptual feature: complex symmetry, interweaving all the while without touching, allowing air, light, and sound to travel through narrow gaps in a state that is both open and likewise tending toward closure." Continuous lighting around the base of each parasol "reveals the geometric intricacy of the pavilion and highlights the overall architectural form in calligraphic arcs." Displaying an obvious connection to Hadid's architecture and design work, the *Lilas* installation generated flowing, continuous space, punctuated by the parasol elements, whose connection to the natural setting was sublimated to create sculptural objects. Zaha Hadid had already designed a summer pavilion for the Serpentine in 2000, but in this instance she agreed to intervene at the last minute when it became apparent that the 2007 pavilion, a design by Olafur Eliasson and Snøhetta's lead architect Kjetil Thorsen, would not be completed on schedule.

Die für die Sommerparty errichtete Installation bestand im Kern aus drei identischen Schirmen aus Textilmaterial. Die drei frei stehenden, 5,5 m hohen Schirme waren um einen zentralen Punkt auf einem von allen Seiten zugänglichen Podest mit einer Gesamtfläche von 310 m² angeordnet. Hadid erklärte: „Jeder Schirm entwickelt sich skulptural von einer kleinflächigen, gegliederten Basis zu einer großflächigen, auskragenden Diamantform. Inspiriert von komplexen natürlichen Geometrien wie Blütenblättern, überschneiden sich die drei Schirme und erzeugen so das konzeptuelle Hauptmerkmal des Pavillons: komplexe Symmetrie und Überschneidung ohne Berührung. So können Luft, Licht und Klang durch die schmalen Zwischenräume dringen; es entsteht ein offener Zustand, der zugleich nach Geschlossenheit strebt." Kontinuierliche Lichtbänder an der Basis der Schirme „betonen die architektonische Gesamtform in kalligrafischen Bögen". *Lilas,* eine Installation, die offenkundig an Hadids architektonische und Designentwürfe anknüpft, erzeugte einen fließenden Raum, der von den Schirmelementen punktuell durchbrochen wurde. Die Verwandtschaft der Schirme mit ihrem natürlichen Umfeld wurde sublimiert, um skulpturale Objekte zu schaffen. Hadid hatte bereits 2000 einen Sommerpavillon für die Serpentine gestaltet, erklärte sich jedoch in letzter Minute bereit einzuspringen, als deutlich wurdc, dass der Pavillon 2007 von Olafur Eliasson und Kjetil Thorsen nicht rechtzeitig fertig würde.

Mise en place pour la réception d'été de la Serpentine Gallery, cette installation se composait pour l'essentiel de trois parasols identiques en toile tendue. Ces structures de 5,5 mètres de haut s'élevaient du centre d'une plate-forme de 310 mètres carrés accessible de tous côtés. « Chaque parasol se développe à la manière d'une sculpture, partant d'une petite base articulée pour constituer un grand auvent en porte-à-faux dont la forme rappelle celle d'un diamant. Inspirés de constructions géométriques naturelles complexes, comme celles des feuilles ou des pétales de fleurs, ces trois éléments se chevauchent pour matérialiser le propos conceptuel principal du pavillon : complexité, symétrie, imbrication sans contact permettant à l'air, à la lumière et au son de se glisser à travers d'étroits passages, l'ensemble dans un état à la fois ouvert et tendant vers la fermeture. » Un éclairage continu installé à la base de chaque parasol « souligne l'imbrication géométrique du pavillon et met en valeur la forme architecturale d'ensemble qui décrit des arcs calligraphiques ». *Lilas,* Fortement liée aux travaux d'architecture et de dessin d'Hadid, l'installation *Lilas* donnait ainsi naissance à un flux d'espace continu, cadré par ces éléments en parasol dont le lien avec l'environnement naturel se voyait sublimé en objets sculpturaux. Zaha Hadid avait déjà conçu un pavillon pour la Serpentine en 2000, mais accepta ici d'intervenir en urgence lorsqu'il apparut que le Pavillon 2007, projet d'Olafur Eliasson et de Kjetil Thorsen (agence Snøhetta), ne serait pas prêt à temps.

The three identical 5.5-meter-high parasols are arrayed around a central point on a low platform that provides a total floor area of 310 square meters.

Die drei identischen, 5,5 m hohen Schirme waren um einen zentralen Punkt auf dem niedrigen Podest mit einer Gesamtfläche von 310 m² angeordnet.

Les trois parasols identiques de 5,5 mètres de haut se répartissaient dans l'espace à partir du centre d'un podium surbaissé de 310 mètres carrés de surface.

A sketch and a very similar photographic view show the three parasol forms as they interact. The structures overlap but do not touch in a pattern of "complex symmetry."

Eine Skizze und eine sehr ähnliche Fotografie veranschaulichen das Zusammenspiel der drei Schirme. Die Konstruktionen überschneiden sich, berühren sich jedoch nicht und bilden ein Muster „komplexer Symmetrie".

Un croquis et une vue photographique très similaires montrent l'interaction des trois formes en parasols qui s'imbriquent, mais ne se touchent pas dans un jeu de « symétrie complexe ».

The architect also designed a bench and sculptures for the installation that was placed on a lawn to the south of the Gallery from 12 to 21 July 2007.

Die Architektin entwarf zudem Bänke und Skulpturen für die Installation, die vom 12. bis 21. Juli 2007 auf dem Rasen südlich der Galerie stand.

L'architecte avait également dessiné un banc et des sculptures pour cette installation mise en place sur la pelouse sud de la galerie du 12 au 21 juillet 2007.

PLANS, DRAWINGS AND MODELS

Architect Zaha Hadid
Design Team Jim Heverin

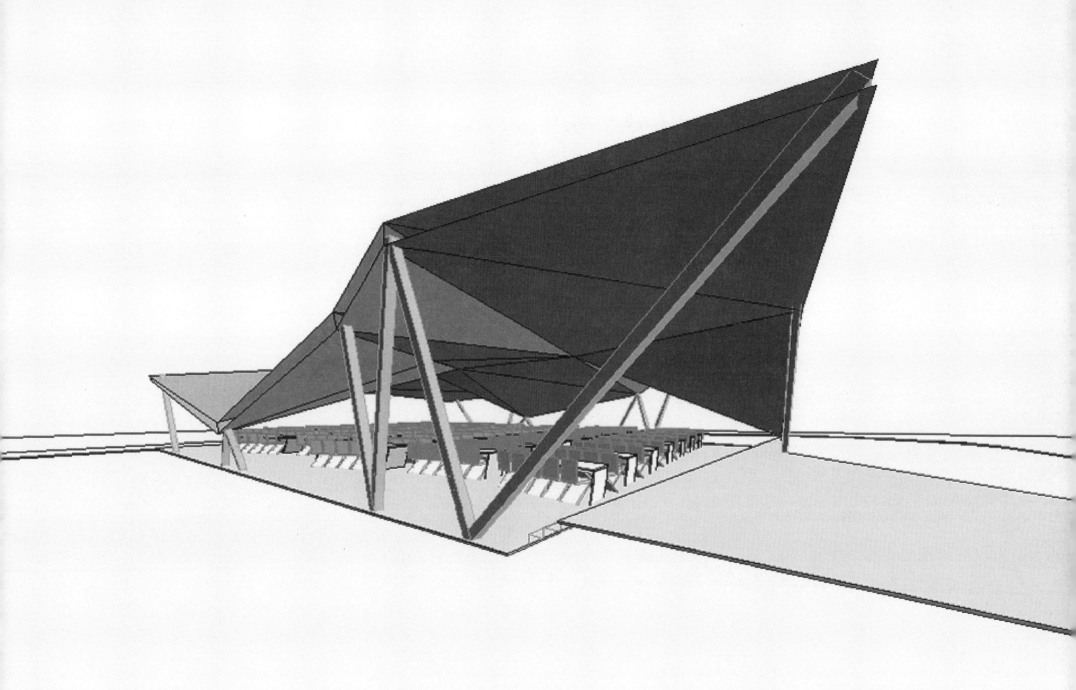

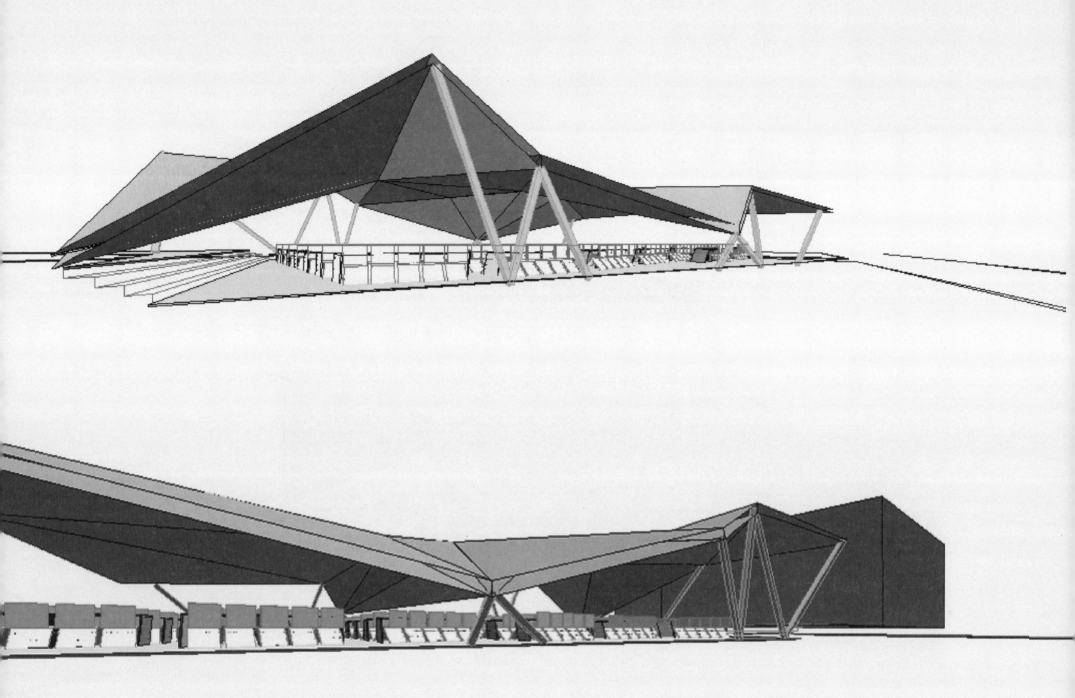

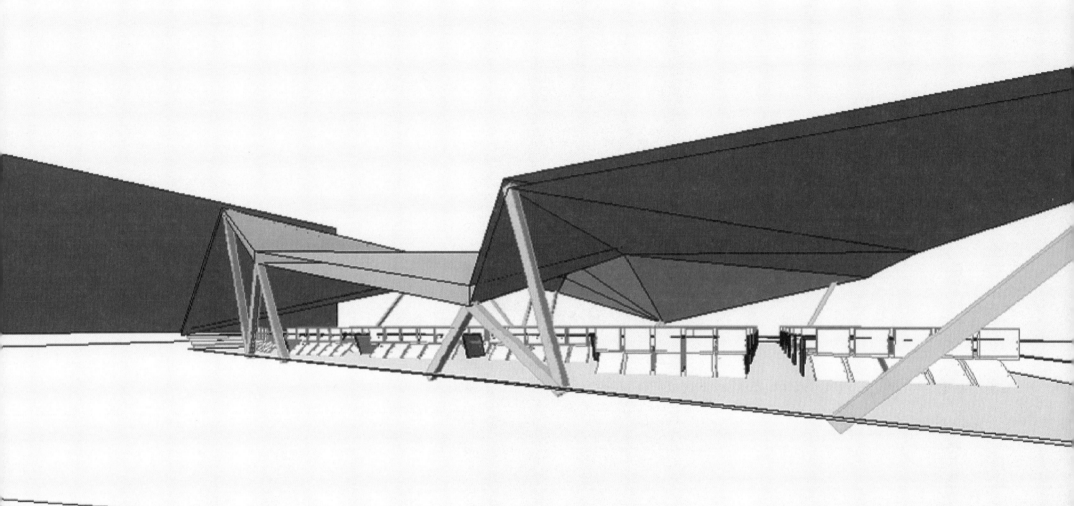

Drawings clearly show the folding rises and falls of the roof, which forms the pavilion's essential presence since there are no walls to speak of, only the irregular and visible supports.

Zeichnungen illustrieren die Faltung des auf- und absteigenden Pavillondachs, das den Bau entscheidend prägt. Hier gibt es keine Wände im eigentlichen Sinn, sondern lediglich unregelmäßig angeordnete, offen sichtbare Stützen.

Ces dessins illustrent les pliages des plans ascendants et descendants de la toiture qui constituent l'essentiel du pavillon en dehors de quelques supports répartis de façon irrégulière. Les murs sont pratiquement absents.

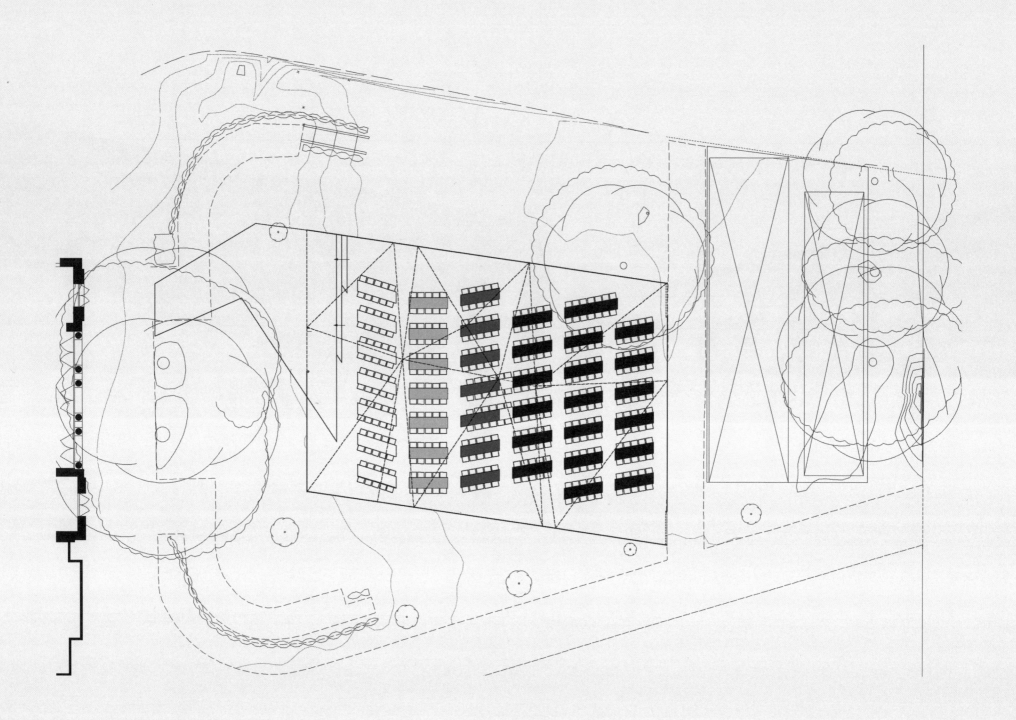

A plan shows the angled alignment of the
Hadid-designed tables within the space
of the pavilion. A determined regularity is
inscribed here within forms that are light
and simple.

Ein Grundriss zeigt die schräge
Platzierung der von Hadid entworfenen
Tische im Innenraum des Pavillons. Die
leichten, schlichten Formen sorgen für
eine deutliche Regelmäßigkeit.

Plan de l'alignement en biais des tables
dessinées par Hadid à l'intérieur du
pavillon. Cette régularité voulue s'inscrit
dans un ensemble de formes simples et
légères.

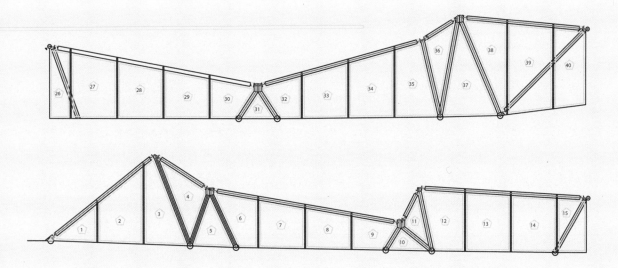

Elevation drawings of the roof structure
and its supports show how it rises and
falls all the way to the ground. Below,
a perspective drawing of the interior of
the pavilion with its furniture in place.

Aufrisse der Dachkonstruktion und ihrer
Stützen veranschaulichen die Auf- und
Abbewegung des Dachs bis zum Boden.
Unten eine Perspektivzeichnung vom
Innenraum des Pavillons mit Mobiliar.

Élévations de la structure de couverture
et de ses supports montrant comment
elle s'élève et plonge jusqu'au sol. En bas,
une perspective de l'intérieur du pavillon
avec le mobilier en place.

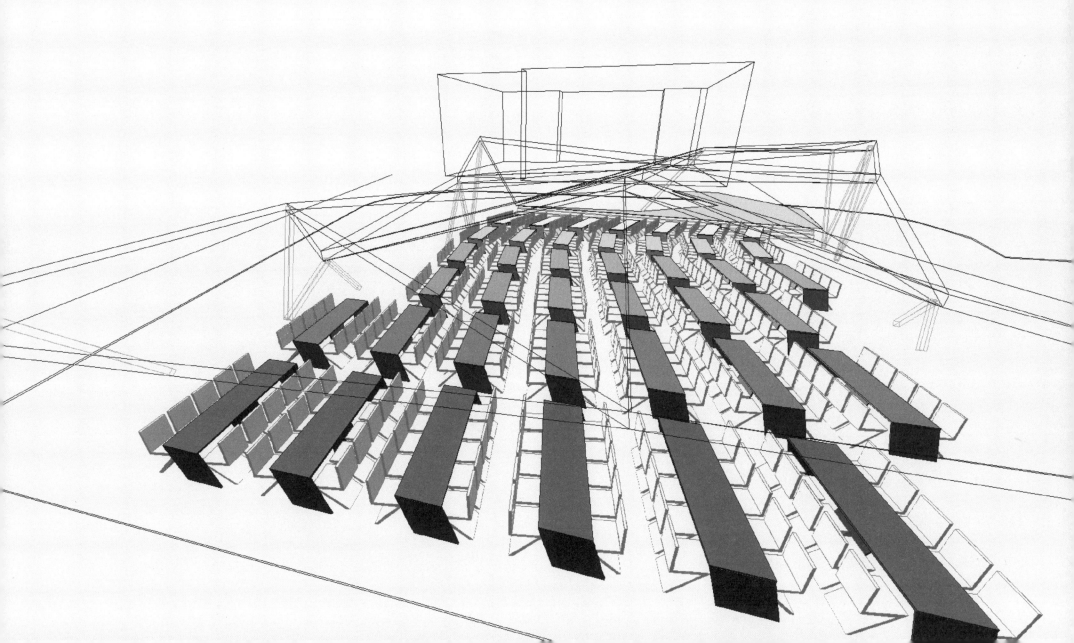

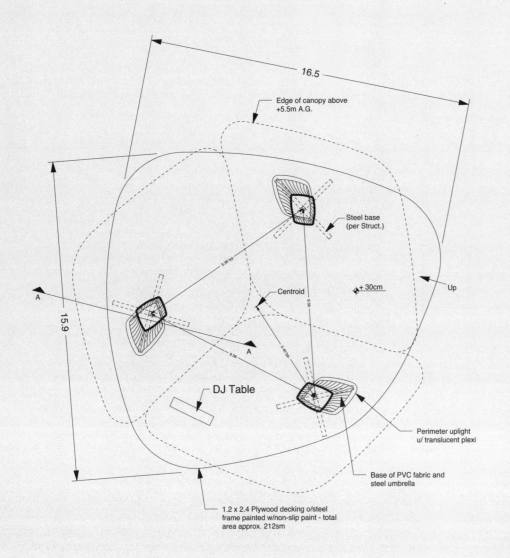

16.5

Edge of canopy above
+5.5m A.G.

Steel base
(per Struct.)

15.9

Centroid

+ 30cm

Up

A

A

DJ Table

Perimeter uplight
u/ translucent plexi

Base of PVC fabric and
steel umbrella

1.2 x 2.4 Plywood decking o/steel
frame painted w/non-slip paint - total
area approx. 212sm

A plan and section of the *Lilas* installation
show that its deceptively simple forms are
carefully designed and relate (especially
in section) to treelike forms, or perhaps
mushrooms in this instance. The human
scale and carefully centered design are
emphasized in these drawings.

Ein Grundriss und ein Querschnitt der
Installation illustrieren, wie detailliert
die täuschend einfachen Formen von
Lilas geplant wurden und (besonders im
Querschnitt) formal an Bäume oder auch
Pilze erinnern. Die Zeichnungen betonen
die auf den Menschen abgestimmten
Größenverhältnisse und das präzise
zentrierte Design.

Plan et coupe de l'installation *Lilas* montrant l'étude soignée de cette structure
d'une simplicité trompeuse qui renvoie
(surtout en coupe) à une forme d'arbre,
ou peut-être ici de champignon. L'échelle
humaine du projet et le centrage précis
du plan sont mis en valeur par ces
dessins.

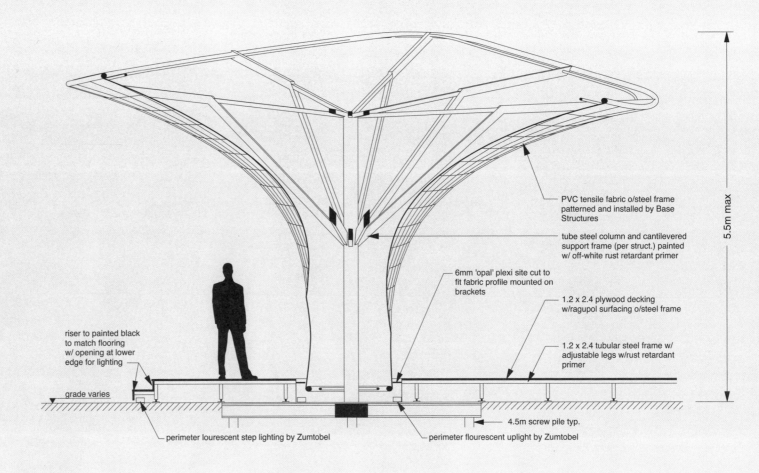

PVC tensile fabric o/steel frame
patterned and installed by Base
Structures

tube steel column and cantilevered
support frame (per struct.) painted
w/ off-white rust retardant primer

6mm 'opal' plexi site cut to
fit fabric profile mounted on
brackets

1.2 x 2.4 plywood decking
w/ragupol surfacing o/steel frame

1.2 x 2.4 tubular steel frame w/
adjustable legs w/rust retardant
primer

5.5m max

riser to painted black
to match flooring
w/ opening at lower
edge for lighting

grade varies

perimeter lourescent step lighting by Zumtobel

4.5m screw pile typ.

perimeter flourescent uplight by Zumtobel

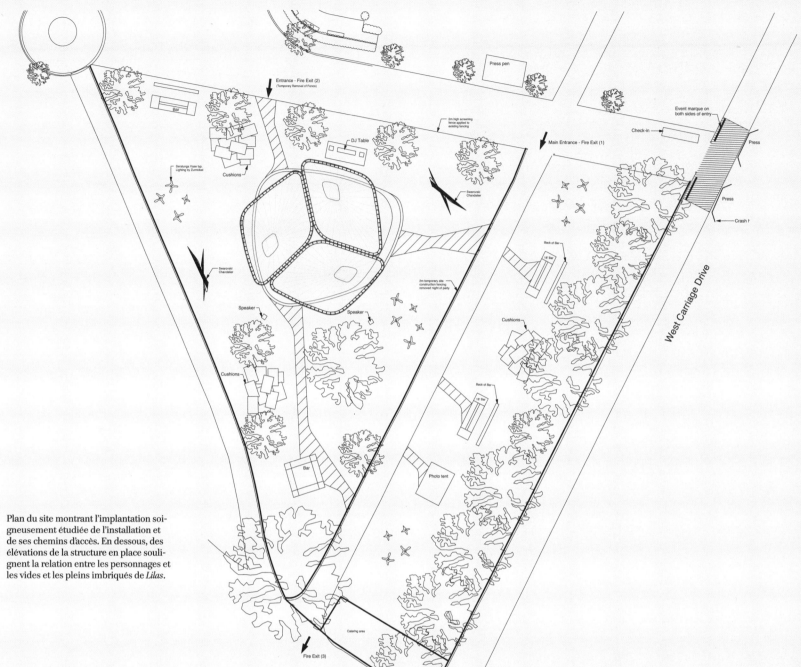

Entrance - Fire Exit (2)
(Temporary Removal of Fence)

Press pen

2m high screening
fence applied to
existing fencing

Main Entrance - Fire Exit (1)

Event marque on
both sides of entry

Check-in

Press

DJ Table

Cushions

Bar

Swarovski
Chandelier

Press

Senklungs Vase typ.
Lighting by Zumtobel

Crash t

Back of Bar

Swarovski
Chandelier

2m temporary site
construction fencing
removed night of party

Speaker

of Bar

Speaker

Cushions

Cushions

West Carriage Drive

Back of Bar

of Bar

Bar

Photo tent

A site plan showing the carefully measured placement of the installation and its approach paths. Below, elevations of the complete structure show the relation of human figures to the voids and overlapping solids of *Lilas*.

Ein Plan veranschaulicht die sorgsam abgewogene Platzierung der Installation und der Zugangswege. Aufrisse (unten) illustrieren das Verhältnis der Besucher zu den Zwischenräumen und den sich überschneidenden Volumina von *Lilas*.

Plan du site montrant l'implantation soigneusement étudiée de l'installation et de ses chemins d'accès. En dessous, des élévations de la structure en place soulignent la relation entre les personnages et les vides et les pleins imbriqués de *Lilas*.

Catering area

Fire Exit (3)

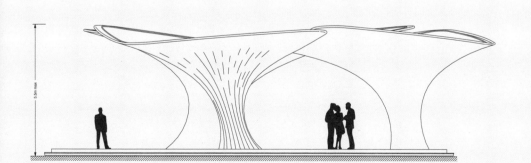

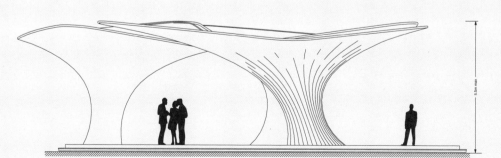

DANIEL LIBESKIND

2001

DANIEL
LIBESKIND

2001

DANIEL LIBESKIND

Studio Daniel Libeskind, Architect LLC
2 Rector Street, 19th Floor
New York, NY 10006
USA

Tel: +1 212 497 9154
Fax: +1 212 285 2130
E-mail: info@daniel-libeskind.com
Web: www.daniel-libeskind.com

Born in Poland in 1946 and a US citizen since 1965, Daniel Libeskind studied music in Israel and New York before taking up architecture at Cooper Union in New York, obtaining a B. Arch (1970). He received a postgraduate degree in the history and theory of architecture (School of Comparative Studies, Essex University, UK, 1972). His work includes the much-published Jewish Museum in Berlin (Germany, 1989–2001). Libeskind has had a considerable influence through his theory and his proposals and more recently with his built work. The city museum of Osnabrück in Germany, the Felix Nussbaum Haus, was inaugurated in 1998. In 2002, the Imperial War Museum North in Manchester (UK) opened to the public. The Danish Jewish Museum was completed in 2004, the extension to the Denver Art Museum in 2006, and the extension to Toronto's Royal Ontario Museum in 2007. His 2003 victory in the competition to design the former World Trade Center site in New York put him at the forefront of contemporary architecture, despite changes afterwards that caused him to largely withdraw from the project. Recent work includes a residential tower in Warsaw, Poland; Crystals at CityCenter shopping center in Las Vegas (Nevada, USA, 2009); the redevelopment of the historic Fiera Milano Fairgrounds (Milan, Italy, 2014); Archipelago 21, the Masterplan for the Yongsan International Business District (Seoul, South Korea, 2009–24); and the Institute For Democracy and Conflict Resolution, University of Essex (Essex, UK, 2010–).

Daniel Libeskind, 1946 in Polen geboren und seit 1965 Bürger der USA, studierte zunächst Musik in Israel und New York und dann Architektur an der Cooper Union in New York (B. Arch, 1970) sowie Architekturgeschichte und -theorie an der School of Comparative Studies der Universität Essex (Großbritannien, 1972). Weithin publiziert ist sein Jüdisches Museum in Berlin (1989 bis 2001). Das Felix-Nussbaum-Haus des Kulturgeschichtlichen Museums Osnabrück wurde 1998 eingeweiht. 2002 öffnete das Imperial War Museum North in Manchester seine Türen. 2004 wurde das Dänische Jüdische Museum fertiggestellt (Kopenhagen), 2006 die Erweiterung des Denver Art Museum (Colorado, USA) sowie ein Anbau an das Royal Ontario Museum in Toronto (Kanada) 2007. Dass Libeskind sich 2003 im Wettbewerb um die Gestaltung des ehemaligen Standorts des World Trade Centers in New York durchsetzte, katapultierte ihn an die Spitze zeitgenössischer Architektur, auch wenn spätere Änderungen ihn letzten Endes bewogen, sich weitgehend von diesem Projekt zurückzuziehen. Zu seinen jüngsten Projekten zählen ein Wohnhochhaus in Warschau (Polen), das Crystals im CityCenter Einkaufszentrum in Las Vegas (Nevada, USA, 2009), die Neugestaltung des historischen Mailänder Messegeländes (Italien, 2014), der Masterplan *Archipelago 21,* für den Yongsan International Business District (Seoul, Südkorea, 2009–24) sowie das Institute For Democracy and Conflict Resolution, University of Essex (seit 2010).

Né en Pologne in 1946 et citoyen américain depuis 1965, Daniel Libeskind étudie la musique en Israël et à New York avant d'opter pour l'architecture à la Cooper Union à New York (B. Arch., 1970). Il est diplômé d'études supérieures en histoire et théorie de l'architecture (École d'études comparatives, université de l'Essex, GB, 1972). Son œuvre comprend entre autres le Musée juif de Berlin (1989–2001), une extension du musée de Berlin. Par ses recherches théoriques et ses propositions, et plus récemment par ses réalisations, Libeskind a exercé une influence considérable. Le musée municipal d'Osnabrück (Allemagne) et la Felix Nussbaum Haus, ont été inaugurés en 1998 et, en 2002, son Imperial War Museum North à Manchester, GB, a été ouvert au public. Le Musée juif danois a été achevé en 2004; son extension du Denver Art Museum en 2006 et celle du Royal Ontario Museum de Toronto en 2007. En 2003, sa victoire au concours pour le site de l'ancien World Trade Center à New York l'a placé au premier rang des grands créateurs contemporains, même s'il a ensuite dû se retirer du projet. Parmi ses travaux récents: un immeuble résidentiel de grande hauteur à Varsovie; le centre commercial Crystals au City Center à Las Vegas (Nevada, 2009); Fiera Milano, rénovation des installations historiques de la Foire de Milan (2014); Archipelago 21, plan directeur du site du quartier d'affaires international de Yongsan (Séoul, Corée du Sud, 2009–24) et l'Institut pour la démocratie et la résolution des conflits, université de l'Essex (GB, 2010–).

Although the 2000 Pavilion by Zaha Hadid was the first of its genre, the Serpentine announced with the choice of Daniel Libeskind in 2001 that his temporary structure would be part of an "ongoing series." Open from 17 June to 9 September 2001, Libeskind's work, entitled *18 Turns*, corresponded in time partially to a Dan Flavin show at the Serpentine, and just preceded the Gallery's commission to Doug Aitken which involved a use of the entire building. Libeskind's aluminum panel structure was inspired in part by the Japanese art of paper folding, origami. In May 2001 Libeskind wrote of the work: "*18 Turns* is a special place of discovery, intimacy, and gathering. The space is seen as part of an infinitely accessible horizon between the Gallery and the landscape. Though the structure will disappear with the onset of autumn, it will leave a sharp afterimage and the ineffable resonance of a unique space." Debates on urban design organized with the Architecture Foundation and a series of BBC Proms Poetry Readings animated the space during the summer, a precursor to the even more active schedule of events programmed for later pavilions. It can be noted that the first two architectural choices of the Serpentine, Hadid and Libeskind, were both veterans of the 1988 Museum of Modern Art show on Deconstructivist architecture, though neither had had occasion at the beginning of the 21st century to build in the UK as yet. Libeskind had stirred a certain amount of controversy with his 1996 proposal to add a striking entrance to the Exhibition Road side of the Victoria and Albert Museum in London, just down the road, as it happens, from Hyde Park and the Serpentine Gallery.

Der Pavillon von Zaha Hadid im Jahr 2000 war der erste seiner Art, doch mit der Wahl von Daniel Libeskind 2001 erklärte die Serpentine, dass sein temporärer Bau Teil einer „fortlaufenden Serie" sei. Libeskinds Bau *18 Turns* war vom 17. Juni bis 9. September 2001 geöffnet; zu Beginn dieser Zeit zeigte die Galerie noch eine Dan-Flavin-Ausstellung, gleich danach entstand eine Auftragsarbeit von Doug Aitken für die Serpentine, für die das gesamte Gebäude genutzt wurde. Libeskinds Konstruktion aus Aluminiumpaneelen war unter anderem von der japanischen Papierfaltkunst Origami inspiriert. „*18 Turns*", schrieb Libeskind im Mai 2001, „ist ein besonderer Ort der Entdeckungen, der Intimität und Begegnung. Ich verstehe den Ort als Teil eines uneingeschränkt zugänglichen Horizonts zwischen Galerie und Landschaft. Obwohl der Bau zum Herbstbeginn verschwinden wird, wird er ein deutliches Nachbild und den unbeschreiblichen Nachhall eines einzigartigen Ortes haben." Im Lauf des Sommers belebten Diskussionsveranstaltungen zur Stadtplanung, organisiert von der Architecture Foundation, sowie Dichterlesungen im Rahmen der BBC Proms den Pavillon: Vorläufer des noch umfassenderen Programms, das für spätere Pavillons zusammengestellt wurde. Wie Hadid hatte auch Libeskind an der Ausstellung über dekonstruktivistische Architektur am Museum of Modern Art (1988) teilgenommen und keiner von beiden hatte zu Beginn des 21. Jahrhunderts in Großbritannien gebaut. Schon 1996 hatte Libeskind für Kontroversen gesorgt: mit seinem Entwurf für einen Erweiterungsbau am Victoria & Albert Museum an der Exhibition Road – ganz in der Nähe der Serpentine Gallery.

Si le pavillon 2000 signé Zaha Hadid fut le premier du genre, ce n'est qu'en 2001 que la Serpentine Gallery annonça à la fois le choix de Daniel Libeskind et de sa construction temporaire comme faisant partie d'une « série en développement ». Ouverte au public du 17 juin au 9 septembre 2001, l'œuvre de Libeskind intitulée *18 Turns* était visible pour un temps, parallèlement à une exposition de Dan Flavin organisée à la Serpentine, et précédait une commande passée à Doug Aitken. La structure de Libeskind en panneaux d'aluminium était en partie inspirée de l'art japonais de l'origami. « *18 Turns* », écrivait l'architecte en mai 2001, « est un lieu particulier destiné à la découverte, à l'intimité et au rassemblement. L'espace doit se voir comme élément d'un horizon accessible de tous côtés entre la galerie et le paysage. Bien que ce pavillon doive disparaître à l'automne, il laissera une image forte et la résonance subtile d'un espace unique. » Pendant l'été, le lieu fut animé par des débats sur l'urbanisme organisés en collaboration avec l'Architecture Foundation et une série de lectures de poésie de la BBC, manifestations annonçant le riche programme d'activités des pavillons à venir. Les deux premiers architectes choisis par la Serpentine, Hadid et Libeskind, avaient tous deux participé à la fameuse exposition sur l'architecture déconstructiviste organisée par le Musée d'art moderne à New York. Ni l'un ni l'autre n'avaient encore eu l'occasion de construire au Royaume-Uni. Libeskind avait cependant déjà suscité une controverse autour de son étonnant projet d'entrée latérale pour le Victoria and Albert Museum sur Exhibition Road, non loin d'Hyde Park et de la Serpentine Gallery.

Developing on the idea of a folded band of metal, Daniel Libeskind relates his structure *18 Turns* to the site and to its proximity with the Serpentine Gallery.

Daniel Libeskind entwickelt sein Konzept eines gefalteten Metallbands und setzt seine Konstruktion *18 Turns* in Beziehung zum Umfeld und zur benachbarten Serpentine Gallery.

Partant de l'idée d'un bandeau de métal plié, Daniel Libeskind fait un lien entre son projet *18 Turns*, le site et la proximité de la Serpentine Gallery.

The angled metallic surfaces of the pavilion offer the public a chance to be in contact with cutting-edge architecture in the heart of London, and also give the public a convivial space to gather (right).

Die schiefen Metallflächen des Pavillons bieten dem Publikum Gelegenheit, mitten in London Avantgarde-Architektur zu erleben, und sind zugleich ein kommunikativer Treffpunkt (rechts).

Les surfaces métalliques inclinées du pavillon donnaient au public l'occasion d'entrer en contact avec une architecture d'avant-garde au cœur même de Londres, tout en lui offrant un espace convivial (à droite).

"Temporary structures like Eighteen Turns are great additions to our parks and cityscapes; they can offer us adventurous, alternative and even radical impressions of what a new architecture might be."

THE GUARDIAN

Clad in aluminum, the pavilion presents a surface punctuated with small rivets, giving some relief to the otherwise sheer metallic planes.

Die Oberfläche des mit Aluminium verblendeten Pavillons ist mit kleinen Nieten besetzt, wodurch die ansonsten puristischen Metallflächen aufgelockert werden.

Habillé d'aluminium, le pavillon se présentait sous la forme d'une surface ponctuée de petits rivets donnant un certain relief à ces plans purement métalliques.

The rather complex folding of the structure alternates voids with solid, reflective surfaces that invite the public both to explore the new architecture and to reconsider the park itself and the placement of the gallery within the greenery.

Durch das komplexe Faltschema der Konstruktion ergibt sich ein Wechselspiel aus Zwischenräumen und massiven, spiegelnden Flächen. Sie laden das Publikum ein, die neuartige Architektur zu entdecken und den Park sowie die Lage der Galerie mitten im Grünen mit neuen Augen zu betrachten.

Le pliage assez complexe de la structure alternait les vides et les pleins. Ses plans réfléchissants invitaient le public à explorer cette architecture nouvelle mais aussi à regarder d'un œil neuf le parc lui-même et l'implantation de la Serpentine Gallery dans la verdure.

Although metal surfaces might at first seem closed, the structure's bending, folding volumes invite visitors to explore the interior, as do the warmer wooden floors.

Obwohl die metallischen Oberflächen zunächst geschlossen wirken, laden die geneigten, gefalteten Volumina die Besucher ein, den Innenraum zu erforschen. Dasselbe gilt für die warmen Holzböden.

Si les surfaces métalliques semblaient au premier regard fermées, le pliage du volume invitait les visiteurs à découvrir l'intérieur du pavillon, de même que les planchers en bois d'une teinte chaleureuse.

Using his vocabulary of sharply angled surfaces, the architect actually challenges the idea of inside and outside, letting one flow into the other. Likewise, walls and ceilings are not found in their usual locations in this pavilion.

Mit extrem schiefwinkligen Flächen – seiner typischen Formensprache – hinterfragt der Architekt im Grunde die Vorstellung von Außen- und Innenraum und lässt sie stattdessen fließend ineinander übergehen. Folglich befinden sich Wände und Decken in diesem Pavillon nicht am üblichen Ort.

Recourant à un vocabulaire à base de plans fortement inclinés, l'architecte remet en question les notions d'intérieur et d'extérieur, traités ici comme des flux s'interpénétrant. De même, les murs et les plafonds du pavillon bousculent les solutions classiques.

Simple wooden chairs and tables occupy the interior of the pavilion, giving an informal atmosphere to what might otherwise seem an aggressive display of metallic strength.

Schlichte Holzstühle und -tische im Innern des Pavillons sorgen für eine informelle Atmosphäre, wo durchaus auch der Eindruck metallischer Strenge hätte entstehen können.

De simples meubles et tables en bois occupaient l'intérieur du pavillon et créaient une atmosphère informelle dans un assemblage métallique qui aurait pu paraître par ailleurs agressif.

The generous space of the interior of the pavilion allows views out to the Serpentine Gallery itself (left), again encouraging visitors to look once more at the older building. With its lack of interior wall and ceiling cladding, the pavilion reveals its structural realities.

Der großzügige Innenraum des Pavillons bietet einen Blick auf die Serpentine Gallery (links) und ermutigt die Besucher einmal mehr, sich das alte Gebäude genauer anzuschauen. Da Wände und Decken unverschalt sind, bleibt die Konstruktion des Pavillons sichtbar.

Le généreux volume intérieur du pavillon offrait des perspectives sur la Serpentine Gallery, encourageant une fois encore le visiteur à regarder différemment le bâtiment ancien. Par l'absence de murs intérieurs et d'habillage des plafonds, le pavillon ne cachait rien de sa construction.

PLANS, DRAWINGS
AND MODELS

Architectural Design Daniel Libeskind/Cecil Balmond
Design Team Thore Garbers, Studio Daniel Libeskind
Structural Engineering Francis Archer, Arup
Project Management Eric Gabriel

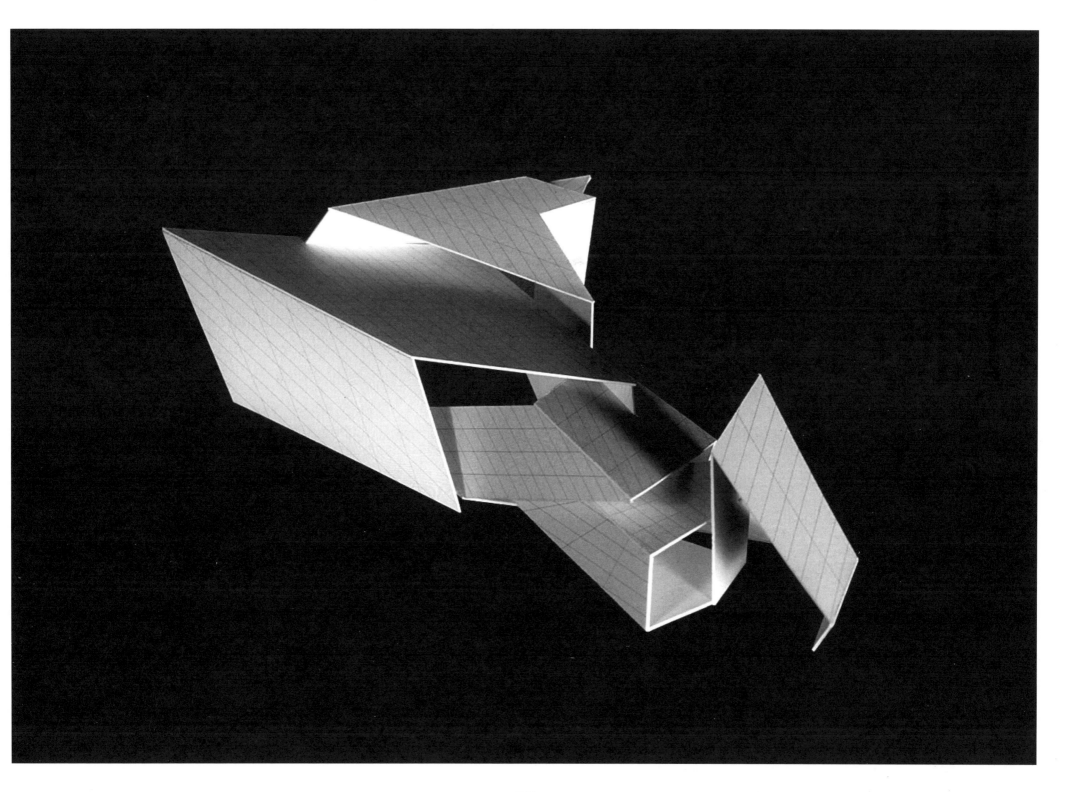

A model shows how the pavilion is
assembled from a sequence of angled,
metallic planes. The structure gives
little hint of its function in this form,
appearing more like a sculpture.

Ein Modell veranschaulicht die Kompo-
sition des Pavillons aus einer Sequenz
schiefwinkliger Metallebenen. Formal
lässt der Bau kaum Rückschlüsse auf
seine Funktion zu und wirkt eher wie
eine Skulptur.

Maquette montrant comment le pavillon
est un assemblage de plans métalliques
inclinés. La structure qui ressemble davantage à une sculpture qu'à un pavillon,
ne laisse guère deviner sa fonction.

The design of *18 Turns* is based on the idea of folding encountered in the Japanese art of origami. Seen from a ground perspective, the model (above) begins to illustrate how the folding process is resolved into a usable pavilion.

Der Entwurf von *18 Turns* geht auf ein Faltkonzept zurück, wie man es aus der japanischen Kunst des Origami kennt. Betrachtet man das Modell aus der Bodenperspektive (oben), wird deutlich, wie der Faltprozess zu einem nutzbaren Pavillon aufgelöst wird.

La conception de *18 Turns* repose sur l'idée de pliage, base de l'art japonais de l'origami. Vue au niveau du sol, la maquette (ci-dessus) illustre comment ce processus de pliage va aboutir à la proposition d'un pavillon parfaitement fonctionnel.

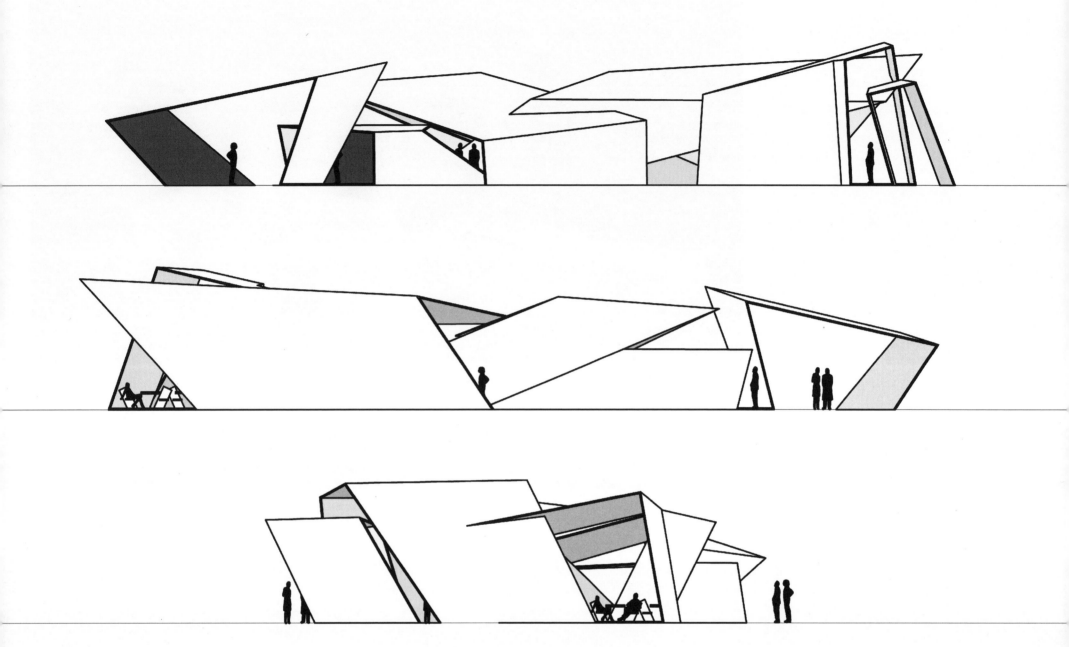

Elevation views show the relative
height of visitors and illustrate how
the externally closed metal surfaces
lift and bend to provide access.

Aufrisse illustrieren die Größenverhältnisse der Besucher zum Bau sowie das
Auf und Ab der hermetisch wirkenden
Metallflächen, durch das Zugänge
entstehen.

Ces élévations montrent le rapport
entre le pavillon et la taille des visiteurs
et comment les plans de métal fermés
se soulèvent et s'inclinent pour leur en
offrir l'accès.

The drawing below clearly demonstrates the architect's concern with both the volumes and the proximity of the Serpentine Gallery itself.

Die Zeichnung unten zeigt deutlich, wie sich der Architekt mit den Volumina des Pavillons sowie seiner Nähe zur Serpentine Gallery auseinandergesetzt hat.

Le dessin ci-dessous démontre clairement le double souci de l'architecte des volumes et de la proximité de la Serpentine Gallery.

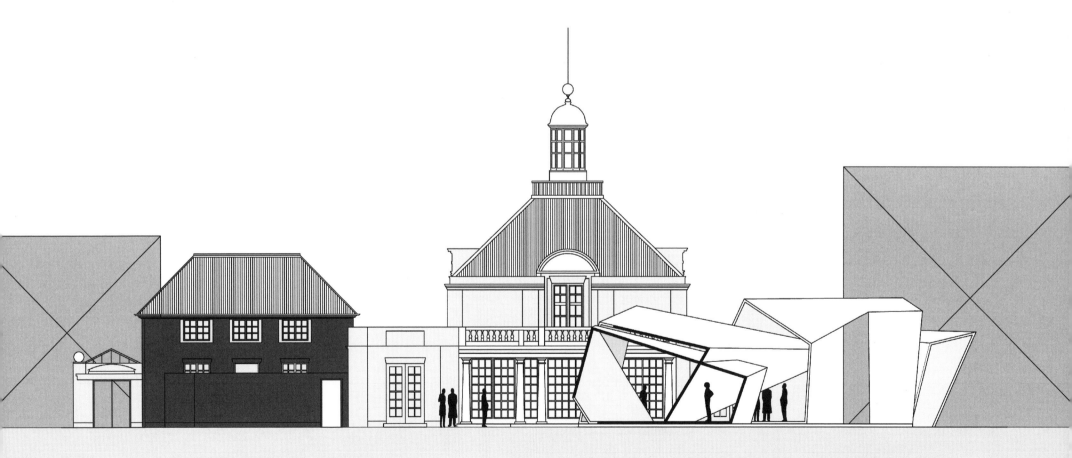

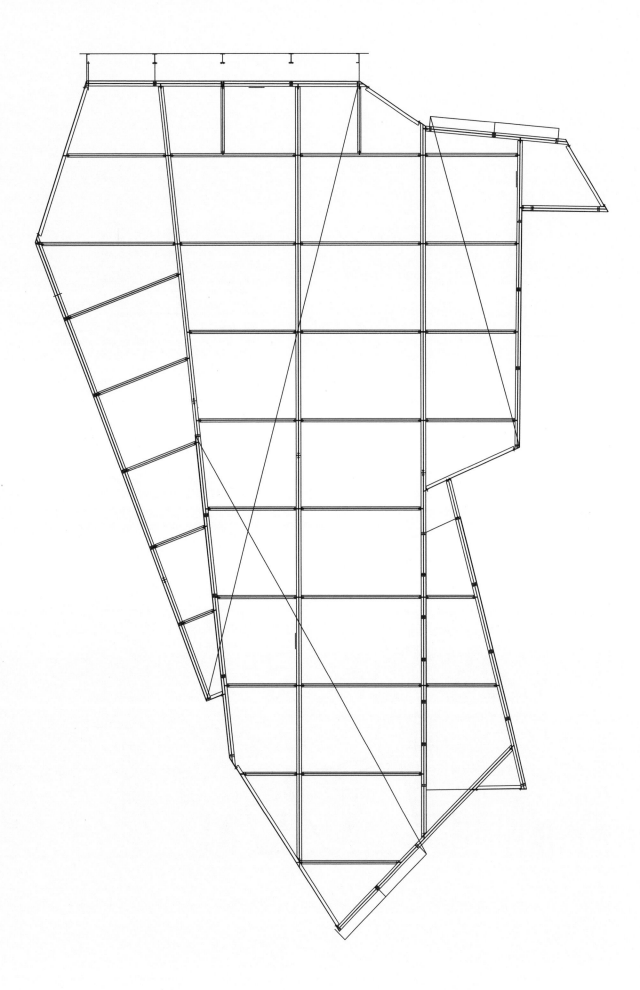

Plans and drawings show how basic
geometric forms, such as the triangle
and the rectangle, are used to assemble
a structure that appears to move and
resolve itself in complex, irregular ways.

Grundrisse und Zeichnungen
veranschaulichen, wie mit einfachen
geometrischen Formen wie Dreiecken
und Rechtecken gearbeitet wird, um eine
Konstruktion zu realisieren, die voller
Dynamik scheint und sich zu komplexen, unregelmäßigen Formen auflöst.

Plans et dessins montrent comment des
formes géométriques de base, comme
le triangle et le rectangle, peuvent
s'assembler pour constituer une structure
semblant à la fois évoluer et se transformer de manière complexe et irrégulière.

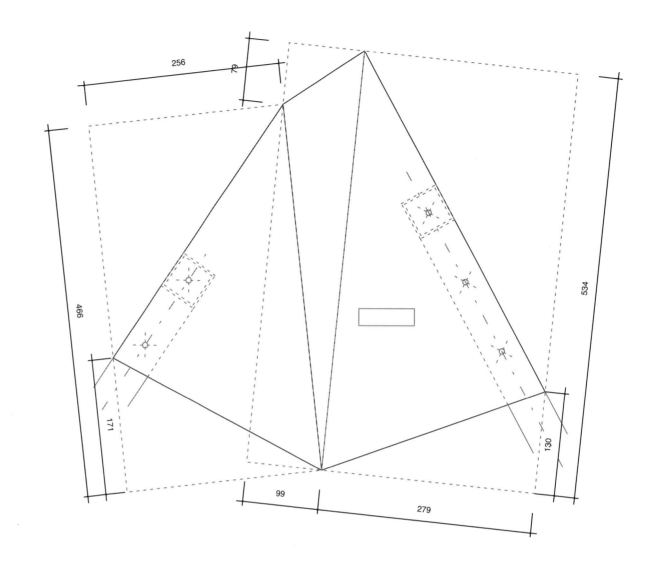

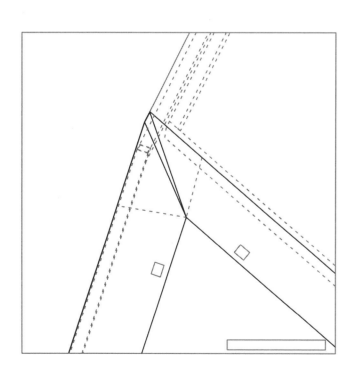

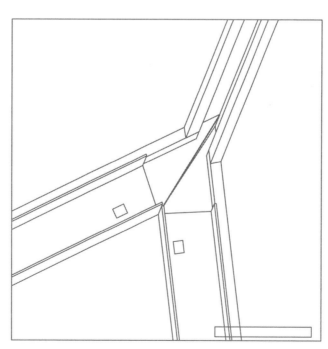

II.31

2002

2002

Toyo Ito & Associates, Architects
1–19–4 Shibuya, Shibuya-ku
Tokyo 150–0002
Japan

Tel: +81 33 409 5822
Fax: +81 33 409 5969

Born in 1941 in Seoul, South Korea, Toyo Ito graduated from the University of Tokyo in 1965 and worked in the office of Kiyonori Kikutake until 1969. He created his own office Urban Robot (URBOT) in Tokyo in 1971, which assumed the name of Toyo Ito Architect & Associates in 1979. His completed work includes his own Silver Hut Residence (Nakano, Tokyo, 1982–84); the Tower of the Winds (Yokohama, Kanagawa, 1986); and the Yatsushiro Municipal Museum (Yatsushiro, Kumamoto, 1989–91). Other projects include his Odate Jukai Dome Park (Odate, Akita, 1995–97) and Nagaoka Lyric Hall (Nagaoka, Niigata, 1995–97), all in Japan. One of his most successful and widely published projects, the Mediatheque in Sendai, was completed in 2001. This structure blends his sharp sense of modernity with a branching, almost natural idea of structure. He received the Golden Lion for Lifetime Achievement from the 8th International Venice Architecture Biennale, the same year he built the Serpentine Pavilion (2002), and the RIBA Gold Medal in 2006. More recently, Toyo Ito has completed the TOD'S Omotesando Building (Shibuya-ku, Tokyo, 2002–04); the Island City Central Park GRIN GRIN (Fukuoka, Fukuoka, 2003–05); Tama Art University Library (Hachioji City, Tokyo, 2005–07); and the Main Stadium for the World Games 2009, Kaohsiung (Taiwan, Republic of China, 2006–09).

Toyo Ito wurde 1941 in Seoul, Korea, geboren und schloss sein Studium 1965 an der Universität Tokio ab. Bis 1969 arbeitete er im Büro von Kiyonori Kikutake. Sein eigenes Büro Urban Robot (URBOT) gründete er 1971 in Tokio, ab 1979 firmiert er unter dem Namen Toyo Ito Architect & Associates. Zu seinen realisierten Bauten zählen sein eigenes Wohnhaus Silver Hut (Nakano, Tokio, 1982–84), Tower of the Winds (Yokohama, Kanagawa, 1986) und das Stadtmuseum Yatsushiro (Yatsushiro, Kumamoto, 1989–91). Weitere Projekte sind sein Odate Jukai Dome Park (Odate, Akita, 1995–97) und die Nagaoka Lyric Hall (Nagaoka, Niigata, 1995–97), alle in Japan. Eines seiner bekanntesten und meistpublizierten Projekte, die Mediathek in Sendai, konnte 2001 fertiggestellt werden. Es ist ein Bauwerk, in dem sich Itos ausgeprägter Sinn für Modernität mit einer verzweigten, fast natürlichen baulichen Ästhetik verbindet. Auf der 8. Architekturbiennale in Venedig wurde Ito mit dem Goldenen Löwen für sein Lebenswerk ausgezeichnet, im selben Jahr, in dem er den Serpentine-Pavillon baute (2002), sowie 2006 mit der RIBA-Goldmedaille. In jüngster Zeit realisierte er das Omotesando Building für TOD'S (Shibuya-ku, Tokio, 2002–04), den Island City Hauptpark GRIN GRIN (Fukuoka, 2003–05), die Universitätsbibliothek der Tama Art University (Hachioji City, Tokio, 2005–07) sowie die Sportarena für die World Games 2009 (Kaohsiung, Taiwan, 2006–09).

Né en 1941 à Séoul (Corée), Toyo Ito reçoit son diplôme d'architecte de l'université de Tokyo en 1965 puis travaille pour l'agence de Kiyonori Kikutake jusqu'en 1969. Il crée sa propre agence, Urban Robot (URBOT), en 1971, qui prend le nom de Toyo Ito Architect & Associates en 1979. Parmi ses réalisations: sa propre résidence, la maison Silver Hut (Nakano, Tokyo, 1982–84); la Tour des vents (Yokohama, Kanagawa, 1986) et le musée municipal de Yatsushiro (Kumamoto, 1989–91). Parmi ses projets récents: le Jukai Dome Park (Odate, Akita, Japon, 1995–97) et la salle de concerts lyriques de Nagaoka (Niigata, Japon, 1995–97). Une de ses réalisations les plus réussies et la plus médiatisée est la médiathèque de Sendai (2001). Ce bâtiment associe son sens aigu de la modernité à un concept presque naturaliste de la structure en branches. En 2002, il a conçu le Pavillon d'été temporaire pour la Serpentine Gallery à Londres et a reçu un Lion d'or pour sa carrière lors de la VIIIe Biennale internationale d'architecture de Venise avant la médaille d'or du RIBA en 2006. Plus récemment, il a réalisé l'immeuble TOD's d'Omotesando (Shibuya-ku, Tokyo, 2002–04); le parc central GRIN GRIN (Fukuoka, 2003–05); la bibliothèque de l'Université d'art Tama (Hachiogi City, Tokyo, 2005–07) et le stade principal des Jeux mondiaux 2009 (Kaohsiung, Taïwan, 2006–09).

Toyo Ito's 309-square-meter, single-story structure was covered in aluminum panels and glass. The 5.3-meter-high pavilion was formed by a steel grillage of flat bars. The 17.5 x 17.5-meter footprint consisted of a "latticed frame of 550-millimeter-deep flat plates, shop welded into 26 discrete panels which are then bolted together on site to form the roof and the wall planes." The concept was to create a column-less structure that was not dependent on an orthogonal grid system, making an open space to be used during the summer months as a café and the required event space. The seemingly random structure was determined by an algorithm derived from the rotation of a single square. Each piece of the structure functioned so that all elements combined to form a complex, mutually interdependent whole. The point, as explained by the architect, was "to render visible again the systems that make the most basic conditions of architecture possible but which were being obscured by a rationalism obsessed with uniformity." The £600 000 pavilion, designed with Arup, had painted structural plywood floors and three-millimeter-aluminum panels for the walls and ceiling and was left in place for three months. Toyo Ito had seen the 2001 Pavilion by Daniel Libeskind and said that he had hardly dared to imagine that he might one day be asked to design such a pavilion. He also made clear that he greatly appreciated the occasion to work with the engineer Cecil Balmond. Commenting on his own ideas in 2002, Toyo Ito wrote: "A curious art object that is clearly architecture, yet at the same time non-architecture. While offering the bare minimum of functions as a space for people, it has no columns, no windows, no doors—that is, it has none of the usual architectural elements. Does this cube hint at a new vision of architecture to come? The question already has us thinking about what comes next."

Toyo Itos 309 m² großer, einstöckiger Bau war mit Aluminiumpaneelen und Glas verblendet. Der 5,3 m hohe Pavillon basierte auf einem Raster aus Flachstahl. Die 17,5 x 17,5 m große Grundfläche bestand aus einem „gitterartigen Rahmen aus 550 mm starken Platten, die in einer Werkstatt zu 26 Einzelpaneelen verschweißt und auf der Baustelle zu Dach- und Wandsegmenten verbolzt wurden". Es sollte eine stützenfreien Konstruktion werden, die nicht auf ein orthogonales Rastersystem angewiesen war, sodass ein offener Raum entstand, der im Sommer als Café und Veranstaltungsort diente. Die vermeintlich willkürliche Konstruktion ergab sich aus einem Algorithmus, der sich aus der Drehung eines einzelnen Würfels ableitete. Jedes Element des Baus trug dazu bei, dass alle Teile zusammen ein komplexes Ganzes bildeten. Dabei wollte der Architekt, wie er selbst ausführt, „erneut jene Systeme sichtbar zu machen, die die zentralen Grundvoraussetzungen von Architektur ermöglichen, jedoch von einem von Uniformität besessen Rationalismus verdeckt wurden". Der 600 000 Pfund teure, mit Arup geplante Pavillon hatte Böden aus gestrichenem Sperrholz und Wände und Decke aus 3 mm starkem Aluminium. Er bestand drei Monate. 2001 hatte Toyo Ito den Pavillon von Daniel Libeskind besichtigt und gesagt, er wage nicht zu hoffen, eines Tages selbst den Auftrag für einen solchen Pavillon zu erhalten. Er betonte auch, wie gern er mit Cecil Balmond als Ingenieur arbeiten wolle. 2002 kommentierte Toyo Ito seine Ideen so: „Ein seltsames Kunstobjekt, das eindeutig Architektur, aber auch keine Architektur ist. Zwar ist es mit dem Nötigsten ausgestattet, doch hat es keine Stützen, keine Fenster, keine Türen – also keine der üblichen baulichen Elemente. Ist dieser Kubus die Andeutung einer Architektur der Zukunft? Diese Frage lässt uns schon jetzt darüber nachdenken, was als Nächstes kommt."

Le pavillon de Toyo Ito (309 mètres carrés) était fait de panneaux de verre et d'aluminium. De 5,3 mètres de haut pour une emprise au sol de 17,5 x 17,5 mètres, il s'appuyait sur une trame en poutres d'acier. La construction consistait en « une ossature triangulée de plaques de 55 centimètres de large, soudées en usine en 26 panneaux, puis boulonnées sur place pour former le toit et les murs ». Ce concept de structure sans colonnes, libre de toute trame orthogonale, permettait d'obtenir un espace très ouvert utilisable pendant les mois d'été comme café et lieu d'accueil pour diverses manifestations. La construction d'organisation apparemment aléatoire suivait en fait un algorithme dérivé du principe de la rotation d'un carré. Chaque partie de la structure participait à l'ensemble global, complexe et interdépendant. Comme l'explique l'architecte, l'idée était « de faire réapparaître des systèmes qui conditionnent fondamentalement l'architecture, mais ont été masqués par un rationalisme obsédé d'uniformité ». Ce pavillon édifié pour 600 000 £ et conçu en collaboration avec Arup, était doté d'un sol en contreplaqué structurel peint, tandis que des panneaux d'aluminium de 3 millimètres d'épaisseur habillaient les murs et le plafond. Toyo Ito, qui avait vu le pavillon de Libeskind en 2001, avait confié qu'il n'osait imaginer qu'on puisse lui confier un jour ce projet. Il apprécia beaucoup sa collaboration avec Cecil Balmond. Commentant son approche, il écrivait en 2002 : « C'est un curieux objet d'art qui est clairement de l'architecture, mais en même temps une non-architecture. Tout en assurant le minimum de fonctions nécessaires pour un espace destiné à recevoir du public, il ne possède ni colonnes, ni fenêtres, ni portes, c'est-à-dire aucun des éléments habituels d'une architecture. Ce cube apporte-t-il une vision nouvelle d'une architecture à venir ? La question même nous fait réfléchir à ce qui peut advenir. »

With its dramatic geometric openings, the pavilion gives the impression that it is not supported in the usual way. The openings, some covered with glass, offer open views of the Park and the Serpentine.

Dank seiner dramatischen Öffnungen scheint der Pavillon ohne das übliche Tragwerk auszukommen. Die zum Teil verglasten Öffnungen bieten Ausblicke auf den Park und die Serpentine Gallery.

Ponctué d'ouvertures géométriques spectaculaires, le pavillon donne l'impression de se passer de tout support classique. Ces ouvertures, dont certaines sont fermées d'un panneau de verre, offrent des vues cadrées sur le parc et la Serpentine.

With its ostensibly solid thick walls,
the pavilion looks more compact from
certain angles than from others, yet
always appears to be fragmented.

Mit seinen scheinbar massiven Wänden
wirkt der Pavillon aus manchen Blickwinkeln kompakter als aus anderen, jedoch
stets fragmentiert.

Sous certains angles, l'épaisseur appa-
rente des murs donne au pavillon une
allure compacte, bien qu'il conserve
toujours son aspect fragmenté.

*"Why can't all new buildings be this good?
Toyo Ito's magical summer pavilion at
the Serpentine Gallery is a lesson in imagination."*
EVENING STANDARD

Photos from both the interior, with its
furniture designed by the architect, and
the exterior of the pavilion give a feeling
of a structure in a state of suspended
animation, in perilous equilibrium.

Aufnahmen vom Innenraum des avillons
mit dem vom Architekten gestalteten
Mobiliar sowie Ansichten des Außenbaus
vermitteln den Eindruck einer Konstruktion in dynamischer Spannung, in einem
fragilen Gleichgewicht.

Les photos de l'intérieur (au mobilier
dessiné par l'architecte), comme celles
de l'extérieur, donnent l'impression
d'une structure dynamique figée dans un
équilibre perilleux.

The contrast of void and white solid arranged by the architect encourages visitors not only to look out in a horizontal direction but also up to the sky.

Der vom Architekten konzipierte Kontrast von Aussparungen einerseits und geschlossenen weißen Flächen andererseits lädt die Besucher ein, nicht nur geradeaus hinauszublicken, sondern auch nach oben, in den Himmel.

Les contrastes entre les pleins et les vides mis en scène par l'architecte incitent les visiteurs à regarder le Pavillon horizontalement mais aussi verticalement, vers le ciel.

The furniture placed by the architect in the pavilion interior creates a comfortable feeling. The ambiguity between interior and exterior spaces is a frequent point of interest of Japanese architects.

Das vom Architekten im Pavillon platzierte Mobiliar sorgt für freundliche Stimmung. Die Ambiguität von Innen- und Außenraum ist für japanische Architekten von großem Interesse.

Le mobilier installé par l'architecte à l'intérieur du pavillon crée un sentiment de confort. L'ambigüité entre les espaces intérieurs et extérieurs intéresse beaucoup les architectes japonais.

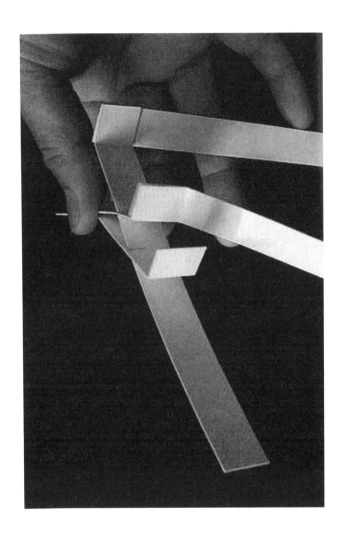

PLANS, DRAWINGS AND MODELS

Architectural Design Toyo Ito/Cecil Balmond
Design Team Toyo Ito & Associates
Takeo Higashi, Hiromi Hosoya, Takayuki Miyoshi
Integrated Design Arup
Charles Walker, Project Director
Daniel Bosia, Project Engineer and Algorithm

Elaborate, handmade models are used to configure the forms of the pavilion and to orchestrate the large number of openings.

Die formale Konfiguration des Pavillons und die Orchestrierung der zahlreichen Öffnungen wurde mithilfe aufwendiger handgearbeiteter Modelle entworfen.

Des maquettes élaborées, réalisées manuellement, ont servi à configurer les formes du pavillon et à orchestrer la répartition de ses multiples ouvertures.

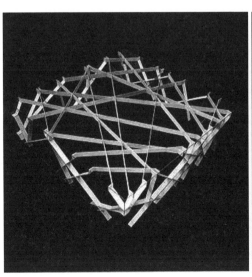
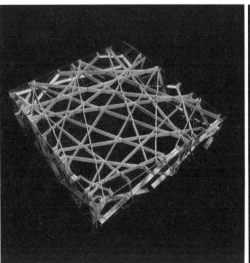
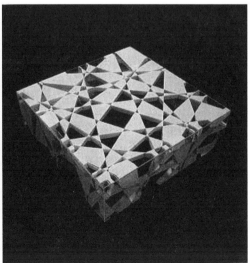

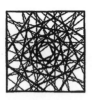 

 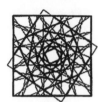 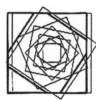 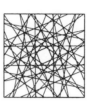

Successive drawings show the result of the rotation of deformation of square patterns, creating a kind of irregular spider's web of lines.

Weitere Zeichnungen illustrieren das Resultat einer Rotation oder Verformung quadratischer Grundmuster, aus denen ein unregelmäßiges Spinnennetz aus Linien entsteht.

La succession de dessins montre les effets de la rotation et de la déformation du modèle du carré, qui créent une sorte de toile d'araignée de lignes.

  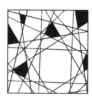

A ground level view of a model shows the degree of piercing imagined by Toyo Ito for this 310-square-meter steel-frame structure.

Eine Modellansicht aus Bodenperspektive illustriert, bis zu welchem Grad Toyo Ito plante, seine 310 m² große Stahlrahmenkonstruktion zu durchbrechen.

Une vue d'une maquette prise du niveau du sol montre le degré d'ouverture imaginé par Toyo Ito pour cette structure en acier de 310 mètres carrés.

A densely woven web of intersecting lines generates triangles and trapezoids that can either be transparent or opaque. The one-story structure thus has five surfaces (walls and roof) that are pierced to the maximum permissible degree.

Durch ein dichtes Netz einander kreuzender Linien entstehen Dreiecke und Trapezoide, die entweder transparent oder opak gehalten sind. Der einstöckige Bau verfügt über fünf Oberflächen (Wände und Decke), die bis zum höchstmöglichen Grad durchbrochen wurden.

Un réseau dense de lignes s'entrecoupant génère des triangles et des trapèzes transparents ou opaques. Les cinq surfaces (murs et toits) de cette structure de plain-pied sont percées au plus haut degré possible.

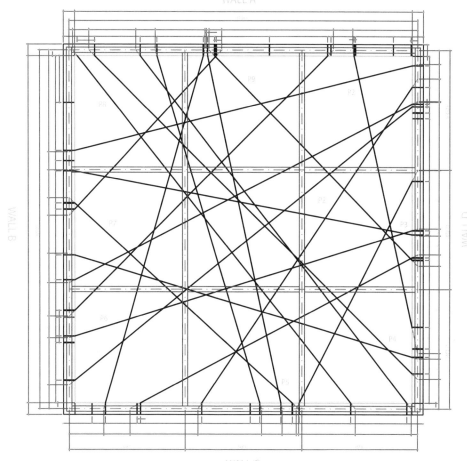

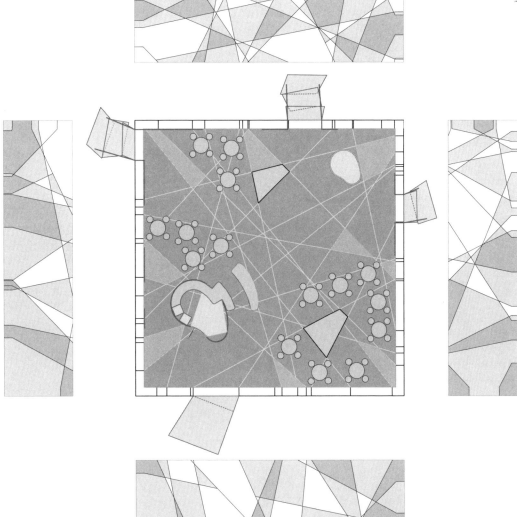

An artistic pattern of geometric forms emerges, but, despite the handmade appearance of the whole in these images, an algorithm of a cube that is expanded and rotated is at the base of this solution.

Es entsteht ein kunstvolles Muster aus geometrischen Formen, doch trotz der handwerklichen Anmutung des Gesamtbaus auf diesen Bildern liegt der Lösung vielmehr der Algorithmus eines Würfels zugrunde, der auseinandergezogen und rotiert wurde.

Un motif de nature géométrique et artistique peut parfois apparaître, mais malgré l'impression d'une intervention humaine, c'est bien un algorithme de cube développé et mis en rotation qui est à la base de la solution choisie par Toyo Ito.

OSCAR NIEMEYER

2003
**OSCAR
NIEMEYER**

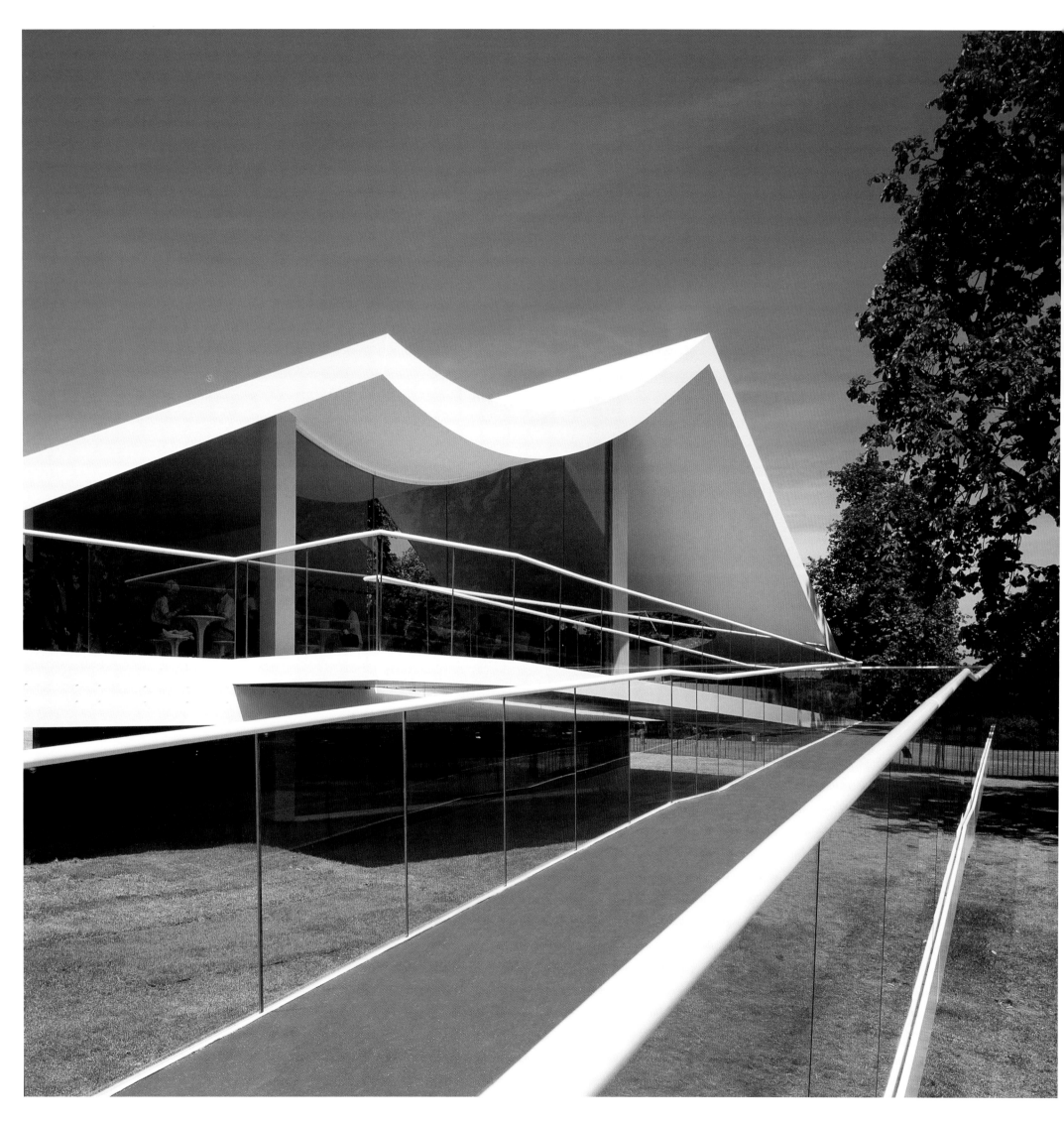

2003 OSCAR NIEMEYER

Oscar Niemeyer
Avenida Atlantica 3940
Rio de Janeiro 22070–002
Brazil

Tel: +55 21 523 4890
Fax: +55 21 267 6388
Web: www.niemeyer.org.br

Born in Rio de Janeiro in 1907, Oscar Niemeyer studied at the Escola Nacional de Belas Artes. He graduated in 1934 and joined a team of Brazilian architects collaborating with Le Corbusier on the new Ministry of Education and Health in Rio de Janeiro. It was Lucio Costa, for whom he worked as an assistant, who introduced Niemeyer to Le Corbusier. Between 1940 and 1954, his work was based in three cities: Rio de Janeiro, São Paulo, and Belo Horizonte. In 1956 Niemeyer was appointed architectural advisor to Nova Cap—an organization responsible for implementing Lucio Costa's plans for Brazil's new capital. The following year, he became its chief architect, designing most of Brasilia's important buildings. In 1964 he sought exile in France for political reasons. There, among other structures, he designed the French Communist Party Headquarters, in Paris. With the end of the dictatorship he returned to Brazil, immediately resuming his professional activities. He was awarded the Gold Medal of the American Institute of Architecture in 1970 and the 1988 Pritzker Prize (with Gordon Bunshaft). This was a vindication of sorts given that he had long been banned from visiting the United States because of his Communist sympathies. A master of curving lines, a quintessentially Brazilian architect, Oscar Niemeyer has continued to work beyond his hundredth birthday. For those who have seen his work in Brazil, in particular in Brasilia, there can be no doubt that Niemeyer was one of the greatest architects of the 20th century. His lyrical modernity undoubtedly influenced the later work of Le Corbusier more than the reverse. Having a pavilion designed by Oscar Niemeyer at the Serpentine was one of the most brilliant gestures of Julia Peyton-Jones, though it is hard to imagine that he never built anything else in the United Kingdom.

Der 1907 in Rio de Janeiro geborene Oscar Niemeyer studierte an der Escola Nacional de Belas Artes. Er machte seinen Abschluss 1934 und schloss sich einem Team brasilianischer Architekten an, die mit Le Corbusier beim Bau eines neuen Ministeriums für Erziehung und Gesundheit zusammenarbeiteten. Er war Assistent bei Lucio Costa, der ihn Le Corbusier vorstellte. Zwischen 1940 und 1954 arbeitete er in Rio de Janeiro, São Paulo und Belo Horizonte. 1956 wurde Niemeyer zum architektonischen Berater von Nova Cap berufen, einer Organisation, die für die Umsetzung von Lucio Costas Plänen für Brasilia, die neue Hauptstadt Brasiliens, verantwortlich war. Im folgenden Jahr wurde er leitender Architekt von Nova Cap und entwarf die meisten Hauptbauten der Stadt. Aus politischen Gründen ging er 1964 ins Exil nach Frankreich. Dort entwarf er unter anderem das Gebäude der Kommunistischen Partei Frankreichs in Paris. Nach dem Ende der Diktatur in Brasilien kehrte er dorthin zurück. 1970 erhielt er die Goldmedaille des American Institute of Architecture und 1988 den Pritzker-Preis (mit Gordon Bunshaft). Dies war in gewisser Weise eine Rehabilitation, nachdem ihm Reisen in die USA wegen seiner kommunistischen Sympathien lange verwehrt geblieben waren. Niemeyer, ein Meister der geschwungenen Linien und ein zutiefst brasilianischer Architekt, praktizierte noch über seinen 100. Geburtstag hinaus. Für alle, die sein Werk in Brasilien und insbesondere in Brasília gesehen haben, besteht kein Zweifel, dass Niemeyer einer der größten Architekten des 20. Jahrhunderts ist. Seine lyrische Moderne hat fraglos eher das Spätwerk von Le Corbusier beeinflusst als umgekehrt. Es war brillant von Julia Peyton-Jones, einen Pavillon von Oscar Niemeyer entwerfen zu lassen, der seltsamerweise nie etwas anderes in Großbritannien gebaut hat.

Né à Rio de Janeiro en 1907, Oscar Niemeyer y fait ses études à l'École nationale des beaux-arts. Diplômé en 1934, il fait partie de l'équipe d'architectes brésiliens qui collabore avec Le Corbusier au projet du nouveau ministère de l'Éducation et de la Santé à Rio. Lucio Costa, dont il est assistant, l'introduit auprès de Le Corbusier. De 1940 à 1954, il intervient essentiellement dans trois villes : Rio de Janeiro, São Paulo et Belo Horizonte. En 1956, il est nommé conseiller pour l'architecture de Nova Cap, organisme chargé de la mise en œuvre des plans de Costa pour la nouvelle capitale, Brasilia. L'année suivante, il en devient l'architecte en chef, dessinant la plupart de ses bâtiments importants. En 1964, il s'exile en France pour des raisons politiques, où il construit entre autres le siège du parti communiste à Paris. À la fin de la dictature, il retourne au Brésil et reprend immédiatement ses activités professionnelles. Il reçoit la médaille d'or de l'American Institute of Architecture en 1970 et le prix Pritzker en 1988, alors qu'il lui avait été longtemps interdit d'entrer aux États-Unis pour cause de sympathies communistes. Maître des lignes courbes, architecte au profond enracinement brésilien, Oscar Niemeyer continue à travailler bien qu'il soit plus que centenaire. Pour ceux qui ont vu son œuvre au Brésil, et en particulier à Brasilia, il ne fait aucun doute qu'il est un des plus grands architectes du XXᵉ siècle. Sa modernité lyrique a certainement influencé les œuvres ultimes de Le Corbusier, plutôt que le contraire. Obtenir qu'Oscar Niemeyer conçoive un pavillon pour la Serpentine est une des plus brillantes actions de Julia Peyton-Jones. Il reste difficilement imaginable qu'il n'ait rien construit d'autre au Royaume-Uni.

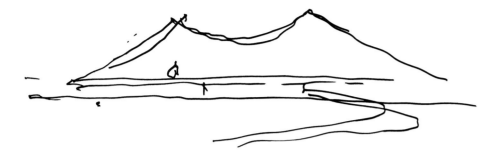

"I am delighted to be designing the Serpentine Gallery Pavilion, my first structure in the United Kingdom," wrote Oscar Niemeyer. "My idea was to keep this project different, free, and audacious. That is what I prefer. I like to draw; I like to see from the blank sheet of paper a palace, a cathedral, the figure of a woman appearing. But life for me is much more important than architecture." In these times of computer-generated architecture, it is a rare privilege to see a recent design of an architect who worked with Le Corbusier in the mid 1930s. Niemeyer was 95 when he agreed to design this project. The pavilion he created for the Serpentine Gallery does have much of the spirit of one of his own sketches brought to life. After first refusing to design this small structure, Oscar Niemeyer accepted when the director of the Serpentine, Julia Peyton-Jones, went to Rio to meet him. One of his long-time collaborators, the engineer José Carlos Sussekind, and Arup in London made certain that the pavilion was built according to the design of the master. Made of concrete and steel, the structure looked more like a permanent addition to the Kensington Gardens than it was. "My architecture followed the old examples," said Niemeyer when he received the 1988 Pritzker Prize. "The beauty prevailing over the limitations of the constructive logic. My work proceeded, indifferent to the unavoidable criticism set forth by those who take the trouble to examine the minimum details, so very true of what mediocrity is capable of." It appears that at his advanced age and in these circumstances Niemeyer wanted to create nothing else than a summing up of his own style. "I wanted to give a flavor of everything that characterizes my work," he said to the *Financial Times*. "The first thing was to create something floating above the ground. In a small building occupying a small space, using concrete, and few supports and girders, we can give an idea of what my architecture is all about." Although translation may take something away from the flow of Niemeyer's Portuguese, his words nonetheless point to the originality of this work: "The architectural lightness of the building, which hangs on columns, with eight-meter metal cantilevers, has assured a different architectural form, creating a feeling of surprise. From our viewpoint this kind of surprise is indispensable in any work of art. The great salon opens to the landscape, without the limits that buildings of permanent character usually require."

„Ich freue mich sehr, den Pavillon der Serpentine Gallery entwerfen zu können, meinen ersten Bau in Großbritannien", schrieb Oscar Niemeyer. „Meine Idee war es, das Projekt anders, frei und kühn zu halten. Das ist mir am liebsten. Ich zeichne gern; mir gefällt es, wenn auf dem weißen Blatt ein Schloss, eine Kathedrale, die Gestalt einer Frau erscheint. Und doch ist das Leben für mich weitaus wichtiger als die Architektur." In Zeiten computergenerierter Architektur ist es ein seltenes Privileg, den neuen Entwurf eines Architekten zu sehen, der schon Mitte der 1930er-Jahre mit Corbusier gearbeitet hat. Niemeyer war 95, als er sich bereit erklärte, das Projekt zu planen. Der Pavillon für die Serpentine Gallery wirkt, als sei eine seiner Zeichnungen zum Leben erwacht. Um Oscar Niemeyer zu gewinnen, musste die Direktorin der Serpentine Gallery, Julia Peyton-Jones, nach Rio reisen. Einer seiner langjährigen Partner, der Ingenieur José Carlos Sussekind, und das Büro Arup in London stellten sicher, dass der Pavillon getreu dem Entwurf des Meisters gebaut wurde. Die Konstruktion aus Stahl und Beton wirkte, als solle sie dauerhaft in den Kensington Gardens stehen. „Meine Architektur folgt den alten Vorbildern", sagte Niemeyer, als er 1988 den Pritzker-Preis erhielt, „der Schönheit, die die Grenzen konstruktiver Logik überwindet. Mein Werk wurde auch von der unvermeidlichen Kritik jener nicht gebremst, die sich die Mühe machen, selbst das kleinste Detail zu untersuchen, was so typisch dafür ist, wozu Mittelmäßigkeit fähig ist." Es scheint, als habe Niemeyer angesichts seines hohen Alters und der Umstände nichts weniger als die Essenz seines persönlichen Stils bauen wollen. „Ich wollte einen kleinen Eindruck davon geben, was mein Werk auszeichnet", sagte er der *Financial Times*. „Der erste Schritt war, etwas zu entwerfen, das schwebt. Mit einem kleinen Gebäude auf kleinem Raum, das nur Beton, wenige Stützen und Träger braucht, können wir eine Vorstellung davon vermitteln, worum es in meiner Architektur geht." Seine Worte geben einen Eindruck von der Originalität seines Werks: „Die architektonische Leichtigkeit des Bauwerks, an Stützen abgehängt und mit Auslegern von 8 m Länge, behauptet sich als ganz eigene architektonische Form und hat etwas Überraschendes. Wir betrachten dieses Überraschungsmoment als unverzichtbar für jedes Kunstwerk. Der große Salon öffnet sich zur Landschaft ohne die Einschränkungen, denen feste Bauten üblicherweise unterworfen sind."

« Je suis ravi de pouvoir concevoir le pavillon de la Serpentine Gallery, ma première réalisation au Royaume-Uni », a écrit oscar Niemeyer. « Mon idée était de proposer un projet différent, libre et audacieux. C'est ce que je préfère. J'aime dessiner. J'aime voir apparaître sur ma feuille de papier un palais, une cathédrale, la silhouette d'une femme. Mais la vie est pour moi beaucoup plus importante que l'architecture ». À notre époque d'architecture assistée par ordinateur, c'est un privilège rare de voir un dessin récent d'un architecte qui a travaillé avec Le Corbusier au milieu des années 1930. Niemeyer était âgé de 95 ans lorsqu'il accepta de concevoir ce projet. Son pavillon fait penser à l'un de ses croquis qui se serait subitement animé. Après un premier refus, il finit par donner son accord suite à la visite à Rio de la directrice de la Serpentine, Julia Peyton-Jones. L'un de ses collaborateurs de longue date, l'ingénieur José Carlos Sussekind, et l'agence Arup à Londres firent en sorte que le pavillon soit exactement réalisé selon les plans du maître. En béton et acier, il faisait davantage penser à une construction permanente que ce qu'il était en réalité. « Mon architecture suit des exemples anciens », déclara Niemeyer lorsqu'il reçut le prix Pritzker 1988. « La beauté prévaut sur les limites de la logique constructive. Mon œuvre a progressé, indifférente aux critiques inévitables avancées par ceux qui prennent la peine d'examiner les plus petits détails, attitude caractéristique de ce dont la médiocrité est capable. » Il semble qu'à cet âge avancé et dans ces circonstances particulières, Niemeyer ait voulu créer ce qui pourrait passer pour un résumé de son style. « J'ai voulu exprimer le parfum de tout ce qui caractérise mon travail », a-t-il déclaré au *Financial Times*. « D'abord, il fallait créer quelque chose qui flotte au-dessus du sol. Nous voulions donner une idée de ce qu'est mon architecture dans ce petit bâtiment, à l'aide de béton, de quelques supports et de poutres. » Si la traduction appauvrit peut-être le flux de la langue portugaise dans laquelle s'exprime Niemeyer, ses paroles insistent néanmoins sur l'originalité de son œuvre : « La légèreté architecturale du bâtiment, qui s'appuie sur des colonnes, avec ses porte-à-faux de huit mètres, a pris une forme architecturale originale qui crée un sentiment de surprise. De mon point de vue, ce principe de surprise est indispensable dans toute œuvre d'art. Le grand salon s'ouvre sur le paysage, sans les limites qu'un bâtiment à caractère permanent impose habituellement. »

As is usually the case, the design for Oscar Niemeyer's Serpentine Pavilion is related to the architect's drawings that depict other subjects, from the mountains in the case of the drawing on this page, to women's bodies.

Wie auch sonst bei ihm üblich, nimmt Oscar Niemeyers Serpentine Pavilion Bezug auf Zeichnungen des Architekten, die andere Motive zeigen – angefangen von Bergen (Zeichnung auf dieser Seite) bis hin zu weiblichen Akten.

Comme souvent chez Niemeyer, son projet de pavillon pour la Serpentine part de dessins réalisés à partir d'autres sujets, comme les montagnes du petit croquis de cette page, ou le corps féminin.

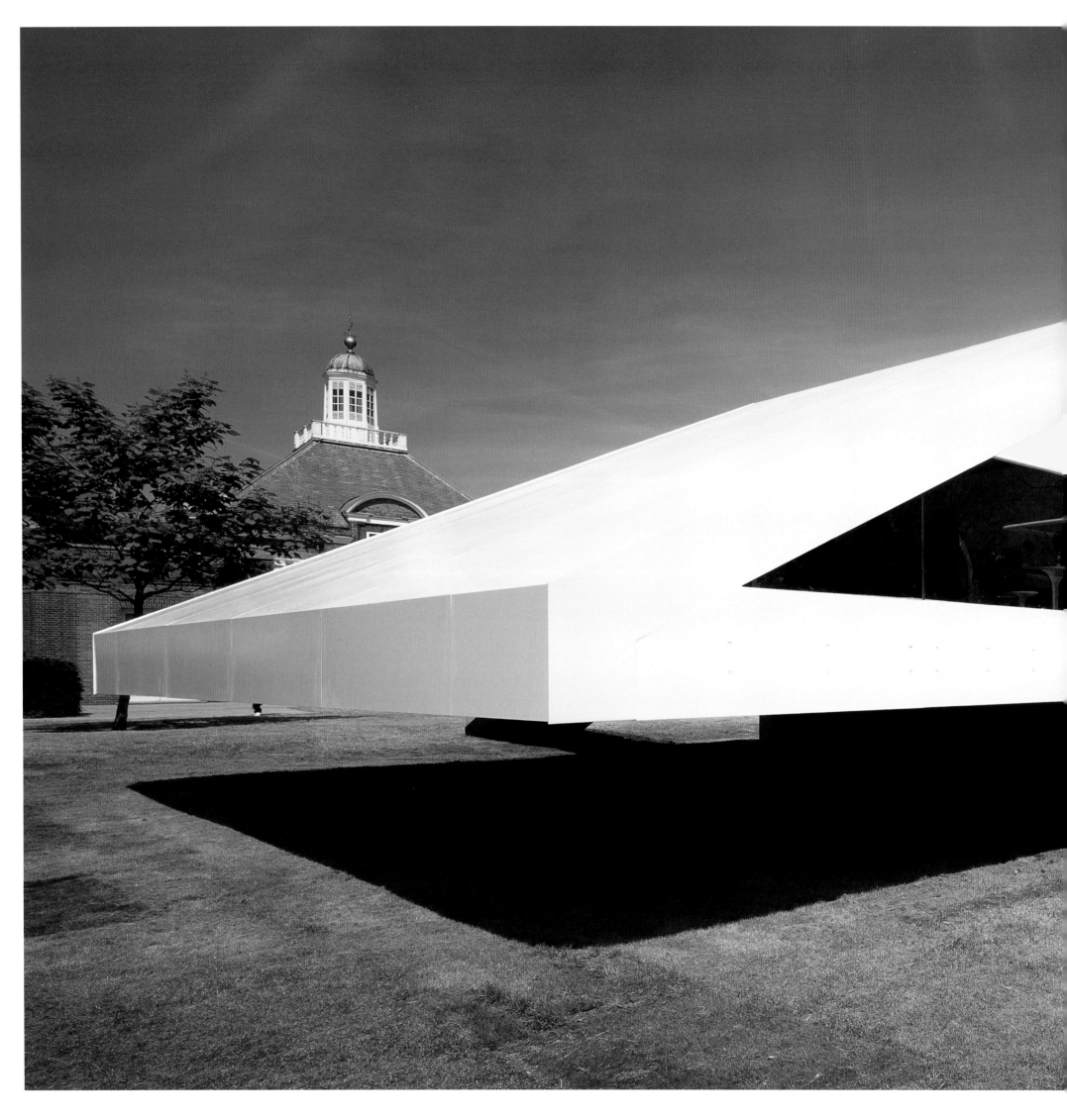

Despite his advanced age, Niemeyer collaborated personally on the project. On this page, his sketches of reclining women, and on the right, the completed Pavilion.

Trotz seines hohen Alters arbeitete Niemeyer persönlich an diesem Projekt. Auf dieser Seite sind seine Skizzen liegender Frauenakte sowie rechts der realisierte Pavillon zu sehen.

Malgré son âge avancé, Niemeyer s'est personnellement beaucoup investi dans ce projet. Sur cette page, ces croquis de femmes allongées et, à droite, le pavillon achevé.

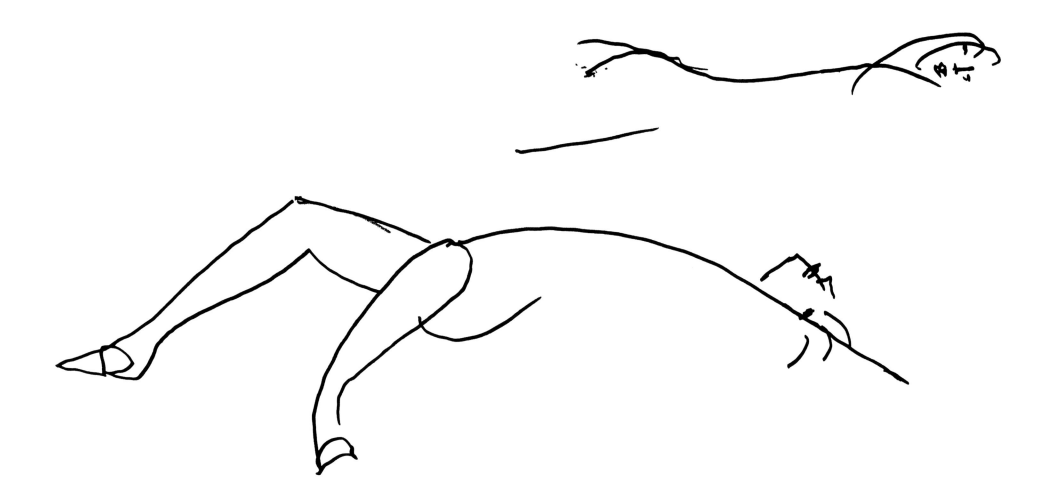

Alternating white curves and red, planar surfaces, the pavilion is made of steel, aluminum, concrete, and glass.

Der Pavillon mit seinen weißen Schwüngen und planen, roten Flächen wurde aus Stahl, Aluminium, Beton und Glas realisiert.

Alternant courbes blanches et plans de couleur rouge, le pavillon a été construit en acier, aluminium, béton et verre.

From this angle, the pavilion brings to mind another building by the Brazilian architect—the Oscar Niemeyer Museum (Curitiba, 2002), which is also lifted off the ground.

Aus dieser Perspektive erinnert der Pavillon an einen anderen Bau des brasilianischen Architekten, das Oscar Niemeyer Museum in Curitiba (2002), das ebenfalls aufgeständert ist.

Vu sous cet angle, le pavillon rappelle d'autres réalisations de l'architecte brésilien comme le musée Oscar Niemeyer à Curitiba (2002), également suspendu au-dessus du sol.

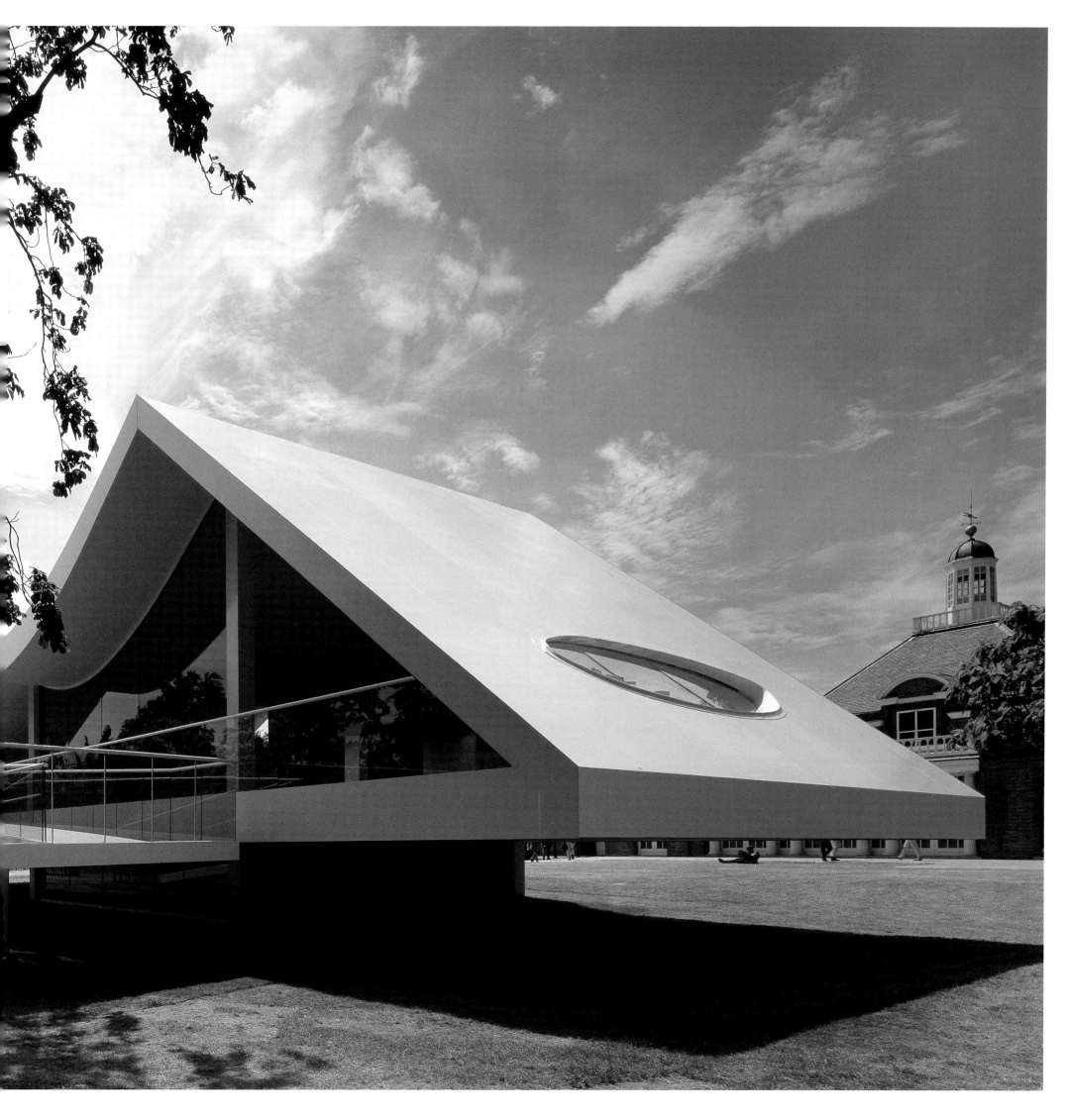

Dramatic curves and a main level that appears to float in the air recall that many of Niemeyer's buildings feature dramatic cantilevers and solid built forms with few visible means of support.

Dramatische Schwünge und eine Hauptebene, die zu schweben scheint, erinnern an zahlreiche Bauten Niemeyers mit spektakulären Auskragungen und massivem Baukörper, jedoch nur wenigen sichtbaren Stützen.

Les courbes spectaculaires de la couverture et la suspension du niveau principal rappellent que nombre de réalisations de Niemeyer présentent des porte-à-faux spectaculaires et des formes pleines avec peu de supports visibles.

The bar inside the pavilion centers on
an elongated oval window that looks out
onto the greenery of Kensington Gardens
in Hyde Park.

Die Bar im Pavillon ist zu einem längli-
chen, ovalen Fenster hin orientiert, das
den Blick auf die Kensington Gardens im
Hyde Park eröffnet.

Le bar de l'intérieur du pavillon est situé
dans l'axe d'une baie en forme d'ovale
étiré qui ouvre sur la verdure des jardins
de Kensington dans Hyde Park.

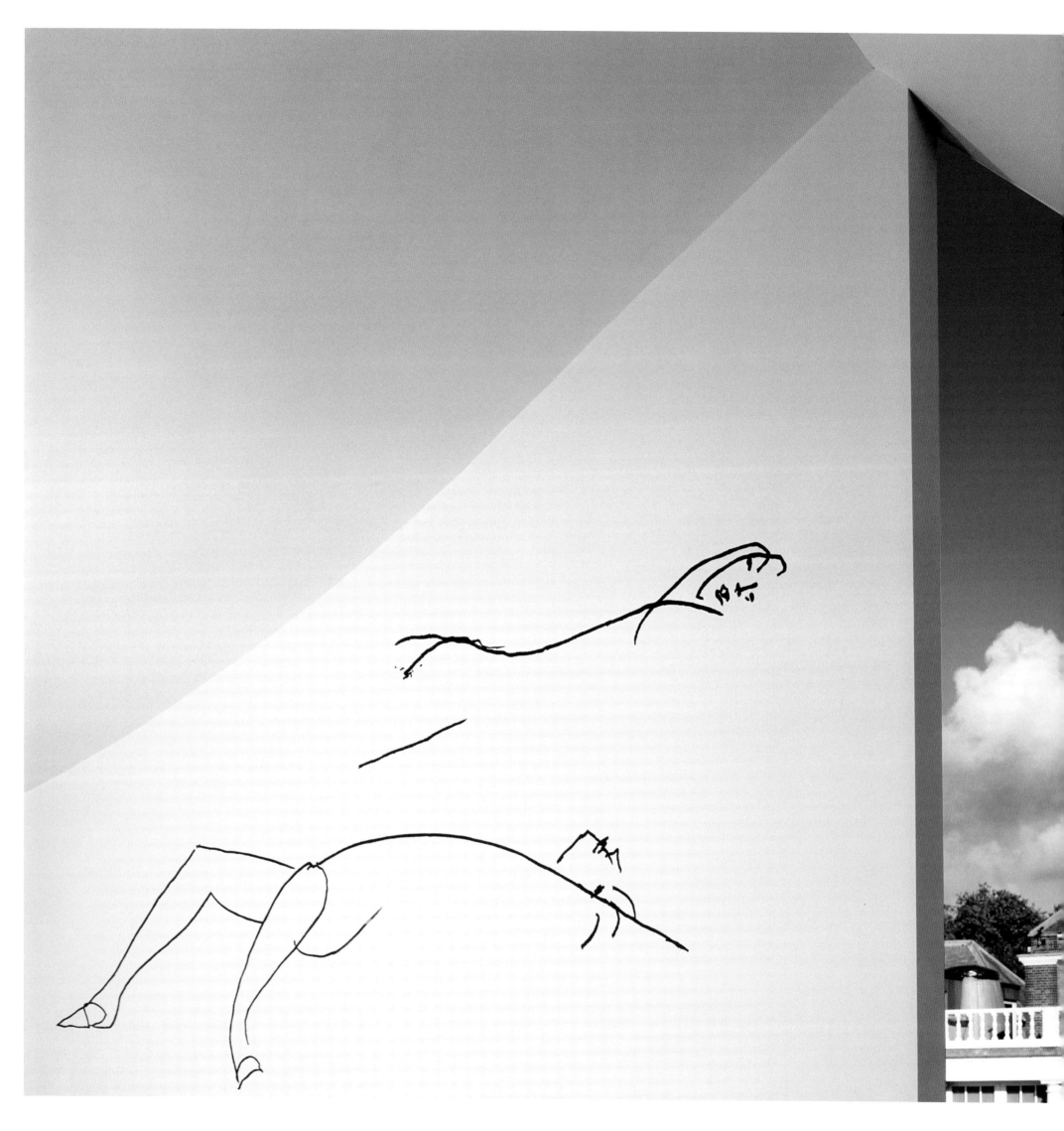

"Imagine Garbo or Sinatra in their prime, and performing now. With this week's opening of the 2003 Serpentine Gallery Pavilion, just such a time-warping miracle is taking place."

EVENING STANDARD

As has been in the case of other buildings of the architect, for example the Teatro Popular in Niterói (2007), Oscar Niemeyer's sketches related to the structure—here showing reclining women—are reproduced on the walls in a view framing the Serpentine Gallery main building.

Wie bei anderen Bauten des Architekten, etwa beim Teatro Popular in Niterói (2007), sind die im Zusammenhang mit dem Bauwerk entstandenen Zeichnungen Oscar Niemeyers – hier liegende weibliche Akte – auf den Wänden wiedergegeben. Diese Ansicht lässt das Hauptgebäude der Serpentine Gallery in einem Rahmen erscheinen.

Comme dans d'autres constructions de l'architecte – tel que dans le Théâtre populaire de Niterói (2007) –, des croquis d'Oscar Niemeyer en rapport avec la création du pavillon sont reproduits sur les murs. Ici, vue de femmes couchées à proximité d'une ouverture encadrant le bâtiment principal de la Serpentine Gallery.

Serpentine Gallery
Pavilion 2003 designed
by Oscar Niemeyer

**PLANS, DRAWINGS
AND MODELS**

Architectural Design Oscar Niemeyer/José Carlos Sussekind
Design Team Jair Valera
Integrated Design Arup
Cecil Balmond/Charles Walker/Hamish Nevile

A drawing reveals the inner design of the
pavilion with the approach walkway and
stairs leading down to the lower level.

Eine Zeichnung zeigt die innere Struktur
des Pavillons mit Zugangsrampe und
Treppen, die ins untere Geschoss führen.

Ce dessin présente le plan intérieur du
pavillon, son allée d'accès et les escaliers
qui descendent vers le niveau inférieur.

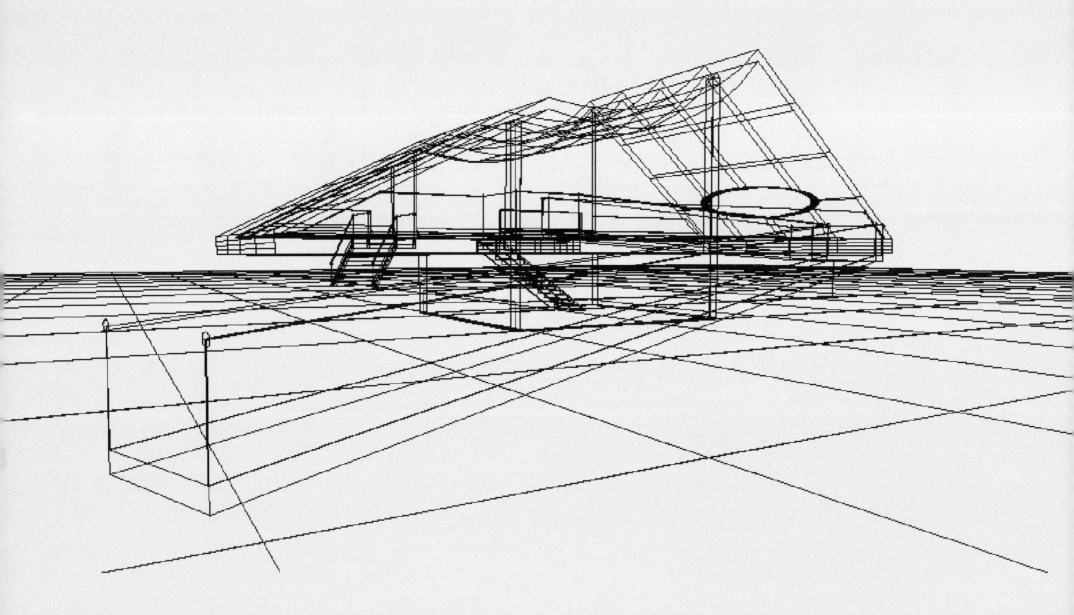

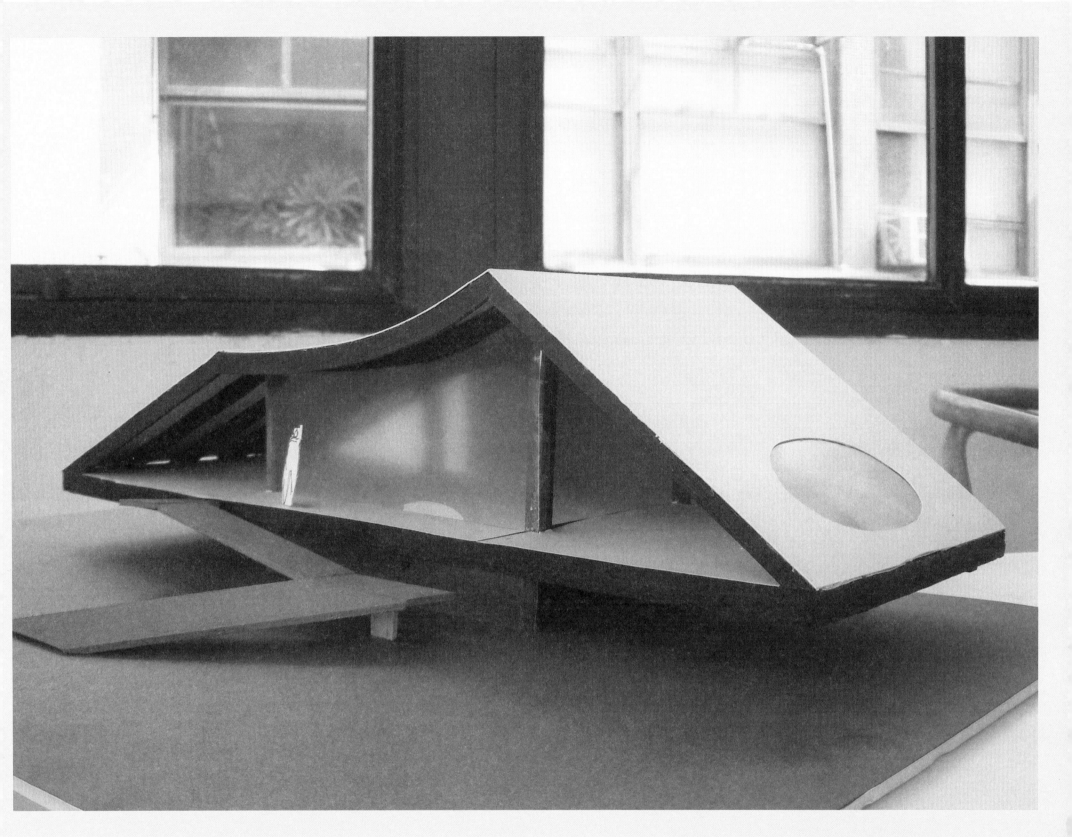

A model demonstrates the great simplicity of the design, with a human-size figure giving the scale. The ideas of a mountain landscape or the form of a reclining woman are sublimated in the roof design.

Ein Modell veranschaulicht die große Schlichtheit des Entwurfs und eine menschliche Figur vermittelt die Dimensionen. Im Dach lässt sich eine Berglandschaft oder die Umrisse eines liegenden Frauenakts entdecken.

Cette maquette illustre la grande simplicité du projet. Le personnage en blanc donne l'échelle. Des images de paysage de montagnes ou de profil de femmes couchées ont été sublimées dans les lignes de la toiture.

Drawings from the office of the engineers Arup demonstrate the extreme simplicity of the structure, relying on a minimum number of points of support. Access to the main level is given by a slanted walkway or stairs.

Zeichnungen des Ingenieurbüros Arup verdeutlichen die ausgeprägte Schlichtheit des Baus, der nur auf eine minimale Anzahl von Stützen angewiesen ist. Der Zugang zur Hauptebene erfolgt über eine schräge Rampe und Treppen.

Cette image de l'agence d'ingénierie Arup montre la simplicité extrême du projet qui repose sur un nombre de points d'appui minimum. L'accès au niveau principal se fait par une rampe ou des escaliers.

Another Arup image relates the scale
and location of the Niemeyer Pavilion
with the Georgian form of the Serpentine
Gallery itself. Neimeyer's curves contrast
with the essentially straight lines of the
earlier building.

Eine weitere Illustration aus dem Büro
Arup setzt Maßstab und Standort des
Niemeyer-Pavillons in ein Verhältnis zur
georgianischen Architektur der Serpentine Gallery. Niemeyers Schwünge
kontrastieren mit der vorwiegenden
Geradlinigkeit des älteren Bauwerks.

Autre image d'Arup montrant le lien
entre l'échelle, la situation du pavillon
Niemeyer et les ormes de style géorgien
de la galerie. Les courbes de l'architecte
contrastent avec le profil essentiellement
rectiligne des bâtiments anciens.

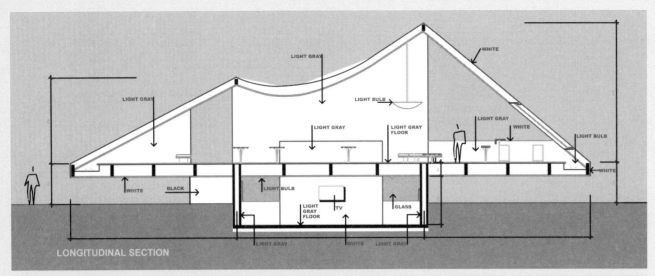

LONGITUDINAL SECTION

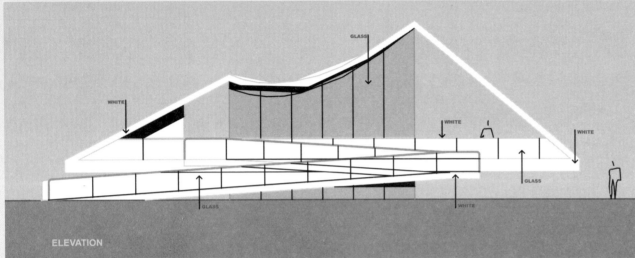

ELEVATION

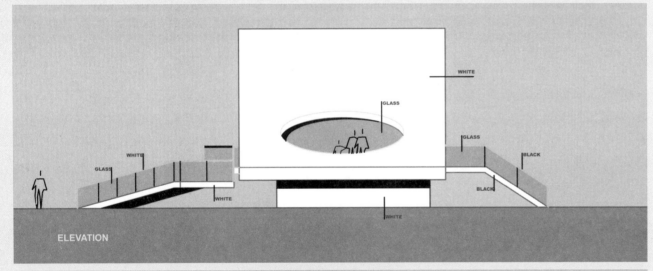

ELEVATION

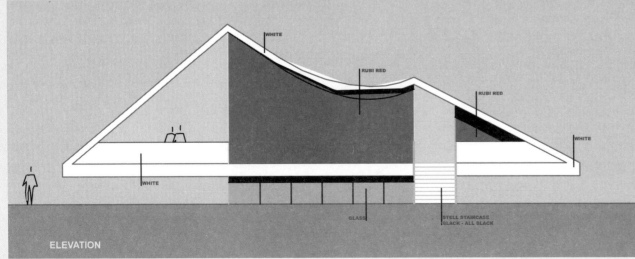

ELEVATION

Drawings show the use of color in the final design ranging from bland and light gray to white and ruby red. The locations of glass surfaces are also indicated.

Zeichnungen zeigen die Zuweisung von Farben im fertigen Entwurf an – von mattem Grau über Hellgrau und Weiß bis hin zu Rubinrot. Auch die Position der Glasflächen ist angegeben.

Ces dessins montrent l'utilisation des couleurs dans le projet final, allant d'un gris neutre et léger à un blanc pur et un rouge rubis. On note aussi l'emplacement des surfaces vitrées.

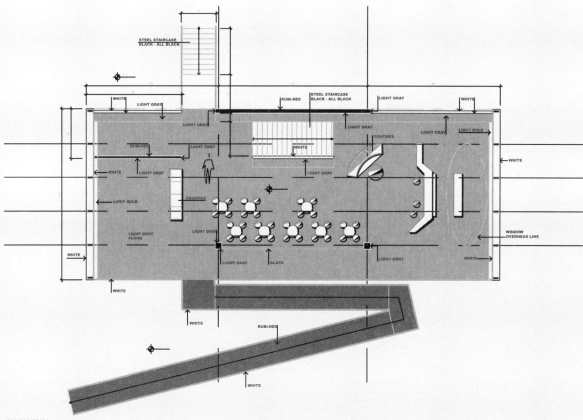

BASEMENT LEVEL

MAIN LEVEL

Another drawing gives the color scheme for the floor surfaces, and shows the placement of furniture in the finished pavilion. The angled walkway is marked to be colored ruby red, a bit like the approach to the Niterói Contemporary Art Museum (1996).

Eine weitere Zeichnung verzeichnet das Farbschema für die Bodenflächen sowie die Platzierung von Einbauten und Möbeln im fertiggestellten Pavillon. Die geneigte Rampe ist rubinrot und erinnert an den Zugang zum Museum für zeitgenössische Kunst in Niterói (1996).

Autre dessin indiquant la gamme chromatique des sols et l'implantation du mobilier dans le pavillon achevé. La rampe inclinée est notée en « rouge rubis », un peu comme pour l'accès du Musée d'art contemporain de Niterói (1996).

IV.31

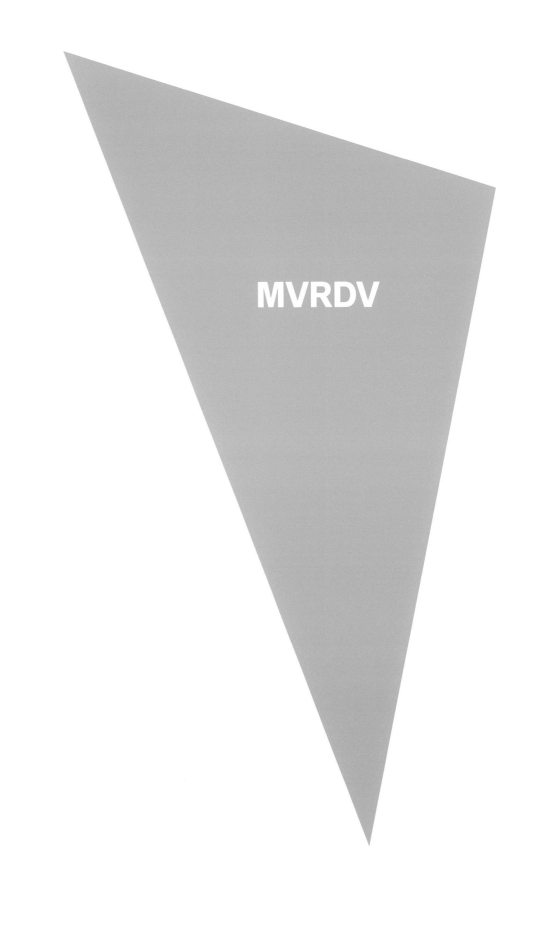

2004
MVRDV

2004 **MVRDV**

MVRDV
Postbus 63136
3002 JC Rotterdam
The Netherlands

Tel: +31 10 477 28 60
Fax: +31 10 477 36 27
E-mail: office@mvrdv.nl
Web: www.mvrdv.nl

MVRDV was created in 1991 by Winy Maas, Jacob van Rijs, and Nathalie de Vries. The name of the firm is made up of the initials of the surnames of the partners. Born in 1959 in Schijndel, Maas studied, like his two partners, at the Technical University in Delft. Jacob van Rijs was born in Amsterdam in 1964, Nathalie de Vries in Appingedam in 1964. Both Maas and Van Rijs worked for Rem Koolhaas in OMA. Maas and de Vries worked in the office of Ben van Berkel before founding MVRDV, and Nathalie de Vries also worked with Mecanoo in Delft. Aside from the Villa VPRO (Hilversum, 1997), the architects designed the spectacular Dutch Pavilion at Expo 2000 in Hanover. MVRDV have also worked on urban development schemes such as their Shadow City Bergen Op Zoom project (1993); the masterplan for Parklane Airport (Eindhoven); and the masterplan for Subdivision 10 in Ypenburg (both in the Netherlands). They also completed the Matsudai Cultural Village Center (Matsudai, Niigata, Japan, 2002–03). More recent work includes the GYRE Building (Shibuya-ku, Tokyo, Japan, 2006–07); Celosía housing in Madrid (Spain, 2001–08); Westerdokseiland housing (Amsterdam, the Netherlands, under construction); and the Torre Huerta (Valencia, Spain, 2007–10).

MVRDV wurde 1991 von Winy Maas, Jacob van Rijs und Nathalie de Vries gegründet. Der Name des Büros besteht aus den Initialen der Partner. Maas, 1959 in Schijndel geboren, studierte ebenso wie seine beiden Partner an der TU Delft. Jacob van Rijs wurde 1964 in Amsterdam geboren, Nathalie de Vries 1964 in Appingedam. Sowohl Maas als auch Van Rijs waren bei OMA für Rem Koolhaas tätig. Maas und De Vries arbeiteten für Ben van Berkel, bevor sie MVRDV gründeten, Nathalie de Vries darüber hinaus für Mecanoo in Delft. Neben der Villa VPRO (Hilversum, 1997) entwarfen die Architekten den spektakulären Niederländischen Pavillon für die Expo 2000 in Hannover. MVRDV arbeitete außerdem an Stadtentwicklungsprogrammen wie dem Projekt *Shadow City Bergen Op Zoom* (1993), dem Masterplan für den Flughafen Parklane (Eindhoven) sowie für Subdivision 10 in Ypenburg (beide in den Niederlanden). Darüber hinaus realisierten sie das Kulturzentrum in Matsudai (Matsudai, Niigata, Japan, 2002–03). Jüngere Projekte sind unter anderem das GYRE Building (Shibuya-ku, Tokio, Japan, 2006–07), die Wohnanlage Celosía in Madrid (Spanien, 2001–08), das Wohnviertel Westerdokseiland (Amsterdam, im Bau) und der Torre Huerta (Valencia, Spanien, 2007–10).

L'agence MVRDV a été créée en 1991 par Winy Maas, Jacob van Rijs et Nathalie de Vries. Son sigle reprend les initiales de noms de famille des associés. Né en 1959 à Schijndel, Maas, comme ses deux partenaires, a étudié à l'Université technologique de Delft. Jacob van Rijs est né à Amsterdam en 1964 et Nathalie de Vries à Appingedam en 1964. Maas et van Rijs ont tous deux travaillé pour OMA, ainsi que dans l'agence de Ben van Berkel, avant de fonder MVRDV. Nathalie de Vries a également travaillé chez Mecanoo à Delft. Parmi leurs réalisations en dehors de la villa VPRO (Hilversum, 1997), ils ont conçu le spectaculaire Pavillon néerlandais à Expo 2000 à Hanovre. MVRDV a également œuvré sur des projets de développement urbain comme « Shadow City Bergen Op Zoom » (1993) ; le plan directeur de l'aéroport Parklane (Eindhoven) et le plan directeur de la Subdivision 10 à Ypenburg. Récemment, l'agence a réalisé le centre culturel du village de Matsudai (Matsudai, Niigata, Japon, 2002–03) ; l'immeuble GYRE (Shibuya-ku, Tokyo, Japon, 2006–07) ; les logements de Celosía à Madrid (Espagne, 2001–08) ; les logements de Westerdokseiland (Amsterdam, Pays-Bas, en construction) et la Torre Huerta (Valencia, Espagne, 2007–10).

The 2004 Summer Pavilion was unique for at least two excellent reasons. First of all, the design proposed to entirely cover the Serpentine Gallery itself with the form of a grass-covered "mountain." It must also remain in a category apart because this ambitious pavilion was never actually built. The structure was to cover even the weathervane of the Serpentine, rising over 23 meters in height, and increase the footprint of the combined structures to 2475 square meters. MVRDV proposed to allow existing park paths to continue up their artificial mountain, and to bring light, air, and even visitors into the "underground" complex through slits. Inside the pavilion, made of galvanized steel, the architects planned a café-auditorium providing space for the Park Nights program of the gallery. Given the subterranean nature of the space thus created, MVRDV paid careful attention to the practical and symbolic impact of interior lighting, stating: "Depending on the requirements of these programs, the lighting can be altered by the use of additional artificial beams of light, which can be directed up at the reflective, galvanized-steel structure creating an artificial sky; or it can be turned downwards, presenting the Gallery beneath like hidden treasure." In more theoretical terms, the architects stated: "All the former Serpentine Pavilions were located on the lawn in front of the Gallery's building, but what would happen if we absorbed the Gallery into the Pavilion. Would it be possible to create a marriage between the two, challenging the art inside the Gallery and forcing new interpretations? The concept intends to forge a stronger relationship between the Pavilion and the Gallery, so that it becomes not a separate structure, but an extension of the Gallery. By subsuming the current building inside the Pavilion, it is transformed into a mysterious hidden space." Indeed, MVRDV have been the only architects to really address the issue of the physical separation of the Serpentine Gallery itself and its Summer Pavilions. Their structure was not content with sitting apart from its "mother" building, preferring instead to swallow it and replace the Serpentine with a new hill in the midst of Hyde Park. The complexities of the design unfortunately caused it not to be built.

Der Sommerpavillon 2004 war aus mindestens zwei guten Gründen einzigartig. Der Entwurf sah vor, die Serpentine Gallery vollständig mit einem grasbewachsenen „Berg" zu überbauen. Darüber hinaus ist der Pavillon auch deshalb ein Sonderfall, weil er nie gebaut wurde. Der „Berg" sollte sogar die über 23 m hohe Wetterfahne der Serpentine überbauen. Damit hätte sich die Grundfläche des gesamten Komplexes auf 2475 m² erhöht. MVRDV wollte die bestehenden Wege im Park über den Berg weiterführen und Licht, Luft und sogar Besucher durch Schlitze in den „unterirdischen" Komplex lassen. Im Pavillon aus verzinktem Stahl planten die Architekten ein Café und ein Auditorium für das *Park-Nights*-Programm der Galerie. Da die Räume unter der Erde lagen, schenkten MVRDV besonders der praktischen und symbolischen Wirkung der Innenbeleuchtung große Aufmerksamkeit: „Je nach Anforderung des Programms lässt sich das Licht durch zusätzliche künstliche Lichtstrahlen verändern, die sich auf die reflektierende Konstruktion aus verzinktem Stahl richten und so einen künstlichen Himmel entstehen lassen oder nach unten gelenkt werden können und das Galeriegebäude als versteckten Schatz erscheinen lassen." Theoretischer formuliert erklärten die Architekten: „Alle bisherigen Serpentine-Pavillons standen auf dem Rasen vor der Galerie, doch was würde geschehen, wenn die Galerie vom Pavillon geschluckt würde? Wäre es möglich, die beiden zu verbinden und so die Kunst in der Galerie zu hinterfragen und neue Interpretationen zu erzwingen? Das Konzept ist darauf angelegt, eine engere Beziehung zwischen Pavillon und Galerie zu schmieden, sodass er kein separater Bau, sondern eine Erweiterung der Galerie wird. Indem das bestehende Gebäude im Pavillon aufgeht, wird es zu einem geheimnisvollen, verborgenen Raum." MRVDV waren die einzigen Architekten, die sich mit dem Thema der Trennung von Galerie und Sommerpavillon auseinandersetzten. Ihre Konstruktion begnügte sich nicht damit, vor dem „Mutterbau" zu stehen, stattdessen wollte sie ihn schlucken und ihn durch einen neuen Hügel mitten in den Kensington Gardens ersetzen. Aufgrund seiner Komplexität konnte der Entwurf leider nicht realisiert werden.

Le Pavillon d'été 2004 est resté unique pour deux raisons. Tout d'abord, ce projet devait entièrement recouvrir la Serpentine Gallery d'une « montagne » semée d'herbe. Ensuite, il fait partie d'une catégorie particulière puisqu'il n'a jamais été réalisé. La structure projetée devait recouvrir jusqu'aux girouettes de la galerie et s'élever à plus de 213 mètres de haut pour une emprise au sol de 2 475 mètres carrés. MVRDV proposa même que les allées du parc se prolongent sur cette colline artificielle et de ne laisser pénétrer la lumière, l'air et même les visiteurs dans ce complexe en quelque sorte « souterrain » que par des fentes. À l'intérieur de cette construction en acier galvanisé, les architectes avaient prévu un café-auditorium pour les programmes des « Park Nights » de la galerie. L'agence avait beaucoup étudié l'impact pratique et symbolique de l'éclairage intérieur : « Selon les besoins des programmes d'animation, l'éclairage peut être modifié par des faisceaux lumineux artificiels additionnels, dirigés sur la structure réfléchissante en acier galvanisé pour créer un ciel artificiel. Ils peuvent aussi s'orienter vers le bas pour faire de la galerie elle-même une sorte de salle du trésor. » En termes plus théoriques, les architectes précisaient que « tous les anciens pavillons de la Serpentine étaient situés sur une pelouse devant le bâtiment de la galerie, mais que se passerait-il si nous absorbions la galerie dans le pavillon ? Serait-il possible de marier les deux, de se confronter aux œuvres d'art exposées dans la galerie et de pousser à de nouvelles interprétations ? Le concept se propose de forger une relation plus forte entre le pavillon et la galerie, celui-ci n'étant plus une construction séparée mais une extension de la galerie. En subsumant les bâtiments actuels à l'intérieur du pavillon, celui-ci se transforme en un mystérieux espace caché ». MVRDV a été la seule agence à aborder sérieusement le problème de la séparation physique de la Serpentine Gallery et des Pavillons d'été. Son projet ne se contentait pas d'une position modeste face au bâtiment « mère » mais préférait l'avaler, le remplacer par une nouvelle colline en plein Hyde Park. Les multiples problèmes que posaient la réalisation de ce projet ont malheureusement empêché sa réalisation.

Our "aim was to devise a Pavilion that would serve not only the Gallery but also the Park by extending them both," say the architects. Their design remained unbuilt.

Unser „Ziel war es, einen Pavillon zu entwickeln, der nicht nur der Galerie, sondern auch dem Park zugute kommen würde, indem er beide erweitert", erklären die Architekten. Ihr Entwurf blieb unrealisiert.

Notre « but était de proposer un pavillon qui soit utile à la fois à la galerie et au parc dans un agrandissement commun », expliquèrent les architectes. Leur projet n'a pu être réalisé.

"*All the former Serpentine pavilions were located on the lawn in front of the Gallery's building, but what would happen if we absorbed the Gallery into the pavilion?*"
MVRDV

Perspective drawings show the extent to which the "pavilion" would have made the Serpentine disappear. "The concept," say the architects, "intends to forge a stronger relationship between the Pavilion and the Gallery, so that it becomes, not a separate structure but an extension of the Gallery. By subsuming the current building inside the Pavilion, it is transformed into a mysterious hidden space."

Perspektivzeichnungen illustrieren, in welchem Ausmaß der „Pavillon" die Serpentine Gallery verschwinden lassen wollte. „Das Konzept", so die Architekten, „ist darauf angelegt, eine engere Beziehung zwischen Pavillon und Galerie zu schmieden, sodass er keine separate Konstruktion, sondern eine Erweiterung der Galerie wird. Indem das bestehende Gebäude im Pavillon aufgeht, wird es zu einem geheimnisvollen, verborgenen Raum."

Ces perspectives reconstituées montrent à quel point le « pavillon » aurait, au final, fait entièrement disparaitre la Serpentine Gallery. « Le concept », ont expliqué les architectes, « se propose de forger une relation plus forte entre le pavillon et la galerie, le premier n'étant plus un bâtiment séparé mais une extension de la galerie. En concentrant le bâtiment actuel à l'intérieur du pavillon, ce dernier en fait un mystérieux espace caché. »

PLANS, DRAWINGS AND MODELS

Architectural Design Winy Maas/Jacob van Rijs/Nathalie de Vries
Integrated design Arup/Rory McGowan/Richard Lawson

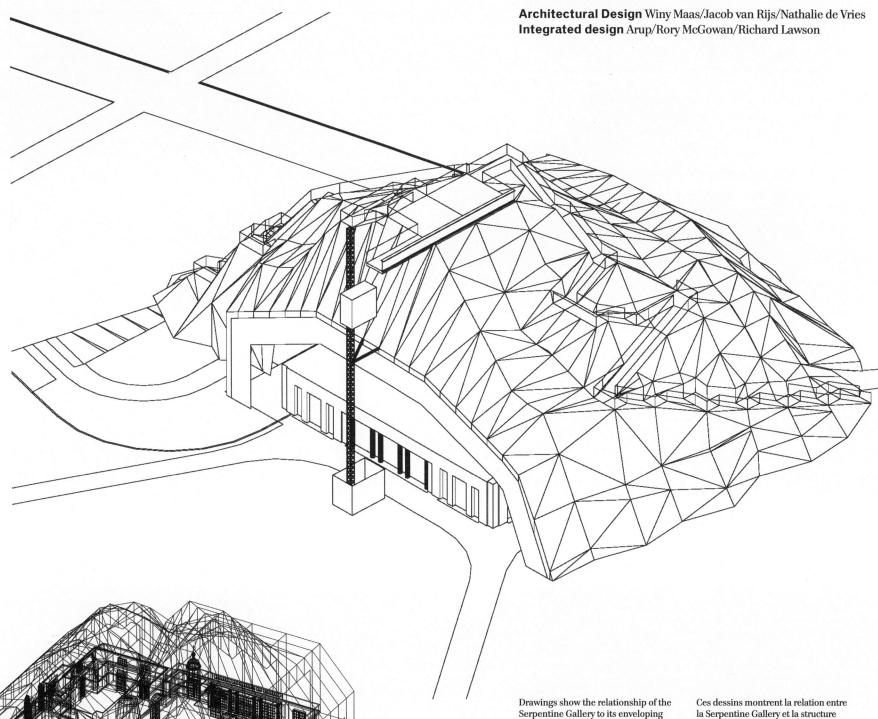

Drawings show the relationship of the Serpentine Gallery to its enveloping structure. "The interior," states MVRDV, "can be seen as a giant three-dimensional 'lobby' in which visitors can also sit. Illumination is provided by an opening in the mountain's surface above the Gallery's existing cupola, which also serves to ventilate the space."

Zeichnungen verdeutlichen das Verhältnis der Serpentine Gallery zu ihrem Überbau. „Der Innenraum", so MVRDV, „lässt sich als monumentale, dreidimensionale ‚Lobby' begreifen, in der die Besucher auch sitzen können. Die Belichtung erfolgt über eine Öffnung an der Spitze des Bergs über der Kuppel des bestehenden Galeriegebäude. Sie dient auch der Belüftung des Raums."

Ces dessins montrent la relation entre la Serpentine Gallery et la structure qui l'enveloppe. « L'intérieur », précise MVRDV, « peut être considéré comme un gigantesque *lobby* en trois dimensions dans lequel les visiteurs peuvent aussi venir s'asseoir. L'éclairage est apporté par une ouverture au sommet de la montagne, au-dessus de la coupole existante de la galerie, qui sert également à la ventilation du volume. »

The architects proposed to create new
paths and stairways along the flanks
of their artificial mountain, as well as
green spaces that they likened to
"alpine meadows."

Die Architekten hatten vorgesehen,
neue Spazierwege und Treppen über die
Hänge ihres künstlichen Bergs zu führen
und Grünflächen anzulegen, die sie mit
„Bergwiesen" verglichen.

Les architectes avaient proposé de créer
des cheminements et des escaliers sur
les pentes de cette montagne artificielle,
ainsi que des espaces verts comparés par
eux à des « alpages ».

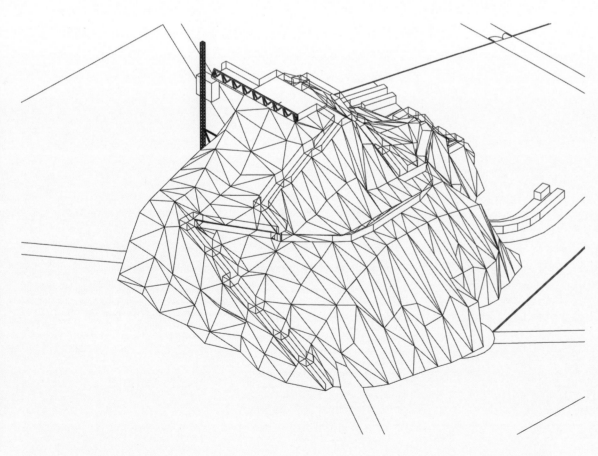

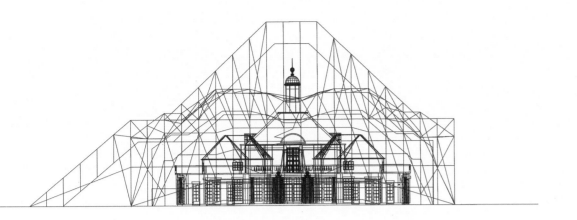

Drawings show that the public would have been allowed quite literally to stand on a platform above the cupola of the old Serpentine Gallery. The project proved to be difficult to carry out and was eventually abandoned.

Zeichnungen belegen, dass die Besucher auf einer Plattform buchstäblich über der Kuppel der alten Serpentine Gallery hätten stehen können. Das Projekt erwies sich in der Umsetzung jedoch als zu problematisch und musste letztendlich aufgegeben werden.

Le public aurait pu accéder à une plate-forme aménagée au-dessus de la coupole de la galerie. Le projet, difficile à mettre en œuvre, a fini par être abandonné.

22

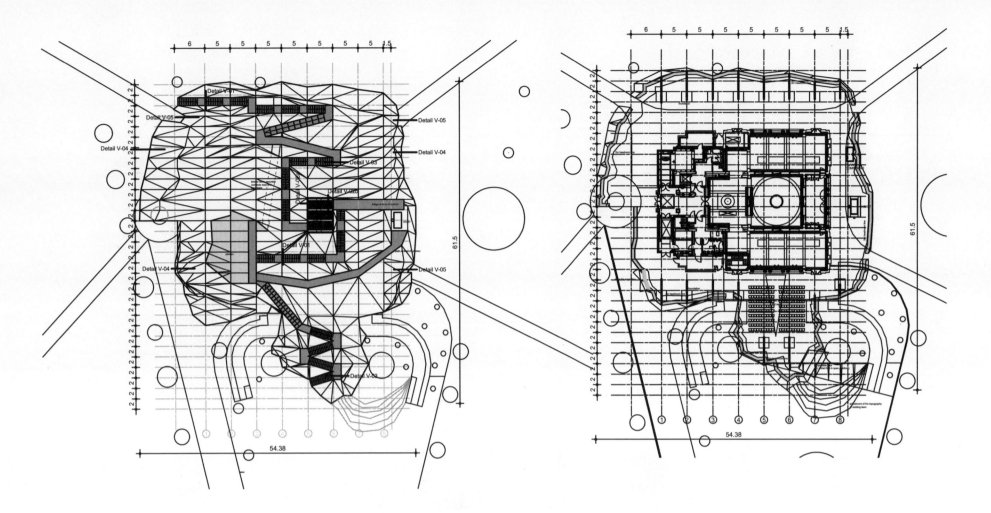

Plans (above) show the way in which the irregular pavilion engulfs the Serpentine. The walkways leading to the summit of the structure are seen in the plan above left and in the section drawing below, with visitors standing above the cupola.

Grundrisse (oben) zeigen, wie stark der unregelmäßige Pavillon die Serpentine vereinnahmt hätte. Die zum Gipfel der Konstruktion führenden Wege sind auf dem Grundriss oben links und dem Querschnitt unten zu erkennen. Dort stehen Besucher über der Kuppel.

Les plans ci-dessus montrent de quelle manière la forme irrégulière du pavillon enveloppe la Serpentine Gallery. Les cheminements d'accès au sommet de la structure apparaissent sur le plan en haut à gauche et dans la coupe ci-dessous, qui montre des visiteurs au-dessus de la coupole.

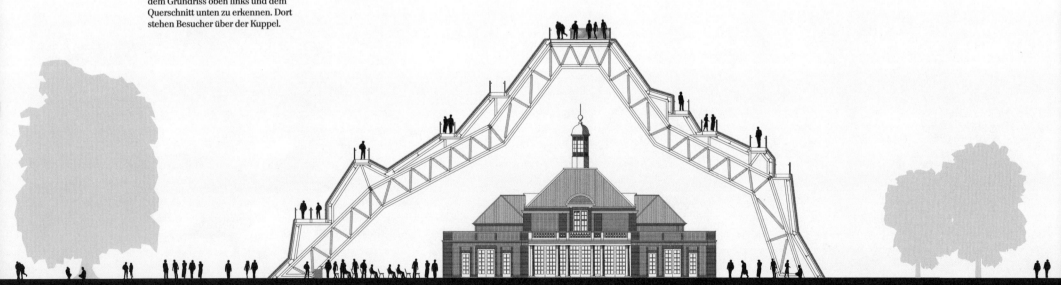

The irregular form of the "mountain" rises high over the roof of the Serpentine, and takes a "natural" irregular form as seen in the site plan to the right. Below, section drawings show the proportions of the Serpentine within the pavilion.

Die unregelmäßige Form des „Bergs" erhebt sich hoch über das Dach der Serpentine und nimmt, wie im Grundriss rechts zu sehen, eine „natürliche" unregelmäßige Form an. Querschnitte (unten) veranschaulichen die Proportionen der Serpentine im Pavillon.

La hauteur de la « montagne » dépasse largement celle de la toiture de la galerie « naturelle », comme le montre le plan de droite. Ci-dessous, une coupe montre les proportions de la galerie à l'intérieur du pavillon.

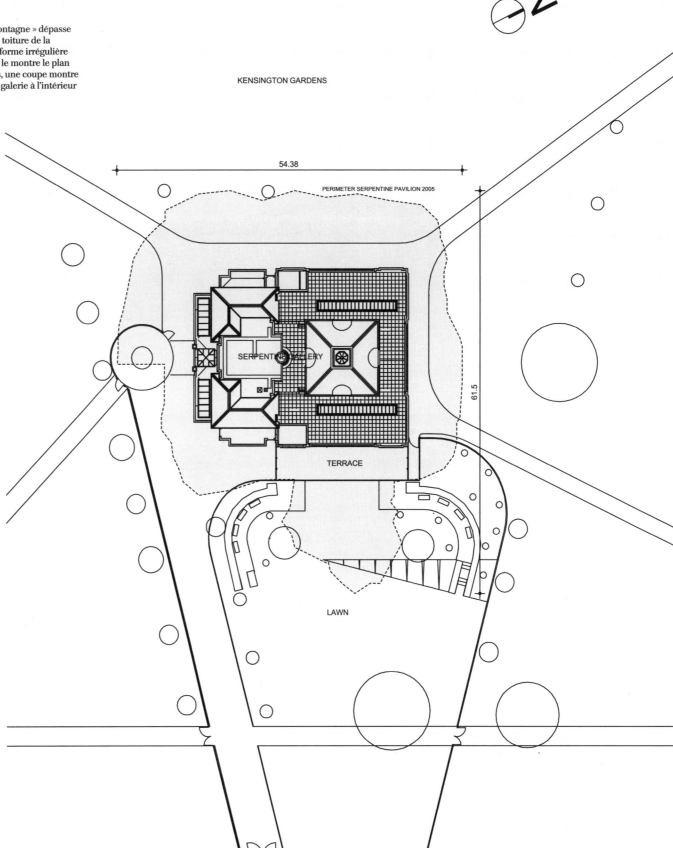

KENSINGTON GARDENS

54.38

PERIMETER SERPENTINE PAVILION 2005

61.5

SERPENTINE GALLERY

TERRACE

LAWN

WEST CARRIAGE DRIVE

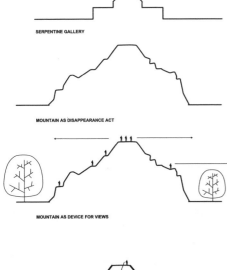

SERPENTINE GALLERY

MOUNTAIN AS DISAPPEARANCE ACT

MOUNTAIN AS DEVICE FOR VIEWS

MOUNTAIN AS DEVICE TO EXPERIENCE THE GALLERY IN NEW WAYS

MOUNTAIN AS DEVICE FOR A NEW INTERIOR

The scale of the MVRDV Pavilion is such that a generous gap between the supporting structure and the Serpentine Gallery itself creates a cavernous interior space, where the "artificial" aspect of the mountain's metallic supports is revealed.

Der MVRDV-Pavillon wäre von so gewaltigen Ausmaßen gewesen, dass schon allein der erhebliche Zwischenraum zwischen Tragwerkskonstruktion und Serpentine Gallery einen mächtigen Innenraum gebildet hätte, in dem die „Künstlichkeit" der Metallträger des Bergs offensichtlich geworden wäre.

L'importance des dimensions du pavillon de MVRDV dégage un vaste volume libre entre la surface de la structure et la galerie, espace caverneux dans lequel se révèle l'aspect « artificiel » des supports métalliques de la « montagne ».

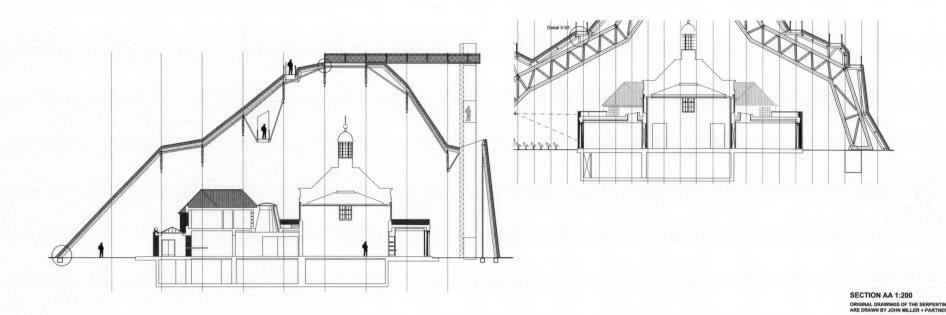

SECTION AA 1:200
ORIGINAL DRAWINGS OF THE SERPENTINE GALLERY
ARE DRAWN BY JOHN MILLER + PARTNERS ARCHITECTS

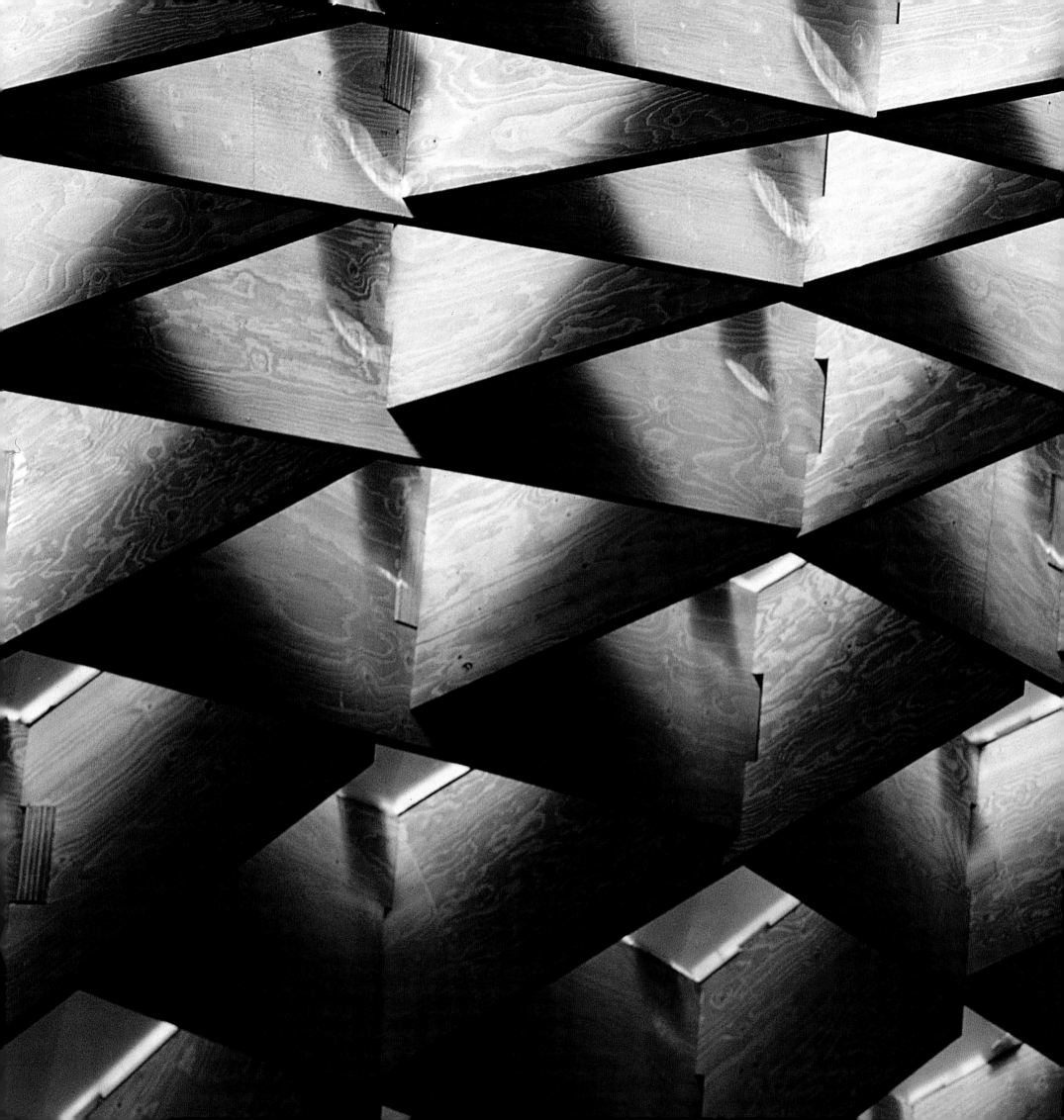

2005

ÁLVARO SIZA &
EDUARDO SOUTO
DE MOURA

2005 ÁLVARO SIZA & EDUARDO SOUTO DE MOURA

Álvaro Siza Arquitecto Lda
Rua do Aleixo, 53–2
4150–043 Porto
Portugal

Tel: +351 22 616 72 70
Fax: +351 22 616 72 79
E-mail: siza@mail.telepac.pt
Web: www.alvarosiza.com/

Souto Moura Arquitectos Lda
R. do Aleixo, 531° A
4150–043 Porto
Portugal

Tel: +351 22 618 75 47
Fax: +351 22 610 80 92
E-mail: souto.moura@mail.telepac.pt

Born in Matosinhos, Portugal, in 1933, Álvaro Siza studied at the University of Porto School of Architecture (1949–55). He created his own practice in 1954, and worked with Fernando Tavora from 1955 to 1958. He has been a professor of Construction at the University of Porto since 1976. He received the European Community's Mies van der Rohe Prize in 1988 and the Pritzker Prize in 1992. He built many small-scale projects in Portugal and worked on the restructuring of the Chiado in Lisbon (Portugal, 1989–); the Meteorology Center in Barcelona (Spain, 1989–92); the Vitra Furniture Factory (Weil am Rhein, Germany, 1991–94); the Porto School of Architecture, Porto University (Portugal, 1986–95); and the University of Aveiro Library (Aveiro, Portugal, 1988–95). His latest projects are the Portuguese Pavilion for the 1998 Lisbon World's Fair (with Eduardo Souto de Moura) and the Serralves Foundation (Porto, 1996–99). Other recent projects include the Aldega Mayor Winery (Campo Maior, Portugal, 2005–06) and the Ibere Camargo Foundation (Porto Alegre, Brazil, 2008). Eduardo Souto de Moura was born in Porto in 1952. He graduated from the School of Architecture of Porto (ESBAP) in 1980. He worked in the office of Álvaro Siza from 1974 to 1979 and created his own office the following year. He received the Pritzker Prize in 2011. His work includes the renovation of the Municipal Market in Braga (1997); the Silo Norte Shopping building; and the project for the Portuguese Pavilion, Expo Hanover (with Álvaro Siza, 1999). Other recent work includes the conversion of the building of the Carvoeira da Foz (Porto); and the Braga Stadium (2004); as well as the Bragança Contemporary Art Museum (Portugal, 2002–08).

Álvaro Siza, geboren 1933 in Matosinhos, Portugal, studierte an der Architekturfakultät der Universität Porto (1949–55). Sein eigenes Büro gründete er 1954, von 1955 bis 1958 arbeitete er mit Fernando Tavora. Seit 1976 ist er Professor für Konstruktionslehre an der Universität Porto. 1988 erhielt er den Mies-van-der-Rohe-Preis der Europäischen Union, 1992 den Pritzker-Preis. Neben vielen kleineren Bauprojekten, die Siza in Portugal realisierte, wirkte er auch bei der Wiederherstellung des Stadtbezirks Chiado mit (Lissabon, Portugal, seit 1989), baute ein Meteorologisches Zentrum (Barcelona, Spanien, 1989–92), eine Produktionshalle für Vitra (Weil am Rhein, Deutschland, 1991–94), die Architekturfakultät der Universität Porto (Portugal, 1986–95) sowie die Universitätsbibliothek von Aveiro (Portugal, 1988–95). Jüngere Projekte sind unter anderem der portugiesische Pavillon für die Expo 1998 in Lissabon (mit Eduardo Souto de Moura) sowie das Museum Serralves (Porto, 1998), das Weingut Adega Mayor in Campo Maior (2005 bis 2006) und die Stiftung Iberê Camargo in Porto Alegre (Brasilien, 2008). Eduardo Souto de Moura wurde 1952 in Porto geboren. Sein Architekturstudium schloss er 1980 an der ESBAP in Porto ab. Von 1974 bis 1979 arbeitete er für Álvaro Siza und gründete 1980 sein eigenes Büro. 2011 erhielt er den Pritzker-Preis. Zu seinen Projekten zählen die Sanierung der städtischen Markthalle in Braga (1997), das Einkaufszentrum Silo Norte Shopping und die Projektplanung des portugiesischen Pavillons für die Expo in Hannover (mit Álvaro Siza, 1999). Zu den jüngeren Projekten zählen der Umbau der Carvoeira da Foz (Porto) und das Stadion in Braga (2004) sowie das Museum für zeitgenössische Kunst in Bragança (2002–08).

Né à Matosinhos au Portugal en 1933, Álvaro Siza a étudié à l'École d'architecture de Porto (1949–55). Il a créé son agence en 1954 et collaboré avec Fernando Tavora de 1955 à 1958. Professeur de construction à l'université de Porto depuis 1976, il a reçu le prix Mies van de Rohe de la Communauté européenne en 1988 et le prix Pritzker en 1992. Parmi ses réalisations : de nombreux projets à petite échelle au Portugal ; la restructuration du quartier du Chiado à Lisbonne (1989–) ; le Centre de météorologie de Barcelone (1989–92) ; une usine de meubles pour Vitra (Weil am Rhein, Allemagne, 1991–94) ; l'École d'architecture de Porto, université de Porto (1986–95) et la bibliothèque de l'université d'Aveiro (Portugal, 1988–95). Plus récemment, il a construit le Pavillon portugais pour l'Exposition universelle de Lisbonne en 1998 (avec Eduardo Souto de Moura) et la Fondation Serralves (Porto, 1996–99). Il est également l'auteur des chais Aldega Mayor (Campo Maior, Portugal, 2005–06) et de la Fondation Ibere Camargo (Porto Alegre, Brésil, 2008). Eduardo Souto de Moura, né à Porto en 1952, est diplômé de l'École d'architecture de Porto (ESBAP, 1980). Il a fait partie de l'agence d'Álvaro Siza de 1974 à 1979 et a créé sa propre agence l'année suivante. Il a reçu le prix Pritzker en 2011. Parmi ses travaux : la rénovation du marché municipal de Braga (Portugal, 1997) ; l'immeuble du centre commercial Silo Norte et le Pavillon portugais pour l'Exposition universelle de Hanovre (avec Álvaro Siza, 1999). Plus récemment, il a réalisé la reconversion de l'immeuble de Carvoeira da Foz (Porto) ; le stade de Braga (2004) ainsi que le Musée d'art contemporain de Bragança (Portugal, 2002–08).

Built between 11 April and 30 June 2005, this 380-square-meter temporary pavilion was the fifth of its kind to be built in Kensington Gardens next to the Serpentine Gallery. With its 22 x 17-meter footprint and maximum height of 5.4 meters, the pavilion was a timber-framed, column-free structure with semi-transparent five-millimeter-thick polycarbonate roofing. Tables and chairs designed by the architects adorned the interior of the building, which was dismantled in October of 2005. Placed in a complex interlocking pattern were 427 unique timber beams, which started in one corner and "radiated out to finish at the opposite extreme." As Hamish Nevile from the engineer's firm Arup explains: "It was created as an evolution of the 'lamella' barrel-vault roofs developed in Germany in the early 1920s. While traditional lamellas were built from identical elements, however, each element of the Pavilion is unique, having a different length and inclination. This geometric freedom enables the precise expression of the complex form demanded by the architects. The reciprocal beam system creates a continuous structure that runs from the roof down to form the walls of the Pavilion." The structure was illuminated by 250 solar-powered lamps and was used for the Time Out Park Nights at the Serpentine Gallery program of talks, films, lectures, and sound events. The pavilion was furnished with 20 tables, 80 chairs, and three chaise longues designed by Siza and Souto de Moura, with a further 200 moveable chairs brought in for the lectures and films. Álvaro Siza saw this pavilion in an unexpected, metaphorical way in relation to the nearby Serpentine: "The Pavilion leans over the neoclassical building like an animal with legs stuck to the ground, tensed with growing hunger, yet held back. His back arched, fur erect. He looks sharply, focusing his whiskers on the building. Forcing it to mark its territory. Locking his legs, lowering his head, restraining a forward leap. Will he eat it one day?" Referring in a less indirect manner to the wooden forms of the Pavilion, Eduardo Souto de Moura said he felt it was "interesting to make something, not an abstract thing like the other architects did but something linked to the trees…" Cecil Balmond, an active participant in this project, described it as a three-way dialogue. In March 2005, he wrote: "A grid curves and escalates, its trajectory a shifting rhythm of material, its skin a studded upholstery of form. With shape and light, material and texture, tradition transcends into a contemporary vernacular on the lawn of the Serpentine Gallery this year."

Der zwischen dem 11. April und 30. Juni 2005 erbaute, 380 m² große Pavillon war der fünfte seiner Art. Bei einer Grundfläche von 22 x 17 m und einer maximalen Höhe von 5,4 m war er eine stützenfreie Holzrahmenkonstruktion mit semitransparenten, 5 mm starken Dachplatten aus Polycarbonat. Tische und Stühle im Pavillon, der bis Oktober 2005 stand, hatten die Architekten selbst entworfen. 427 individuell geformte Holzträger wurden zu einem komplexen Muster verzahnt, das in einer Ecke begann, von dort aus „ausstrahlte und am gegenüberliegenden äußersten Ende" abschloss. Hamish Nevile vom Ingenieurbüro Arup erklärt: „Er war als Weiterentwicklung des Zollinger-Lamellendachs geplant, das in den frühen 1920er-Jahren in Deutschland entwickelt worden war. Während traditionelle Lamellenkonstruktionen aus identischen Elementen bestehen, hatte jedes Element dieses Pavillons seine eigene Form, Länge und Neigung. Diese geometrische Freiheit entsprach genau der von den Architekten geforderten, komplexen Form. Das System aus reziproken Trägern erlaubt eine durchgängige Konstruktion, die vom Dach nahtlos in die Wände des Pavillons übergeht." Der Bau wurde mit 250 Solarleuchten erhellt und für das Programm der *Time Out Park Nights at the Serpentine Gallery* genutzt. Er war mit 20 Tischen, 80 Stühlen und drei Chaiselongues möbliert. Für Vorträge und Filme konnten 200 Stühle aufgestellt werden. Álvaro Siza interpretierte den Pavillon und seine Beziehung zur Serpentine metaphorisch: „Der Pavillon beugt sich zum klassizistischen Bau hinüber, wie ein Tier, das mit den Beinen im Boden feststeckt; gespannt und immer hungriger und doch gebunden. Sein Rücken ist gestreckt, sein Fell aufgestellt. Das Tier lauert, richtet seine Fühler auf das Haus. Zwingt es, sein Terrain abzustecken. Spannt seine Beine an, senkt den Kopf, gestattet sich nicht, vorwärtszuspringen. Wird es den Bau eines Tages fressen?" Eduardo Souto de Moura bezog sich direkter auf die Holzformen des Pavillons und erklärte, für ihn sei es „interessant, etwas zu schaffen – nichts Abstraktes wie die anderen Architekten, sondern etwas, das eine Verbindung zu den Bäumen hat ..." Cecil Balmond, der auch am Projekt beteiligt war, nannte es einen Drei-Wege-Dialog. Er schrieb im März 2005: „Ein Gitter wölbt sich und schwingt sich auf, seine Flugbahn ist ein veränderlicher Rhythmus aus Materialien, seine Haut eine nietenbeschlagene Polsterform. Mit Form und Licht, Material und Textur wächst die Tradition dieses Jahr über sich hinaus, wird zu einer zeitgenössischen Formensprache auf dem Rasen der Serpentine Gallery."

Construit du 11 avril au 30 juin 2005 et démantelé en octobre, ce pavillon temporaire de 380 mètres carrés était le cinquième de la série. D'une surface au sol de 22 x 17 mètres et de 5,4 mètres de hauteur maximum, il présentait une ossature en bois, une toiture en plaques de polycarbonate semi-transparent de 5 millimètres d'épaisseur, et ne comportait aucune colonne. Les 427 poutres de bois avaient été assemblées selon un plan complexe qui partait d'un angle et « rayonnait jusqu'à l'autre extrémité ». Pour Hamish Nevile, de l'agence d'ingénierie Arup : « C'était une évolution des toitures à voûtes en berceau de type *lamella* mis au point en Allemagne au début des années 1920 ». Alors que les *lamellas* étaient assemblées à partir d'éléments identiques, ici chacun est unique, dans sa longueur comme dans son inclinaison. Cette liberté géométrique permet d'exprimer avec précision la forme complexe voulue par les architectes. Le système réciproque de poutraison crée une structure continue qui part du toit et descend vers le bas en formant les murs du pavillon. » La structure éclairée par 250 sources lumineuses alimentées par énergie solaire fut utilisée pour le programme de manifestations « Time Out Park Nights at the Serpentine Gallery ». Le pavillon était meublé de 20 tables, 80 sièges et 3 chaises longues dessinées par Siza et Souto de Moura, sans compter les 200 chaises supplémentaires apportées pour les conférences et les projections de films. Pour Alvaro Siza, ce pavillon est de façon métaphorique et inattendue en relation avec la galerie : « Le pavillon s'incline vers le bâtiment néoclassique, comme un animal dont les pattes seraient prises dans le sol, dans une tension due à un appétit grandissant mais néanmoins contenu. Son dos s'étire, sa peau se dresse. Il observe, concentre ses antennes sur la demeure. Il l'oblige à définir son espace. Il referme les pattes, baisse la tête, s'interdisant d'avancer. Mangera-t-il un jour ? » Se référant de manière moins indirecte à l'utilisation du bois et de ses formes dans ce pavillon, Eduardo Souto de Moura a dit sentir qu'il était « intéressant de faire quelque chose qui ne soit pas abstrait comme ce que nos confrères avaient proposé, mais quelque chose de lié aux arbres … » Cecil Balmond en parle comme d'un dialogue à trois voix. En mars 2005, il écrivait : « Une trame s'incurve et monte, accomplit sa trajectoire dans un rythme marqué par les matériaux, sa peau est un rembourrage capitonné. Par la forme et la lumière, le matériau et la texture, la tradition se transcende cette année en un style vernaculaire contemporain sur la pelouse de la Serpentine Gallery. »

Two hundred and fifty solar-powered lamps are arrayed on the roof of the pavilion, whose unexpected, scaled appearance marked a decided variant on the more clearly "modern" forms of previous summer structures at the Serpentine.

Auf dem Dach des Pavillons, dessen erstaunliche, geschuppte Optik eine deutliche Abweichung von der sonst so dezidiert „modernen" Formensprache früherer Sommerpavillons der Serpentine war, waren 250 Solarleuchten angeordnet.

Deux cent cinquante lampes à alimentation par énergie solaire étaient réparties sur la toiture du pavillon, dont le surprenant aspect écaillé marquait une forte différence par rapport aux projets précédents, plus ouvertement « modernes ».

A sketch by Álvaro Siza relates the form of the pavilion to the presence of the Serpentine itself. Two photos emphasize the studded and ribbed nature of the structure, with its almost reptilian appearance.

Eine Skizze Álvaro Sizas stellt die Form des Pavillons in Bezug zur Serpentine. Die zwei Aufnahmen verdeutlichen die fast reptilienhafte Anmutung des Baus, der mit Nieten beschlagen und von Rippen durchzogen ist.

Un croquis d'Álvaro Siza montre le lien entre la forme du pavillon et la galerie. Les deux photographies font ressortir les nervures et l'aspect « clouté » de la structure qui prend ici une apparence presque reptilienne.

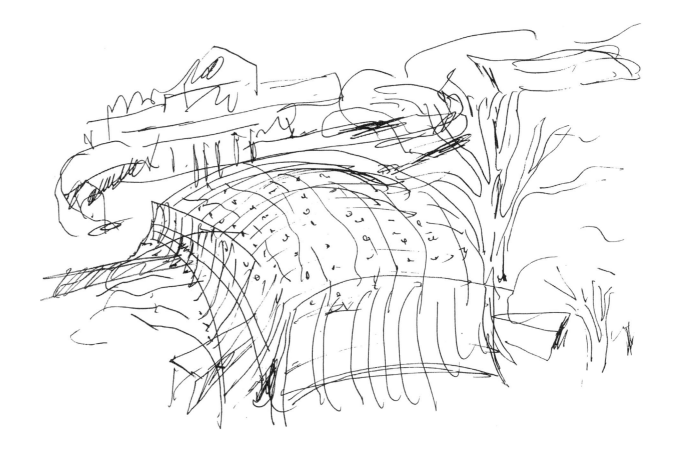

With its generous openings and inward leaning supports, the pavilion takes on something of the appearance of a rather solid tent, with its activities spilling out onto the Kensington Gardens lawns.

Dank der großzügigen Öffnungen und nach innen geneigten Stützen wirkt der Pavillon fast wie ein stabiles Zelt, dessen Betriebsamkeit auf die Rasenflächen der Kensington Gardens übergreift.

Par ses ouvertures généreuses et ses supports inclinés, le pavillon avait l'aspect d'une tente massive dont les activités débordaient sur les pelouses des jardins de Kensington.

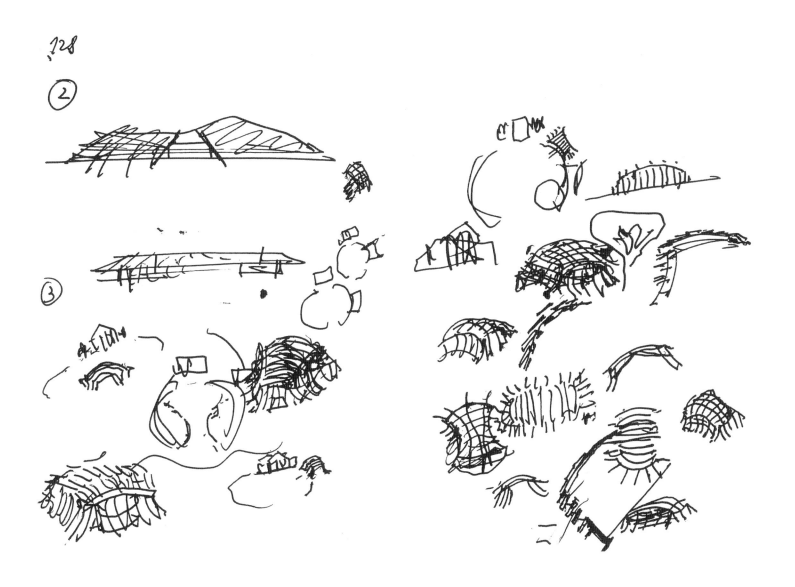

Sketches by the architects and images showing the latticework wooden roof and its column-free interior space amply demonstrate that this design is somewhat out of the mainstream of contemporary architecture, even that usually practiced by the two Portuguese architects involved.

Skizzen der Architekten und Aufnahmen des Pavillons zeigen die hölzerne Gitterkonstruktion des Dachs. Der stützenfreie Innenraum belegt mehr als deutlich, dass dieser Entwurf nicht nur aus dem Mainstream zeitgenössischer Architektur herausfällt, sondern auch aus dem sonstigen Werk der beiden portugiesischen Architekten.

Les croquis des architectes et les photos de la toiture en caissons de bois et de son espace intérieur dégagé de toute colonne montrent à quel point ce projet se situe hors des courants principaux de l'architecture contemporaine, y compris celle pratiquée habituellement par les deux architectes portugais.

The structure of the pavilion was derived from a rectangular grid, which was then "distorted to create a dynamic curvaceous form." It was made of interlocking timber beams, "a material that accentuated the relationship between the Pavilion and surrounding Park."

Die Konstruktion des Pavillons wurde aus einem rechteckigen Raster entwickelt, das anschließend „verformt wurde, um eine dynamisch geschwungene Form zu schaffen". Realisiert wurde sie dank ineinander verzahnter Holzträger, „einem Material, das das Zusammenspiel von Pavillon und umgebender Parklandschaft besonders unterstreicht".

La structure du pavillon est issue d'une trame rectangulaire « déformée pour créer une forme dynamique en courbe ». Elle était en poutres de bois imbriquées, « matériau qui accentuait la relation entre le pavillon et le parc environnant ».

The interior space with its curving bar, architect-designed furniture, and generous glazing is both inviting and open to its environment.

Der Innenraum mit einer geschwungenen Bar, dem von den Architekten entworfenen Mobiliar und großzügiger Verglasung wirkt ebenso einladend wie offen zu seinem Umfeld.

L'espace intérieur, avec son bar incurvé, son mobilier dessiné par les architectes et ses généreux vitrages, était à la fois accueillant et ouvert sur son environnement.

"The temporary pavilion has become unmissable, a rare opportunity to view the work of the finest international architects at first hand. This is how architecture should be exhibited and remembered. See it, and Siza's exquisite space will stay with you."
FINANCIAL TIMES

The arching structure, designed in collaboration with Cecil Balmond of Arup, is emphasized in the performance image to the left.

Bei der Aufführung links im Bild fällt die mit Cecil Balmond entworfene, gewölbte Konstruktion besonders auf.

La forme en arc de la structure, conçue en collaboration avec Cecil Balmond d'Arup, est mise en valeur par l'image de performance reproduite à gauche.

Sketches by Siza and another picture of the prickly skin of the pavilion again call attention to the scaled, tortoise-like armor that constitutes the exterior shell of the structure.

Skizzen von Siza sowie eine weitere Aufnahme der stacheligen Außenhaut des Pavillons lenken nochmals die Aufmerksamkeit auf den geschuppten, schildkrötenartigen Panzer, der die äußere Hülle des Baus bildet.

Les croquis de Siza et une autre image de la peau du pavillon piquetée de luminaires renforcent l'impression de carapace de tortue donnée par l'extérieur de la structure.

PLANS, DRAWINGS
AND MODELS

Architectural Design Álvaro Siza/Eduardo Souto de Moura/Cecil Balmond
Design Team Tiago Figueiredo/Tiago Coelho/Atsushi Ueno
Integrated Design Arup/Hamish Nevile/Martin Self

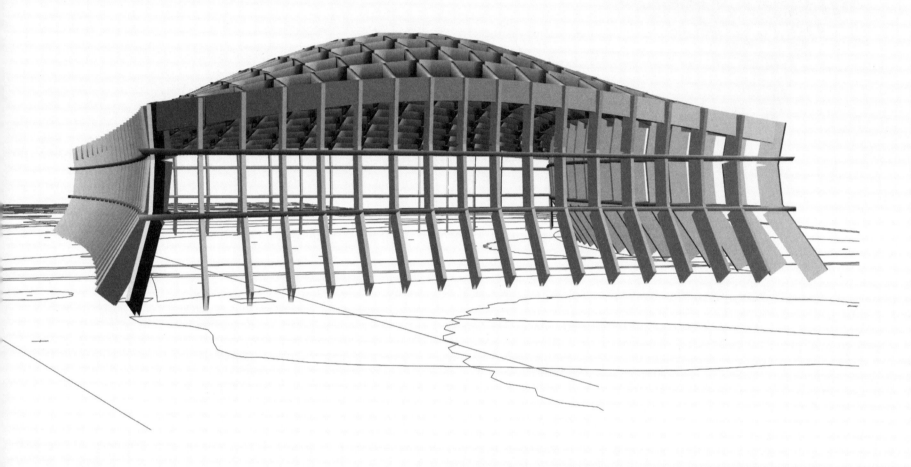

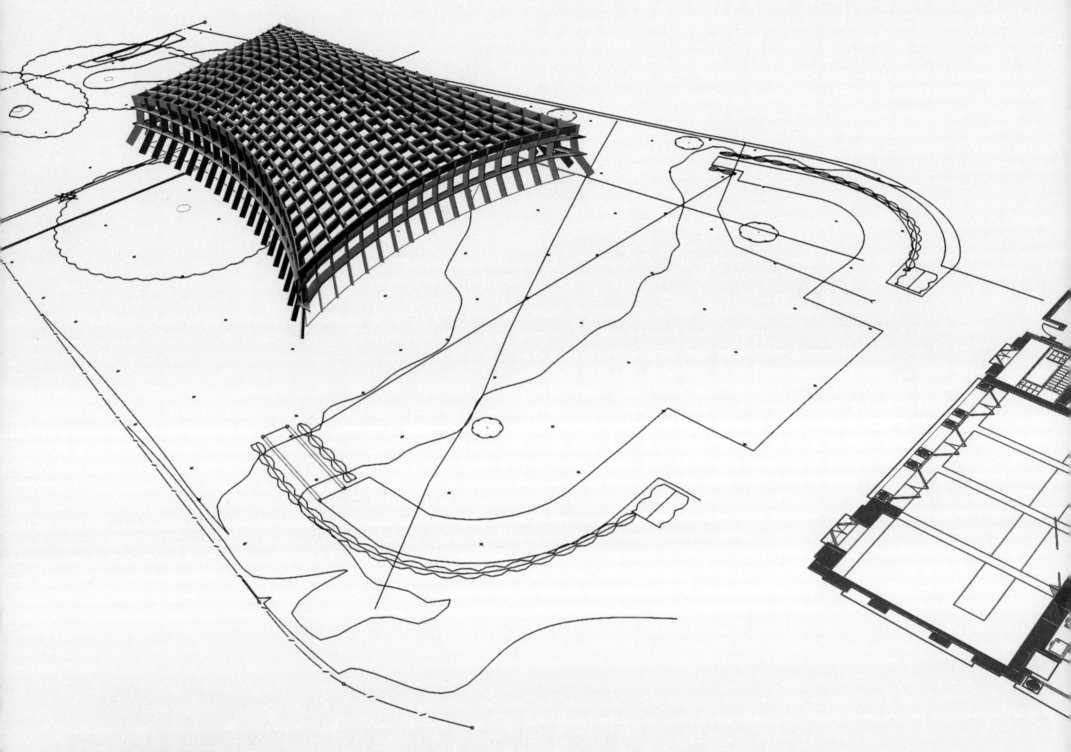

An overall drawing of the pavilion shows
how the originally regular grid employed
by the architects is in some sense
draped over the supports, resulting in
a curving deformation.

Eine Überblickszeichnung des Pavillons
veranschaulicht, wie das von den Architekten verwendete regelmäßige Raster
gewissermaßen über die Stützen drapiert
wurde, wodurch die geschwungene
Verformung entsteht.

Ce dessin du pavillon montre comment
la trame régulière utilisée à l'origine
par les architectes est en quelque
sorte déposée comme un drapé sur
les supports, ce qui produit une
déformation curviligne.

Engineering sketches show the irregular deformation of the original geometric grid and explain that "ETFE strips are cut across the width of the building." ETFE (Ethylene tetrafluoroethylene) is a form of highly resistant plastic.

Bauzeichnungen zeigen die unregelmäßige Verformung des ursprünglich geometrischen Rasters und illustrieren, wie „Streifen aus ETFE den Bau in Querrichtung überziehen". ETFE (Ethylen-Tetrafluorethylen) ist ein hochbeständiger Kunststoff.

Les croquis techniques montrent la déformation irrégulière de la trame géométrique d'origine et la pose de « bandes d'ETFE découpées sur toute la largeur du bâtiment ». L'ETFE (éthylène tétrafluoroéthylène) est un plastique à haute résistance.

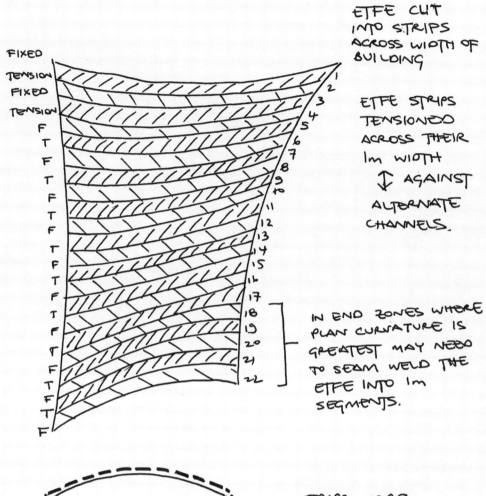

ETFE CUT INTO STRIPS ACROSS WIDTH OF BUILDING

ETFE STRIPS TENSIONED ACROSS THEIR 1m WIDTH

↕ AGAINST ALTERNATE CHANNELS.

IN END ZONES WHERE PLAN CURVATURE IS GREATEST MAY NEED TO SEAM WELD THE ETFE INTO 1m SEGMENTS.

STRIPS WRAP AROUND SIDES TO FORM WALLS SEAMLESS WITH ROOF

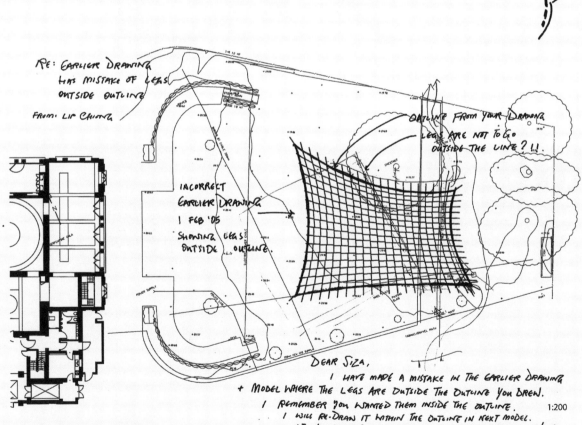

RE: EARLIER DRAWING HAS MISTAKE OF LEGS OUTSIDE OUTLINE

FROM: LIP CHIONG

INCORRECT EARLIER DRAWING 1 FEB '05 SHOWING LEGS OUTSIDE OUTLINE.

OUTLINE FROM YOUR DRAWING

LEGS ARE NOT TO GO OUTSIDE THE LINE ?!!

DEAR SIZA,
I HAVE MADE A MISTAKE IN THE EARLIER DRAWING + MODEL WHERE THE LEGS ARE OUTSIDE THE OUTLINE YOU DREW.
I REMEMBER YOU WANTED THEM INSIDE THE OUTLINE.
I WILL RE-DRAW IT WITHIN THE OUTLINE IN NEXT MODEL.
IT HELPS REDUCE NUMBER OF MEMBERS TOO.   LIP

1:200

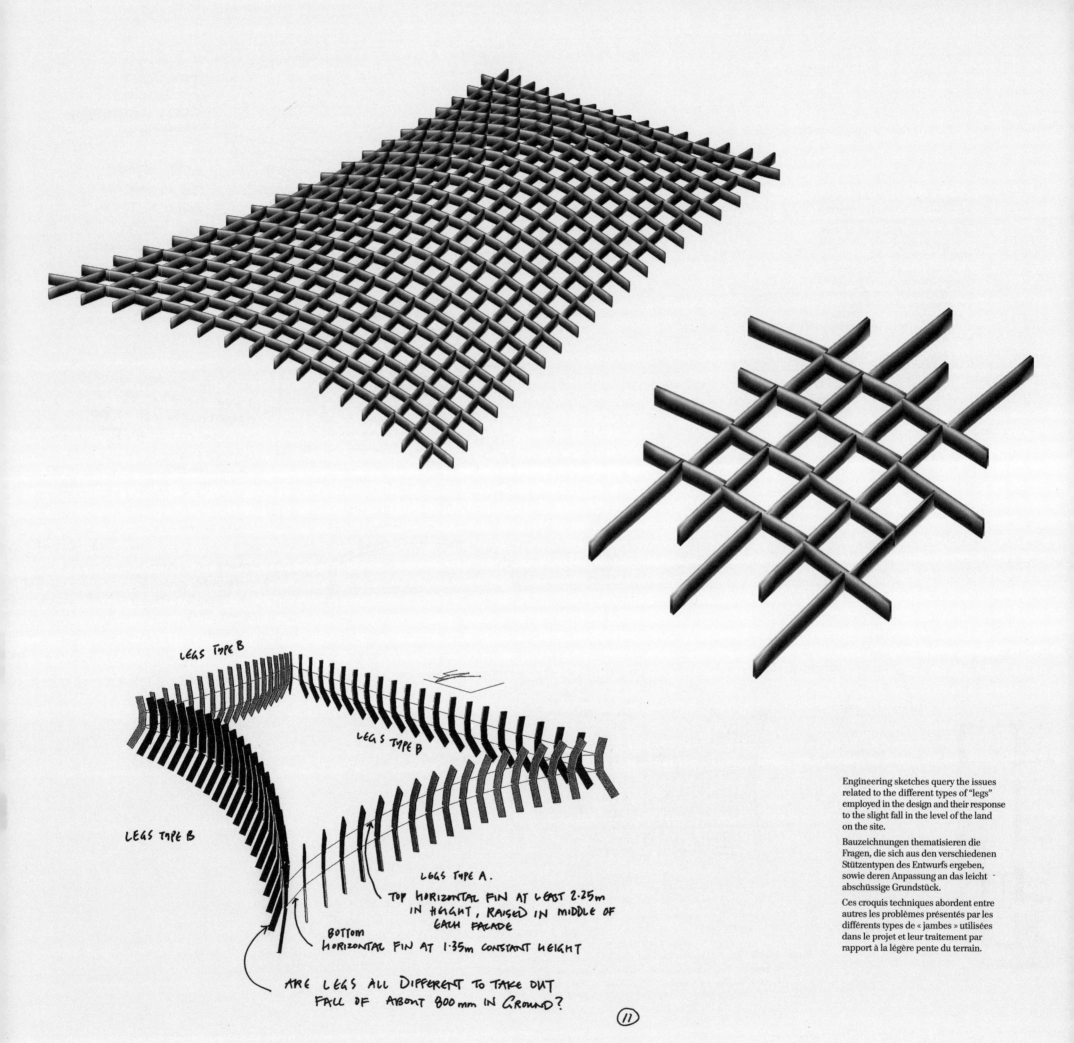

LEGS TYPE B

LEGS TYPE B

LEGS TYPE B

LEGS TYPE A.
TOP HORIZONTAL FIN AT LEAST 2·25m
IN HEIGHT, RAISED IN MIDDLE OF
EACH FACADE

BOTTOM
HORIZONTAL FIN AT 1·35m CONSTANT HEIGHT

ARE LEGS ALL DIFFERENT TO TAKE OUT
FALL OF ABOUT 800mm IN GROUND?

⑪

Engineering sketches query the issues
related to the different types of "legs"
employed in the design and their response
to the slight fall in the level of the land
on the site.

Bauzeichnungen thematisieren die
Fragen, die sich aus den verschiedenen
Stützentypen des Entwurfs ergeben,
sowie deren Anpassung an das leicht
abschüssige Grundstück.

Ces croquis techniques abordent entre
autres les problèmes présentés par les
différents types de « jambes » utilisées
dans le projet et leur traitement par
rapport à la légère pente du terrain.

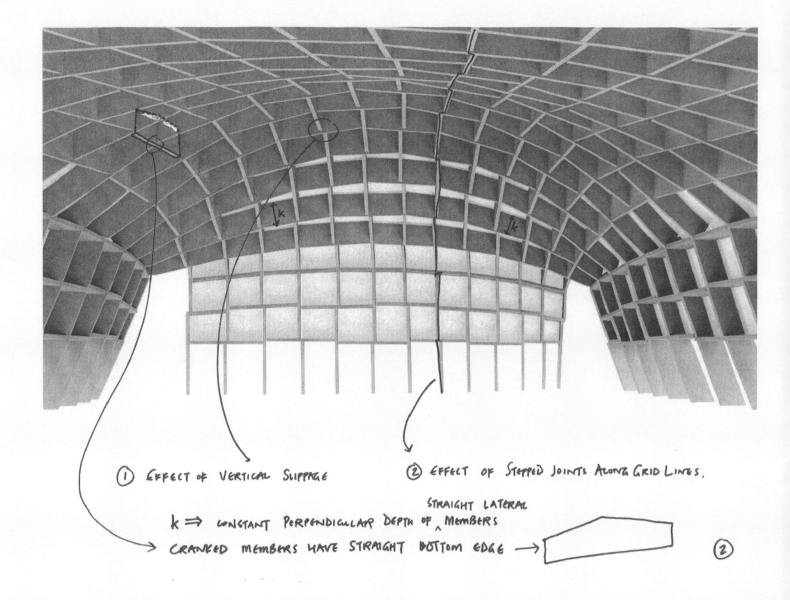

Drawings show the interior of the structure and the engineering issues posed by the deformation of the grid, causing strains or "slippage" that have to be compensated for in the final design.

Zeichnungen zeigen den Innenraum der Konstruktion und illustrieren die bautechnischen Fragen, die sich aus der Verformung des Rasters ergeben, durch die es zu Lasten und „Druckverlusten" kommt und die im endgültigen Entwurf kompensiert werden müssen.

Dessins montrant l'intérieur de la structure et les problèmes techniques posés par la déformation de la trame provoquant des tensions ou des « ripages », qui durent être compensés dans le projet final.

(1) EFFECT OF VERTICAL SLIPPAGE

(2) EFFECT OF STEPPED JOINTS ALONG GRID LINES.

STRAIGHT LATERAL
k ⇒ CONSTANT PERPENDICULAR DEPTH OF MEMBERS
CRANKED MEMBERS HAVE STRAIGHT BOTTOM EDGE → (2)

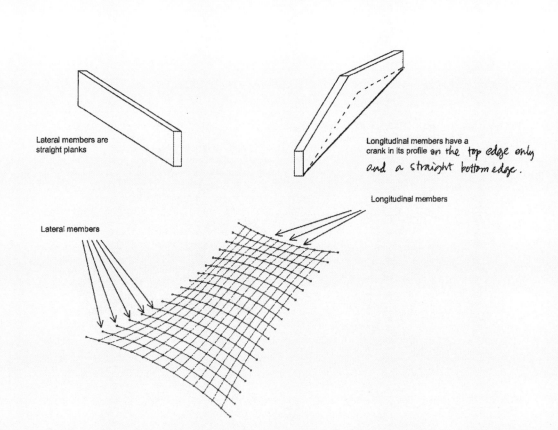

Lateral members are straight planks

Longitudinal members have a crank in its profile on the top edge only and a straight bottom edge.

Longitudinal members

Lateral members

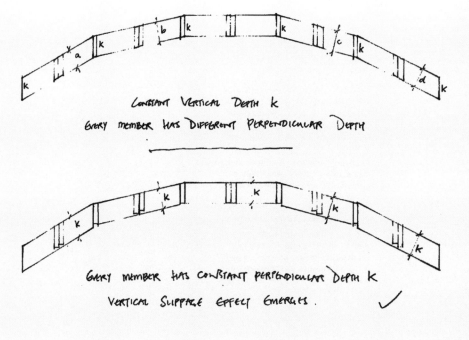

CONSTANT VERTICAL DEPTH k
EVERY MEMBER HAS DIFFERENT PERPENDICULAR DEPTH

EVERY MEMBER HAS CONSTANT PERPENDICULAR DEPTH k
VERTICAL SLIPPAGE EFFECT EMERGES. ✓

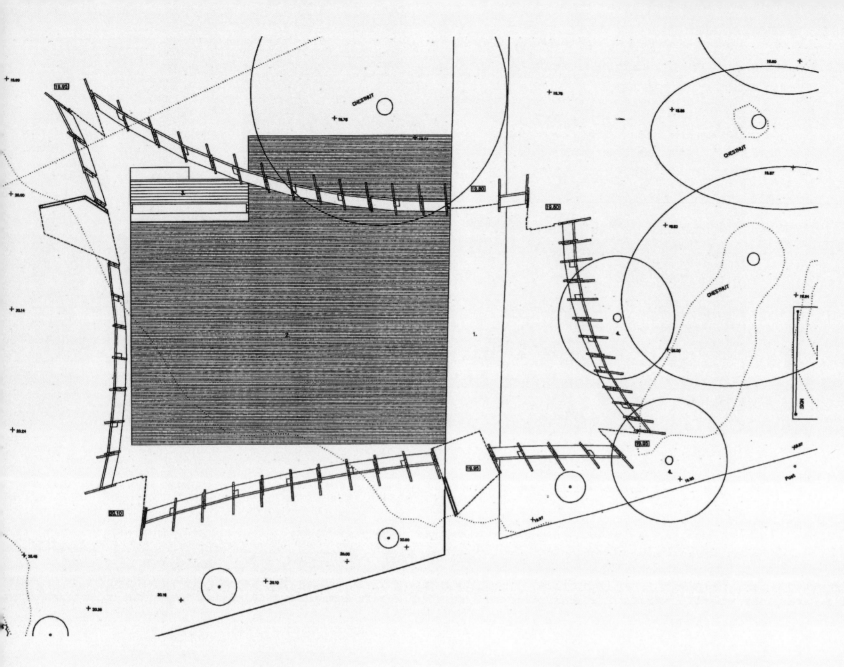

Drawings again emphasize the way in which the original vertical grid is laid over the final shape of the supports much like a bed cover—engendering the deformations that are very much part of the final intent of the architects.

Auch diese Zeichnungen illustrieren, wie das ursprünglich vertikale Raster wie eine Bettdecke über die endgültige Form der Stützen gelegt wird – und so die Verformung erzeugt, die ein entscheidender Aspekt der Pläne der Architekten war.

Ces dessins montrent là encore la façon dont la trame horizontale originale est déposée sur ses supports, un peu comme un couvre-lit, engendrant des déformations qui font partie du propos des architectes.

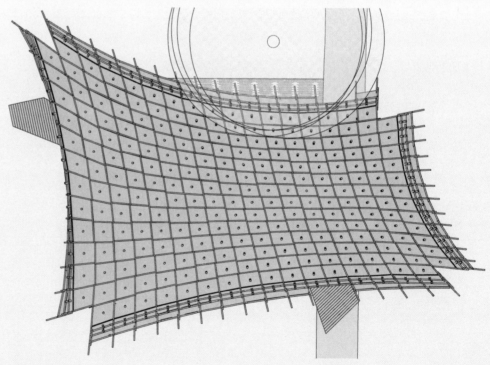

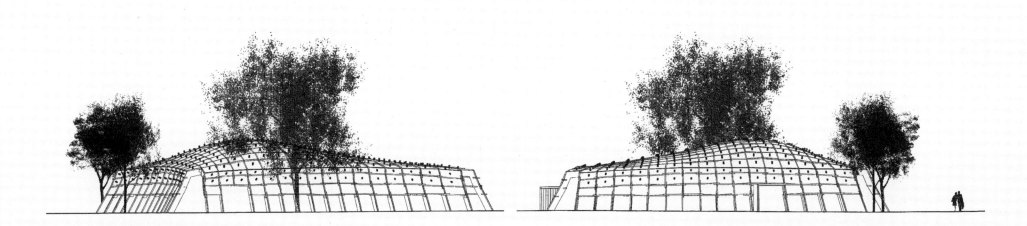

Álvaro Siza stated that he wished to "guarantee that the new building—while presenting a totally different architecture—established a 'dialogue' with the Neoclassical house."

Álvaro Siza erklärte, er wolle „sicherstellen, dass die neue Konstruktion – trotz ihrer vollkommen andersartigen Architektur – einen ‚Dialog' mit dem klassizistischen Gebäude eingeht."

Álvaro Siza a déclaré qu'il avait souhaité « faire en sorte que la nouvelle construction, tout en étant d'une architecture totalement différente, établisse un dialogue avec le bâtiment néoclassique ».

REM KOOLHAAS &
CECIL BALMOND

2006
REM KOOLHAAS &
CECIL BALMOND

2006 REM KOOLHAAS & CECIL BALMOND

OMA
Heer Bokelweg 149
3032 AD Rotterdam
The Netherlands

Tel: +31 10 243 82 00
Fax: +31 10 243 82 02
E-mail: office@oma.com
Web: www.oma.com

Balmond Studio / Unit 9
190a New North Road
London N1 7BJ
UK

Tel: +44 20 70 43 06 51
E-mail: info@balmondstudio.com
Web: www.balmondstudio.com

Rem Koolhaas created the Office for Metropolitan Architecture in 1975 with Elia and Zoe Zenghelis and Madelon Vriesendorp. Born in Rotterdam in 1944, he worked as a journalist for the *Haagse Post* and as a screenwriter before studying at the Architectural Association in London. He became well known after the 1978 publication of his book *Delirious New York*. Rem Koolhaas won the 2000 Pritzker Prize and the 2003 Praemium Imperiale Award. OMA's built work includes the McCormick Tribune Campus Center at the Illinois Institute of Technology (Chicago, Illinois, USA, 2000–03); and the Head-quarters and Cultural Center for China Central Television (CCTV, Beijing, China, 2002–09). The current work of OMA—which is run by seven partners: Rem Koolhaas, Ellen van Loon, Reinier de Graaf, Shohei Shigematsu, Iyad Alsaka, David Gianotten, and managing partner Victor van der Chijs—includes the Taipei Performing Arts Center (Taipei, Taiwan, ROC, 2009–14). Born and educated in Sri Lanka, Cecil Balmond came to London for postgraduate studies and joined Arup in 1968. He is an internationally recognized designer, structural engineer, author, and former deputy chairman of the multidisciplinary engineering firm Arup, where he founded the Advanced Geometry Unit (AGU). Balmond has now set up his own practice called Balmond Studio. Undertaking a variety of design projects, the team is currently involved with a large project viaduct in Milan (Italy), a development in Asia, and a radical proposition for a new kind of modular housing. Balmond's interest lies in the genesis of form using numbers, music, and mathematics as vital sources. Aside from the 2006 Serpentine Pavilion designed with Rem Koolhaas, he worked with the Dutch architect on the Seattle Central Library (Seattle, Washington, USA, 2004); Casa da Música (Porto, Portugal, 2005); and on the CCTV Headquarters building in Beijing (China, 2002–09). He designed the Pedro e Inês Footbridge (Coimbra, Portugal 2006) and the Weave Bridge for the University of Pennsylvania (Philadelphia, USA, 2010). His books include *Number 9: The Search for the Sigma Code* (1998); *Informal* (2002), which explores structure as catalyst in architecture; and *Element* (2007). Balmond has also collaborated on Serpentine Summer Pavilions with Daniel Libeskind (2001), Toyo Ito (2002), and Álvaro Siza and Eduardo Souto de Moura (2005).

1975 gründete Rem Koolhaas mit Elia und Zoe Zenghelis und Madelon Vriesendorp sein Office for Metropolitan Architecture (OMA). Koolhaas, 1944 in Rotterdam geboren, arbeitete als Journalist für die *Haagse Post* und als Drehbuchautor, bevor er an der Architectural Association in London studierte. Bekannt wurde er 1978 mit der Veröffentlichung seines Buchs *Delirious New York*. 2000 gewann er den Pritzker-Preis, 2003 den Praemium Imperiale. Zu OMAs realisierten Bauten zählen das McCormick Tribune Campus Center am Illinois Institute of Technology (Chicago, USA, 2000–03) und die Zentrale mit Kulturzentrum für das chinesische Staatsfernsehen (CCTV, Peking, 2002–09). Ein aktuelles Projekt von OMA, das von sieben Partnern geführt wird – Rem Koolhaas, Ellen van Loon, Reinier de Graaf, Shohei Shigematsu, Iyad Alsaka, David Gianotten und Managing Partner Victor van der Chijs – ist unter anderem das Taipei Performing Arts Center (Taiwan, 2009–14). Cecil Balmond, geboren und ausgebildet in Sri Lanka, kam zu weiterführenden Studien nach London und schloss sich 1968 dem Büro Arup an. Balmond ist ein renommierter Designer, Bauingenieur, Autor und war stellvertretender Vorsitzender des Ingenieurbüros Arup, wo er die Advanced Geometry Unit (AGU) gründete. Heute hat Balmond sein eigenes Büro, Balmond Studio. Das Team arbeitet derzeit an einem großen Viadukt in Mailand, einem Bauvorhaben in Asien sowie einem radikal neuen Konzept für modulare Wohnbauten. Balmond interessiert sich besonders für Formen, die aus Zahlen, Musik und Mathematik generiert werden. Neben dem Serpentine-Pavillon 2006 arbeitete er mit Rem Koolhaas auch an der Seattle Central Library (Washington, USA, 2004), der Casa da Musica in Porto (Portugal, 2005) und der CCTV-Zentrale in Peking (China, 2002–09). Er entwarf die Fußgängerbrücke Pedro e Inês (Coimbra, Portugal, 2006) und die Weave Bridge für die University of Pennsylvania (Philadelphia, USA, 2010). Er veröffentlichte *Number 9: The Search for the Sigma Code* (1998), *Informal* (2002), in dem er sich mit Baukonstruktion als Katalysator in der Architektur beschäftigt, sowie *Element* (2007). Balmond arbeitete darüber hinaus mit Daniel Libeskind (2001), Toyo Ito (2002) sowie Álvaro Siza und Eduardo Souto de Moura (2005) an deren Serpentine Summer Pavilions.

Rem Koolhaas a fondé l'Office for Metropolitan Architecture (OMA) en 1975 en association avec Elia et Zoe Zenghelis et Madelon Vriesendorp. Né à Rotterdam en 1944, il a débuté comme journaliste pour le *Haagse Post* puis a été scénariste, avant d'étudier à l'Architectural Association de Londres. Il s'est fait connaître en 1978 par la publication de son livre *Delirious New York*. Il a remporté le prix Pritzker en 2000 et le Praemium Imperiale en 2003. Parmi les réalisations d'OMA figurent le Centre du campus McCormick Tribune à l'Illinois Institute of Technology (Chicago, Illinois, 2000–03) et le siège et centre culturel de la Télévision centrale de Chine (CCTV, Pékin, 2002–09). L'agence, qui est dirigée par sept partenaires (Rem Koolhaas, Ellen van Loon, Reinier de Graaf, Shohei Shigematsu, Iyad Alsaka, David Gianotten, et le directeur-gérant Victor van der Chijs) travaille actuellement au projet du Centre des arts du spectacle de Taipei (Taïwan, 2009–14). Né et formé au Sri Lanka, Balmond est venu à Londres pour poursuivre des études supérieures et a rejoint l'agence Arup en 1968. Concepteur, ingénieur structurel et auteur de notoriété internationale, il est ex-vice-président de l'agence d'ingénierie multidisciplinaire Arup au sein de laquelle il a fondé l'Advanced Geometry Unit. Il a ensuite fondé sa propre agence, le Balmond Studio, engagée dans des projets très variés dont, actuellement, un grand viaduc à Milan, un nouveau quartier en Asie et une proposition radicale pour un nouveau type de logement modulaire. Balmond s'intéresse à la genèse des formes, utilisant pour sources les mathématiques et la musique. En dehors du Pavillon 2006 de la Serpentine, il a collaboré avec l'architecte néerlandais Rem Koolhaas à la bibliothèque centrale de Seattle (État de Washington, 2004) ; la Casa da Musica à Porto (Portugal, 2005) et le siège de la CCTV à Pékin (2002–09). Il a conçu la passerelle Pedro e Inês (Coimbra, Portugal, 2006) et le Weave Bridge pour l'université de Pennsylvanie (Philadelphie, 2010). Parmi ses livres remarqués figurent *Number 9. The Search for the Signal Code* (1998) et *Informal* (2002) qui explore la structure en tant que catalyseur de l'architecture. Balmond a également collaboré aux pavillons d'été de la Serpentine conçus par Daniel Libeskind (2001), Toyo Ito (2002) et Alvaro Siza et Edouardo Souto de Moura (2005).

Cecil Balmond explains: "These Pavilions have evolved with various structural typologies and materials, provoking a debate on architecture; this year the exploration continues not only with typology and material but with the very definition of Pavilion." Arup described the project, open to the public from 13 July to 15 October 2006, in rather statistical terms: "The *Cosmic Egg* perched five meters above the ground on top of the 18-meter-diameter translucent polycarbonate hub that hosted this year's expanded itinerary of art events." This walled enclosure functioned as a café, as well as hosting two 24-hour interview Marathons convened by Rem Koolhaas and Hans Ulrich Obrist with leading politicians, architects, philosophers, writers, artists, filmmakers, and economists "exposing the hidden and invisible layers of London." The space could seat up to 300 people. The 10-meter width of the platform was calculated in relation to the size of the Serpentine itself. The main hull of the Egg, which was intended to be inflated with 6000 cubic meters of helium and a further 2000 cubic meters of pressurized air, and made to float 10 meters above the ground, consisted of more than one ton of PVC-coated polyester cloth, specially made for the project for its combined transparency and strength. The architects stated that "the aim of translucency and physical lightness inspired the use of new materials in innovative ways." The construction and use of the pavilion coincided with an exhibition of the German artist Thomas Demand (6 June–20 August 2006), part of which was inserted into the pavilion. Koolhaas, in a 2006 interview with Hans Ulrich Obrist, stated: "I thought it was very important not so much to reinvent the tradition of the Pavilion, but to try to do something that was not about space or about materials. I tried to imagine something that was like Yves Klein's Fire Pavilion, on which he collaborated with Claude Parent and Werner Ruhnau, or the one based on air. That work was never realized and obviously won't be this time, but I've always found it incredibly compelling. When I was still studying architecture, I was really baffled by my inability to be deeply enthusiastic about Archigram's less conceptual domes and inflatables, and by my unbelievable excitement about Klein's projects. They're two things that seem very similar but have a huge difference in value. To even raise the word 'inflatable' in England now is either a really radical perversion or a profound irony."

Cecil Balmond erklärt: „Diese Pavillons haben sich anhand verschiedener Typologien und Materialen weiterentwickelt und eine Debatte über Architektur angestoßen. Dieses Jahr geht es aber um die Definition des Pavillons an sich." Arup beschrieb das vom 13. Juli bis 15. Oktober 2006 geöffnete Projekt nüchterner: „Das *Cosmic Egg* (Kosmische Ei) schwebte 5 m über dem Boden auf einer durchsichtigen Nabe aus Polycarbonat mit einem Durchmesser von 18 m, in der das in diesem Jahr erweiterte Kunstprogramm stattfand." Der von Wänden umgebene Raum diente als Café und Veranstaltungsort für zwei 24-stündige Interviewmarathons, einberufen von Rem Koolhaas und Hans Ulrich Obrist, an denen führende Politiker, Architekten, Philosophen, Autoren, Künstler, Filmemacher und Wirtschaftsfachleute teilnahmen und die „die verborgenen, unsichtbaren Schichten Londons aufdeckten". Der Raum fasste 300 Besucher. Das 10 m breite Podium war proportional zur Größe des Serpentinegebäudes konzipiert. Die zentrale Hülle des Eis, die mit 6000 m³ Helium und weiteren 2000 m³ Druckluft gefüllt werden und 10 m über dem Boden schweben sollte, bestand aus über 1 t speziell angefertigtem, mit PVC beschichtetem, transparentem und belastbarem Polyestergewebe. Die Architekten erklärten, „die Zielvorgaben Transluzenz und physische Leichtigkeit inspirierten den innovativen Einsatz neuer Materialien". Bau- und Nutzzeit des Pavillons fielen mit einer Ausstellung des deutschen Künstlers Thomas Demand (6. Juni–20. August 2006) zusammen, die teilweise im Pavillon untergebracht war. 2006 äußerte Koolhaas in einem Interview mit Hans Ulrich Obrist: „Mir schien es besonders wichtig, weniger die Tradition des Pavillons neu zu erfinden als vielmehr etwas zu versuchen, das nichts mit Raum oder Material zu tun hatte. Ich versuchte also, etwas zu erfinden, das Ähnlichkeit mit Yves Kleins Feuerpavillon hatte (zusammen mit Claude Parent und Werner Ruhnau) oder mit Kleins Bau aus Luft. Diese Arbeiten wurden damals und heute nicht realisiert, aber ich fand sie schon immer faszinierend. Als Architekturstudent war ich immer verblüfft darüber, wie wenig ich mich für die weniger konzeptuellen Kuppeln und aufblasbaren Konstruktionen von Archigram zu begeistern konnte und wie fasziniert ich von Kleins Projekten war … Heutzutage ist es in England entweder eine zutiefst radikale Perversion oder eine fundamentale Ironie, den Begriff ‚aufblasbar' auch nur aufzubringen."

Pour Cecil Balmond : « Ces pavillons ont évolué selon des typologies structurelles et des matériaux divers, provoquant un débat sur l'architecture. Cette année, l'exploration se poursuit non seulement dans ces champs, mais dans celui de la définition même du pavillon ». L'agence Arup décrivit ce projet ouvert au public du 13 juillet au 15 octobre 2006 en termes rationnels : « Le *Cosmic Egg* perché à 5 mètres au-dessus du sol, posé sur un volume en polycarbonate translucide de 18 mètres de diamètre, était conçu pour accueillir le vaste programme d'événements artistiques de cette année. » Ce lieu clos accueillant plus de 300 personnes a servi de café, mais aussi de siège des interviews « marathons » de 24 heures de Rem Koolhaas et Hans Ulrbrich Obrist avec d'importants politiciens, architectes, philosophes, écrivains, artistes, réalisateurs et économistes pour « révéler les strates cachées et invisibles de Londres ». Les 10 mètres de large de la plate-forme ont été calculés par rapport aux dimensions de la Serpentine Gallery. Le volume de l'Œuf cosmique gonflé de 6 000 mètres cubes d'hélium et 2 000 mètres cubes d'air pressurisé pour pouvoir flotter à 10 mètres au-dessus du sol, était contenu dans une toile de polyester enduit de PVC d'une tonne, spécialement choisie pour sa transparence et sa résistance. « La volonté de translucidité et de légèreté a conduit à l'utilisation novatrice de matériaux nouveaux », ont expliqué les architectes. Le pavillon accueillait une partie des œuvres de l'exposition parallèle de l'artiste allemand Thomas Demand. Koolhaas, dans un entretien de 2006 avec Hans Ulrich Obrist a précisé : « J'ai pensé qu'il était très important non pas tant de réinventer la tradition du pavillon, que d'essayer de faire quelque chose qui ne porte ni sur l'espace, ni sur les matériaux. J'ai tenté d'imaginer quelque chose qui fasse un peu penser au pavillon de feu d'Yves Klein, pour lequel il avait collaboré avec Claude Parent et Werner Ruhnau, ou à celui basé sur l'air. Cette œuvre ne fut pas réalisée et ne le sera certainement jamais, mais je l'ai toujours trouvée incroyablement séduisante. Lorsque j'étais encore étudiant en architecture, j'étais surpris de mon incapacité à m'enthousiasmer pour les dômes gonflables moins conceptuels d'Archigram, et par mon excitation devant les projets de Klein. Ce sont deux choses qui semblent très similaires mais diffèrent grandement en termes de valeur. Le mot 'gonflable' évoque aujourd'hui en Grande-Bretagne soit une perversion radicale soit une profonde ironie. »

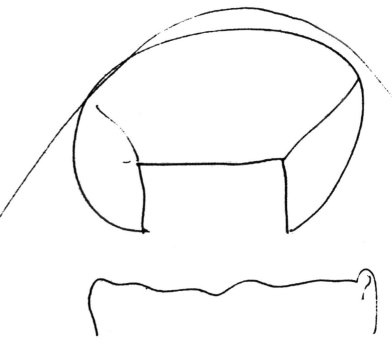

Seen in the context of the Park and the Serpentine Gallery, the translucent inflatable canopy of the pavilion stands out as an unusual presence, inviting passersby to discover its ovoid form from closer in.

In ihrem Kontext aus Park und Serpentine Gallery hebt sich die Dachkonstruktion des Pavillons als außergewöhnliche Präsenz ab und lädt Passanten ein, das eiförmige Volumen aus der Nähe zu erkunden.

Dans le contexte du parc et de la Serpentine Gallery, la toiture translucide gonflable du pavillon lançait un signal surprenant qui invitait les passants à venir découvrir de plus près ce curieux volume ovoïde.

"The 2006 Serpentine Pavilion is defined by events and activities. We are proposing a space that facilitates the inclusion of individuals in communal dialogue and shared experience."

REM KOOLHAAS

Glowing from within at night, the pavilion was meant, as Cecil Balmond stated, to provoke a debate on architecture as well as provide a place for the numerous activities organized by the Gallery for the summer months.

Der nachts von innen leuchtende Pavillon sollte, so Cecil Balmond, sowohl eine Debatte über Architektur auslösen als auch Platz für zahlreiche Veranstaltungen bieten, die von der Galerie für die Sommermonate geplant waren.

Illuminé de l'intérieur pendant la nuit, le pavillon, comme Cecil Balmond l'a expliqué, devait provoquer un débat sur l'architecture et offrir un lieu abrité pour les multiples activités de la galerie pendant les mois d'été.

The ovoid shape of the canopy sitting above its translucent base. Below, a sketch by Cecil Balmond shows the proportions of the pavilion and asks questions about its height and support.

Die eiförmige Dachkonstruktion ruht auf seiner transluzenten Basis. Eine Skizze von Cecil Balmond (unten) zeigt die Proportionen des Pavillons und stellt Fragen zu Höhe und Tragwerk des Pavillons.

La masse ovoïde semble juste posée sur sa base translucide. Ci-dessous, un croquis de Cecil Balmond montre les proportions du pavillon et pose en légende des interrogations sur sa hauteur et son support.

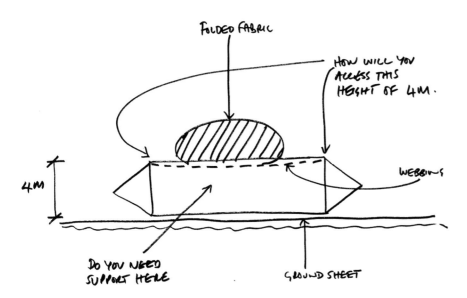

SERPENTINE PAVILION 2006.

FOLDED FABRIC

HOW WILL YOU ACCESS THIS HEIGHT OF 4M.

4M

WEBBING

DO YOU NEED SUPPORT HERE

GROUND SHEET

Seen looming up behind the Serpentine or through its own translucent ground-level walls, the pavilion makes a strong statement: the variable shape of the construction contrasts with the more staid shapes of the older architecture

Der Pavillon – ob hinter der Serpentine aufragend oder durch die transluzenten Wände seiner unteren Ebene gesehen – ist ein klares Statement: Seine variable Konstruktion kontrastiert mit den gesetzteren Formen des älteren Baus.

Qu'il apparaisse surgissant de derrière la Serpentine Gallery ou au travers des murs transparents de sa base, le pavillon s'imposait par ses dimensions et son profil variable face aux contours rigides de l'ancienne architecture.

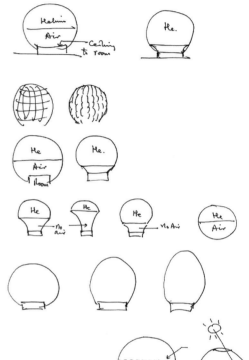

The translucent walls of the pavilion make visible the forms of the neighboring Serpentine Gallery, yet also of passersby. Sketches show the use of helium in the upper part of the canopy to inflate it and make it rise.

Durch die durchscheinenden Wände des Pavillons zeichnen sich die Umrisse der benachbarten Serpentine Gallery sowie von Passanten ab. Skizzen illustrieren die Verwendung von Helium im oberen Teil des Dachs, mit dem es aufgepumpt wird und dann aufsteigt.

Les murs translucides du pavillon laissaient voir les formes de la galerie, mais aussi les silhouettes des passants. Des croquis montrent le gonflement à l'hélium et le développement de la partie supérieure.

VII.17

A simple ring of polycarbonate façade panels circles the main interior space. Sketches show the volume of the inflated Pavilion vis-à-vis its older host building.

Ein schlichter Ring aus Polycarbonat-Platten umfängt den zentralen Innenraum. Skizzen veranschaulichen das Volumen des aufgeblasenen Pavillons vis-à-vis vom älteren Mutterbau.

Un simple anneau en panneaux de façade en polycarbonate clôt l'espace intérieur principal. Les croquis montrent le volume du pavillon une fois gonflé, par rapport au bâtiment ancien de la galerie.

On this page and the preceding double page, the pavilion interior with a frieze designed by the artist Thomas Demand, a first occasion for a direct collaboration between an artist and architects in this context.

Auf dieser und der vorangegangenen Doppelseite ist der Innenraum des Pavillons mit einem Bildfries des Künstlers Thomas Demand zu sehen: Es war dies der erste Fall einer unmittelbaren Zusammenarbeit eines Künstlers mit den Architekten.

Sur cette page et la double page précédente, intérieur du pavillon décoré d'une frise de l'artiste Thomas Demand, première collaboration directe entre un artiste et des architectes dans le contexte des pavillons de la Serpentine Gallery.

The enclosure below the canopy in use as a café and forum for televised and recorded public programs including the *Time Out* magazine's *Park Nights*.

Der umbaute Raum unter der Dachkonstruktion wurde als Café sowie als Forum für öffentliche Programme genutzt, die auch übertragen oder gefilmt wurden, etwa die *Park Nights* des Magazins *Time Out*.

L'espace compris sous la partie gonflable servait de café et de forum pour des programmes télévisés publics enregistrés, dont les *Park Nights* du magazine *Time Out*.

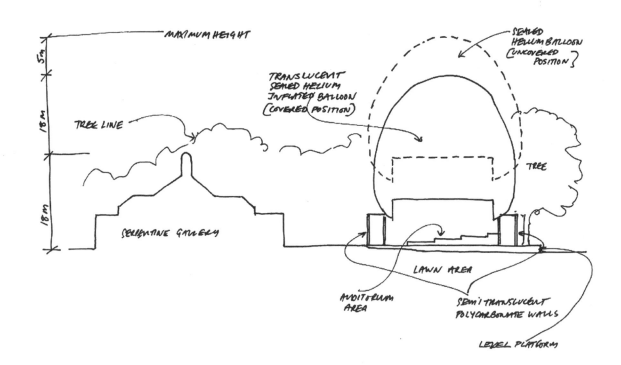

OUTER WALL
TRANSLUCENT
POLYCARBONATE

TREE

SERPENTINE GALLERY.

EAST TERRACE

PUBLIC FLOW

PUBLIC FLOW

CROSS PATH

RAISED PLATFORM.

AUDITORIUM AREA

INNER WALL
TRANSLUCENT
POLYCARBONATE

MAIN DRIVEWAY TO GALLERY

PLANS, DRAWINGS AND MODELS

Architectural Design Rem Koolhaas/Cecil Balmond
Design Team OMA/Clément Blanchet/
Adam Furman/Karel Wuytack/Karen Crequer
Integrated Design Arup/Chris Carroll
Carolina Bartram/Tristan Simmonds

MAXIMUM HEIGHT

SEALED HELIUM BALLOON (UNCOVERED POSITION)

TRANSLUCENT SEALED HELIUM INFLATED BALLOON (COVERED POSITION)

5m

TREE LINE

18m

18m

SERPENTINE GALLERY

TREE

AUDITORIUM AREA

LAWN AREA

SEMI TRANSLUCENT POLYCARBONATE WALLS

LEVEL PLATFORM

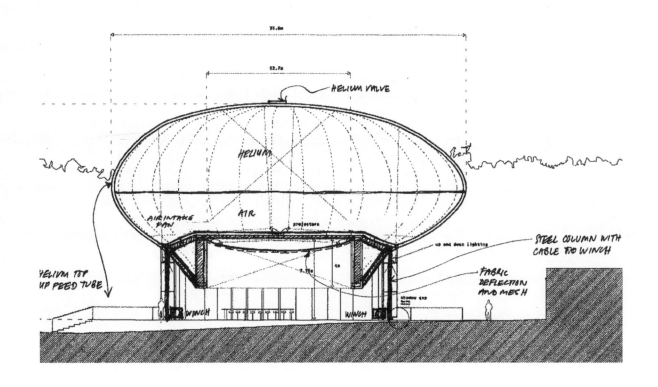

Models and drawings from Cecil Balmond showing the forms of the canopy and the way it was to be filled with helium in the upper section. The helium feed and top valve are indicated in the drawing below.

Modelle und Zeichnungen von Cecil Balmond verdeutlichen die Form der Dachkonstruktion und die für die Befüllung mit Helium vorgesehene obere Zone. Der Heliumzugang sowie das obere Ventil sind in der Zeichnung unten zu sehen.

Des maquettes et des dessins de Cecil Balmond montrent les formes du ballon et la manière dont il était gonflé à l'hélium par la partie supérieure. L'alimentation en hélium et la valve supérieure sont indiquées dans le dessin ci-dessous.

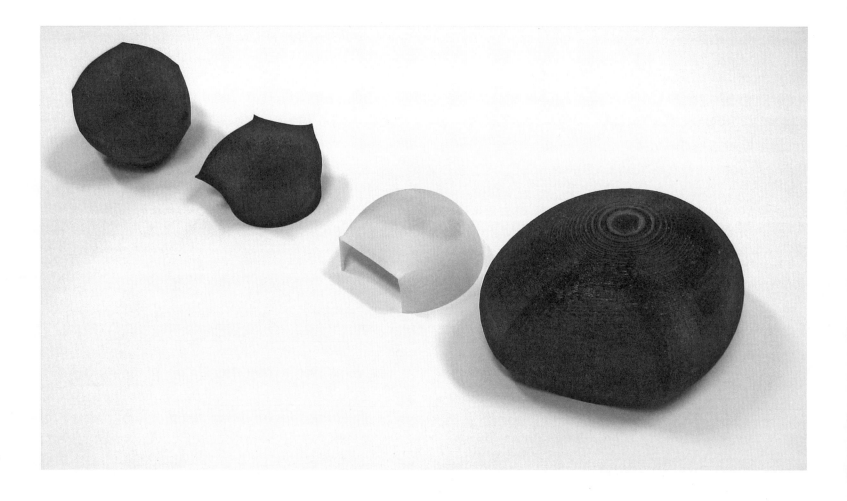

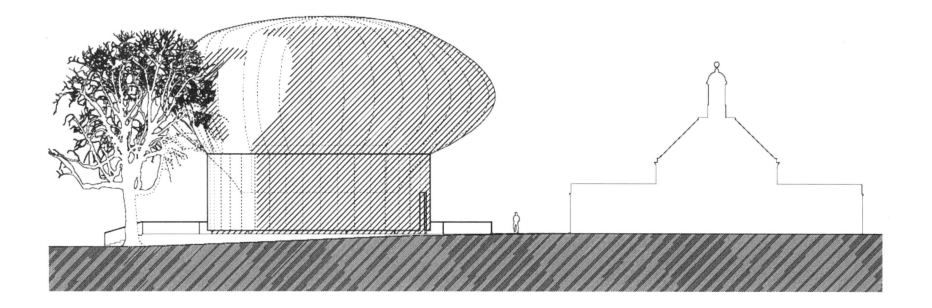

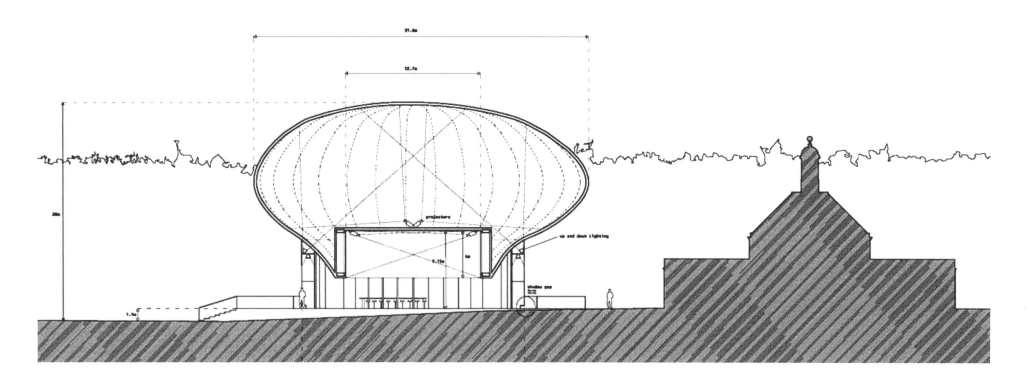

The proportions of the pavilion and its inflatable canopy are studied in these drawings, which show the Serpentine Gallery to the right.

Die Proportionen des Pavillons und die aufblasbare Dachkonstruktion sind auf diesen Zeichnungen detaillierter dokumentiert. Die Serpentine Gallery ist rechts im Bild zu sehen.

Les proportions du pavillon et de son « œuf » gonflable sont étudiées dans ces dessins, qui montrent également la Serpentine Gallery (à droite).

Renderings from the office of Rem Koolhaas show the canopy and the spaces beneath it as being something like evanescent clouds in front of or next to the more solid and less flexible shape of the Serpentine.

Darstellungen aus dem Büro von Rem Koolhaas zeigen die Dachkonstruktion und die darunter gelegenen Räume als eine Art flüchtige Wolke vor bzw. neben dem massiveren und weniger flexiblen Baukörper der Serpentine.

Ces rendus issus de l'agence de Rem Koolhaas montrent le ballon et l'espace qu'il recouvre sous forme de nuages évanescents près de la forme plus massive et moins souple de la galerie.

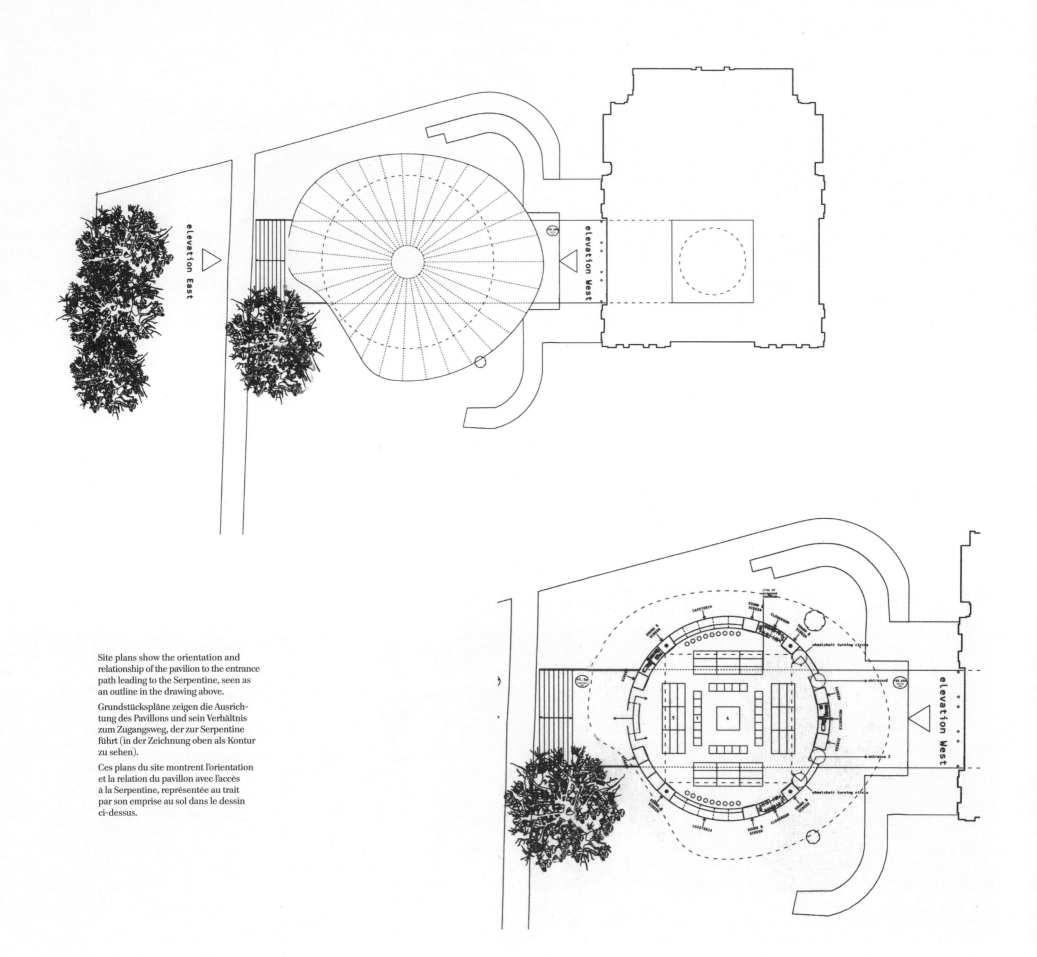

Site plans show the orientation and relationship of the pavilion to the entrance path leading to the Serpentine, seen as an outline in the drawing above.

Grundstückspläne zeigen die Ausrichtung des Pavillons und sein Verhältnis zum Zugangsweg, der zur Serpentine führt (in der Zeichnung oben als Kontur zu sehen).

Ces plans du site montrent l'orientation et la relation du pavillon avec l'accès à la Serpentine, représentée au trait par son emprise au sol dans le dessin ci-dessus.

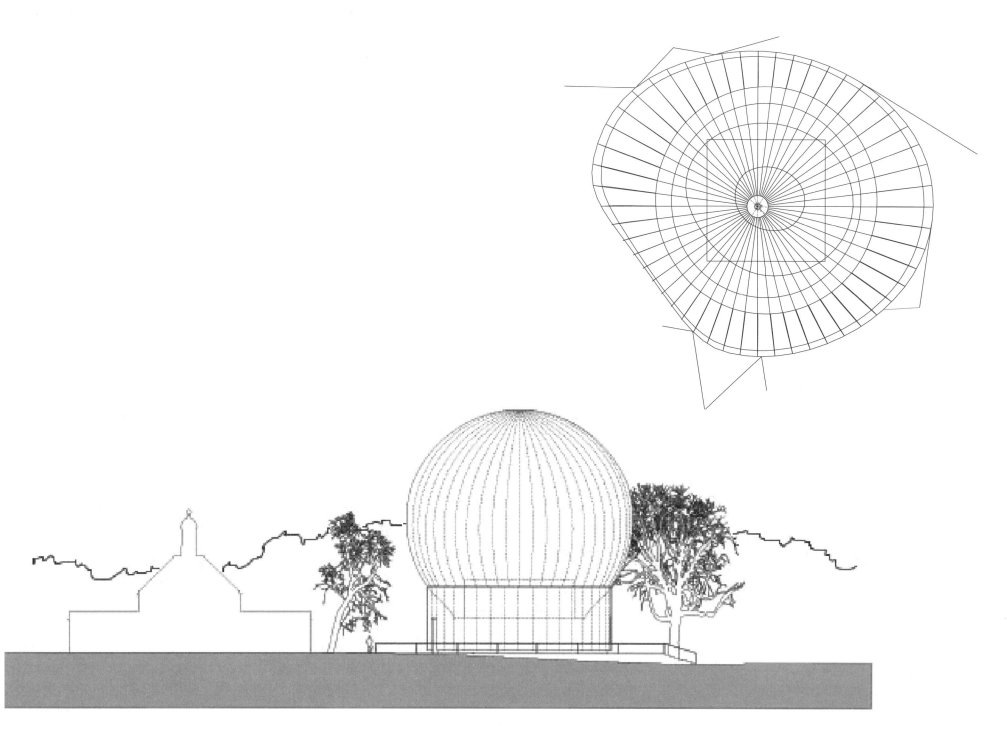

Seen in elevation and section the pavilion
has a balloonlike appearance that stands
well above the old Serpentine building.
In plan, the canopy is a bulbous and
somewhat irregular ovoid.

Aufriss und Querschnitt zeigen, dass der
Pavillon als Ballon den Altbau der Serpentine weit überragt. Auf dem Grundriss wirkt der Dachkorpus wie ein wuch-
tiges, unregelmäßiges Ei.

Vu en coupe et en élévation, le pavillon
se présente sous la forme d'un ballon qui
domine de toute sa hauteur la Serpentine
Gallery. En plan, ce ballon est un ovoïde
bulbeux, légèrement irrégulier.

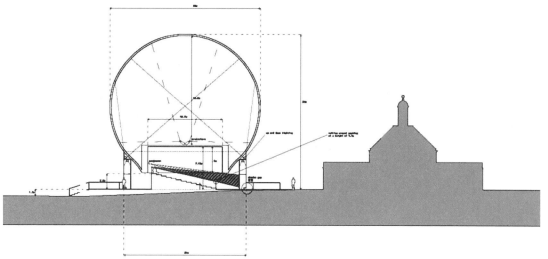

OLAFUR ELIASSON & KJETIL THORSEN

2007

OLAFUR ELIASSON & KJETIL THORSEN

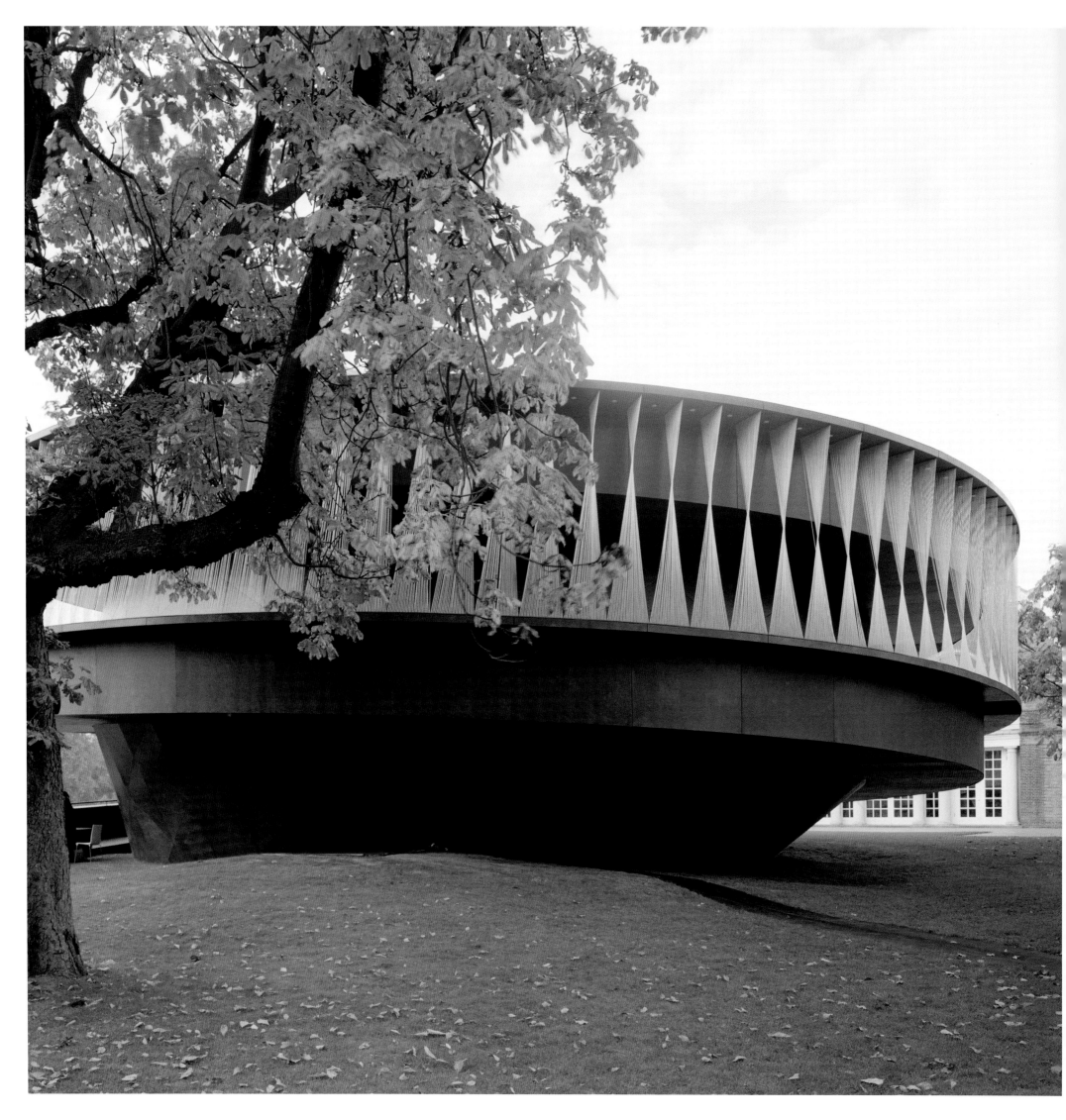

2007 OLAFUR ELIASSON & KJETIL THORSEN

Olafur Eliasson
Studio Olafur Eliasson
Christinenstr. 18/19, Haus 2
10119 Berlin
Germany

E-mail: studio@olafureliasson.net
Web: www.olafureliasson.net

Snøhetta AS
Skur 39, Vippetangen
0150 Oslo
Norway

Tel: +47 24 15 60 60
Fax: +47 24 15 60 61
E-mail: contact@snoarc.no
Web: www.snoarc.no

Olafur Eliasson was born in 1967 in Denmark of Icelandic parents and attended the Royal Academy of Fine Arts in Copenhagen (1989–95). Early in his career he moved to Germany, establishing Studio Olafur Eliasson as an experimental laboratory in Berlin. Eliasson lives and works in Copenhagen and Berlin. He has had solo exhibitions at the Musée d'Art Moderne de la Ville de Paris, the ZKM in Karlsruhe, and the 21st Century Museum of Contemporary Art in Kanazawa; and he represented Denmark in the 2003 Venice Biennale. His installations feature elements appropriated from nature—billowing steam evoking a water geyser, rainbows, or fog-filled rooms. By introducing "natural" phenomena, such as water, mist, or light, into an artificial setting, be it a city street or an art gallery, the artist encourages viewers to reflect on their perception of the physical world. This moment of perception, when viewers pause to consider what they are experiencing, has been described by Eliasson as "seeing yourself sensing." Snøhetta is an architectural practice created in Oslo in 1987. It is directed by Craig Dykers, Christoph Kapeller, and Kjetil Trædal Thorsen, who worked with Olafur Eliasson on the 2007 Serpentine Summer Pavilion. Thorsen was born in Haugesund, Norway, in 1958, and has participated actively in such Snøhetta projects as the art museum built for the Winter Olympics in Lillehammer (1991); the Bibliotheca Alexandrina (Egypt, 1993–2001); the National Opera House in Oslo (Norway, 2000–07); and the museum on the World Trade Center site in Lower Manhattan, New York. A large-scale artwork by Olafur Eliasson was installed in the foyer of the Snøhetta-designed Oslo Opera House. In 2005 Eliasson and Thorsen collaborated on a proposal for Turner Contemporary in Margate.

Olafur Eliasson wurde 1967 als Sohn isländischer Eltern in Dänemark geboren und studierte an der Königlich Dänischen Akademie der Künste in Kopenhagen (1989–95). Bereits früh zog er nach Deutschland und gründete das Studio Olafur Eliasson als experimentelles Labor in Berlin. Heute lebt und arbeitet er in Kopenhagen und Berlin. Er hatte Einzelausstellungen am ZKM in Karlsruhe, dem Musée d'Art Moderne de la Ville de Paris sowie dem 21st Century Museum of Contemporary Art in Kanazawa in Japan und vertrat Dänemark auf der Biennale 2003 in Venedig. Für seine Installationen nutzt er Naturerscheinungen – Wasserdampf, Regenbögen oder Räume voller Nebel. Durch das Versetzen „natürlicher" Phänomene wie Wasser, Dunst oder Licht in künstliche Umgebungen, sei es eine Straße oder eine Galerie, regt der Künstler die Betrachter dazu an, über ihre Wahrnehmung der physischen Welt nachzudenken. Diesen Augenblick, in dem Betrachter darüber nachdenken, was sie gerade erleben, bezeichnete Eliasson als „sich selbst wahrnehmen sehen". Snøhetta ist ein 1987 in Oslo gegründetes Architekturbüro unter der Leitung von Craig Dykers, Christoph Kapeller und Kjetil Trædal Thorsen, der gemeinsam mit Olafur Eliasson am Sommerpavillon der Serpentine Gallery 2007 arbeitete. Thorsen wurde 1958 in Haugesund in Norwegen geboren und war an Snøhetta-Projekten wie dem Kunstmuseum für die Olympischen Winterspiele in Lillehammer (1991), der Bibliotheca Alexandrina (Ägypten, 1993–2001), der Staatsoper in Oslo (2000–07) und dem Museum am Standort des World Trade Center in New York beteiligt. Im Foyer der Osloer Oper wurde ein großformatiges Kunstwerk von Olafur Eliasson installiert. 2005 entwickelten Eliasson und Thorsen gemeinsam einen Entwurf für das Turner-Contemporary-Museum in Margate.

Olafur Eliasson est né en 1967 au Danemark de parents islandais. Il a étudié à l'Académie royale des beaux-arts de Copenhague (1989–95). Très tôt dans sa carrière, il s'est installé en Allemagne ou il a créé son atelier à Berlin, le Studio Olafur Eliasson, laboratoire expérimental. Il a été l'objet d'expositions personnelles au Musée d'art moderne de la Ville de Paris, au ZKM de Karlsruhe, au Musée d'art contemporain du XXIᵉ siècle de Kanazawa (Japon) et a représenté le Danemark à la Biennale de Venise en 2003. Ses installations mettent en scène des éléments tirés de la nature – vapeur évoquant un geyser, arcs-en-ciel, salles envahies de brouillard, lumière, etc. En introduisant ces « phénomènes naturels » dans un cadre artificiel, que ce soit celui d'une rue ou d'une galerie d'art, l'artiste encourage les spectateurs à réfléchir sur leur perception du monde physique. Ce moment de perception, lorsque le spectateur s'arrête pour comprendre ce qu'il est en train d'expérimenter, est décrit par Eliasson par la formule « se voir en train de ressentir ». Snøhetta est une agence d'architecture fondée à Oslo en 1987. Elle est dirigée par Craig Dykers, Christoph Kapeller et Kjetil Trædal Thorsen, qui a travaillé avec Olafur Eliasson sur le projet du Pavillon d'été 2007 de la Serpentine. Thorsen, né à Haugesund (Norvège) en 1958, a participé activement à certains projets de Snøhetta comme le musée d'art édifié pour les Jeux olympiques de Lillehammer (1991) ; la Bibliotheca Alexandrina (Égypte, 1993–2001) ; l'Opéra national d'Oslo (2000–07) et le musée sur le site du World Trade Center à New York. Une œuvre d'Olafur Eliasson de grandes dimensions a été installée dans le foyer de l'Opéra d'Oslo. En 2005, Eliasson et Thorsen ont collaboré sur une proposition pour le musée Turner Contemporary à Margate (GB).

The artist Olafur Eliasson collaborated with the Norwegian architect Kjetil Thorsen, a founder of the Norwegian architectural practice Snøhetta, on the 2007 Pavilion. Made up of a steel structural frame clad in dark timber sheets and a cantilevered walkway, the pavilion featured a timber ramp that spiraled twice around the periphery, rising from the lawn to a high point, offering visitors a view of Kensington Gardens. A sense of unexpected invention inhabited this structure. "We thought it might be interesting to investigate how the body, as a time-based renewable source, is also a pavilion of sorts." For all its originality, the Pavilion also took into account both its site and the history of similar structures. In 2007 Olafur Eliasson stated: "There's the tradition of making pavilions, which in a sense are not real buildings. It's a display-oriented trajectory, from the large exhibitions in the 19th century to modern ones like the Frieze Art Fair. So, throughout the history of the relationship between the park and the city, between the Serpentine and the park, and between the Serpentine and the Pavilion, we see an ongoing negotiation of what constitutes reality. This determines the degree to which we allow people to understand the potential of this construction as a means to re-evaluate themselves in relation to their surroundings." The artist and architect imagined their pavilion in relation to the "permanence" of the Serpentine Gallery itself and also in terms of its spiraling potential for discovery. "We're not attempting to make a picture of time," said Eliasson, "we're trying to be of time," while Thorsen replied, "The only infinite space is inside you." The pair agreed, in an interview with Hans Ulrich Obrist and Julia Peyton-Jones, that they had been influenced by the Austrian–American architect and designer Frederick Kiesler (1890–1965). Eliasson stated: "He's one of the people who has proved the increasingly important point that there's a spatial performativity out there somewhere between art and architecture that has great potential." As Eliasson and Thorsen described it: "Based on the principle of a winding ramp, the 2007 Serpentine Gallery Pavilion explores the idea of vertical circulation within a single space. The aim is to reconsider the traditional, single-level pavilion structure by adding a third dimension: height. The vertical movement of visitors in the Pavilion will complement the horizontal circulation in the exhibition spaces at the adjacent Serpentine Gallery." Olafur Eliasson concludes: "The spiraling form is less about form for its own sake and more about how people move within space."

Für den Pavillon 2007 arbeitete der Künstler Olafur Eliasson mit dem norwegischen Architekten Kjetil Thorsen vom Architekturbüro Snøhetta zusammen. Der Pavillon bestand aus einem tragenden Stahlrahmen, der mit dunklem Holz verblendet war und eine auskragende Rampe hatte, die sich außen zweimal spiralförmig um den Bau wand – vom Rasen bis zum höchsten Punkt mit Ausblick über die Kensington Gardens. Die Konstruktion war von großem Erfindergeist geprägt. „Wir wollten untersuchen, ob auch der Körper als zeitbasierte erneuerbare Ressource eine Art Pavillon sein könnte." Trotzdem berücksichtigte der originelle Pavillon sein Umfeld und auch die Geschichte ähnlicher Bauten. Olafur Eliasson erklärte 2007: „Es gibt eine Tradition, Pavillons zu bauen, die eigentlich keine Gebäude sind. Von den Großausstellungen des 19. Jahrhunderts bis hin zu modernen Varianten wie der Kunstmesse Frieze werden sie entlang von Ausstellungen gebaut. Daher glauben wir, dass sich durch die Geschichte der Beziehung von Park und Stadt, von Serpentine und Park sowie von Serpentine und Pavillon eine ständige Debatte darüber zieht, was Realität konstituiert. Dies bestimmt, inwieweit wir zulassen, dass die Leute das Potenzial dieses Baus verstehen: als Mittel, sich neu in Beziehung zu ihrem Umfeld zu setzen." Künstler und Architekt entwarfen ihren Pavillon sowohl in Bezug auf die „Permanenz" der Serpentine Gallery als auch, um Entdeckungen zu ermöglichen. „Wir versuchen nicht, die Zeit in ein Bild zu fassen", sagte Eliasson, „wir versuchen, in der Zeit zu sein." Thorsen dazu: „Der einzige unendliche Raum liegt in uns selbst." Die beiden sagen, sie seien von dem österreichisch-amerikanischen Architekten und Designer Frederick Kiesler (1890–1965) beeinflusst. Eliasson erklärt: „Er ist einer derjenigen, die die immer wichtiger werdende These bestätigt haben, dass irgendwo zwischen Kunst und Architektur eine räumliche Performativität mit einem großen Potenzial existiert." Eliasson und Thorsen führen aus: „Ausgehend vom Prinzip einer spiralförmigen Rampe ist der Serpentine-Pavillon 2007 eine Auseinandersetzung mit vertikaler Drehung in einem Raum. Die traditionelle einstöckige Pavillonstruktur sollte überdacht werden, indem eine dritte Dimension hinzukam: die Höhe. Die vertikale Bewegung der Besucher im Pavillon wird zum Pendant der horizontalen Bewegung in den Ausstellungsräumen der Serpentine Gallery nebenan." Olafur Eliasson fasst zusammen: „Bei der Spiralform geht es weniger um die Form selbst als vielmehr darum, wie sich Menschen im Raum bewegen."

Le Pavillon 2007 est le fruit de la collaboration de l'artiste Olafur Eliasson et de l'architecte Kjetil Thorsen (Snøhetta). Il se composait d'une ossature en acier habillée de panneaux de bois, d'une passerelle suspendue et d'une rampe en bois tournant à deux reprises sur elle-même en périphérie, partant de la pelouse pour aller jusqu'au point le plus élevé et offrir une vue sur les jardins de Kensington. Cette construction était étonnamment inventive. « Nous avons pensé qu'il serait intéressant d'étudier comment le corps, ressource renouvelable reposant sur le temps, est également en soi une sorte de pavillon. » Le pavillon prenait aussi en compte son site et l'histoire de bâtiments similaires. En 2007, Olafur Eliasson déclarait : « Il existe une tradition de construction de pavillons qui, en un sens, ne sont pas de vrais bâtiments. Il s'agit de projets orientés vers la présentation de produits, celle des grandes expositions du XIXᵉ siècle jusqu'aux plus modernes comme la Frieze Art Fair. Ainsi, tout au long de l'histoire de la relation entre le parc et la ville, entre la Serpentine et le parc et entre la Serpentine et le pavillon, nous constatons une négociation permanente sur ce qui constitue la réalité. Ceci détermine le degré auquel nous permettons au public d'appréhender le potentiel de cette construction en tant que moyen de réévaluation de soi-même par rapport à son environnement. » L'artiste et l'architecte ont imaginé leur pavillon en relation avec la « permanence » de la galerie, et en termes de potentiel de découverte par la spirale. « Nous ne tentons pas de donner une image du temps, explique Eliasson, nous essayons d'être à temps. » Thorsen réplique : « Le seul espace infini est en nous. » Tous deux reconnaissent l'influence de l'architecte et designer austro-américain Frederick Kiesler (1890-1965). Pour Eliasson : « Il est une des personnes qui a démontré un point de plus en plus important, l'existence d'une performativité spatiale entre l'art et l'architecture disposant d'un grand potentiel. » Eliasson et Thorsen présentent leur pavillon : « Reposant sur le principe d'une rampe tournante, le Pavillon 2007 de la Serpentine Gallery explore l'idée de circulation verticale à l'intérieur d'un espace unique. L'objectif est de reconsidérer la structure traditionnelle du pavillon sur un seul niveau en lui ajoutant une troisième dimension : la hauteur. Le mouvement vertical des visiteurs dans le pavillon complètera la circulation horizontale dans les espaces d'exposition de la galerie adjacente. » « La spirale relève moins d'une forme en soi que de la façon dont les gens se déplacent dans cet espace », conclut Olafur Eliasson.

Clad in timber, the 2007 pavilion was in place from 24 August to 5 November of that year, representing a first direct collaboration on the overall design of a Pavilion between an architect (Thorsen) and an artist (Eliasson).

Der holzverschalte Pavillon 2007 stand vom 24. August bis 5. November des Jahres und war das Ergebnis der ersten direkten Zusammenarbeit eines Architekten (Thorsen) und eines Künstlers (Eliasson) an einem Sommerpavillon.

Habillé de bois, le Pavillon 2007 est resté en place du 24 août au 5 novembre de cette même année. Il représentait la première collaboration directe entre un architecte (Thorsen) et un artiste (Eliasson) dans la conception d'un pavillon de la Serpentine.

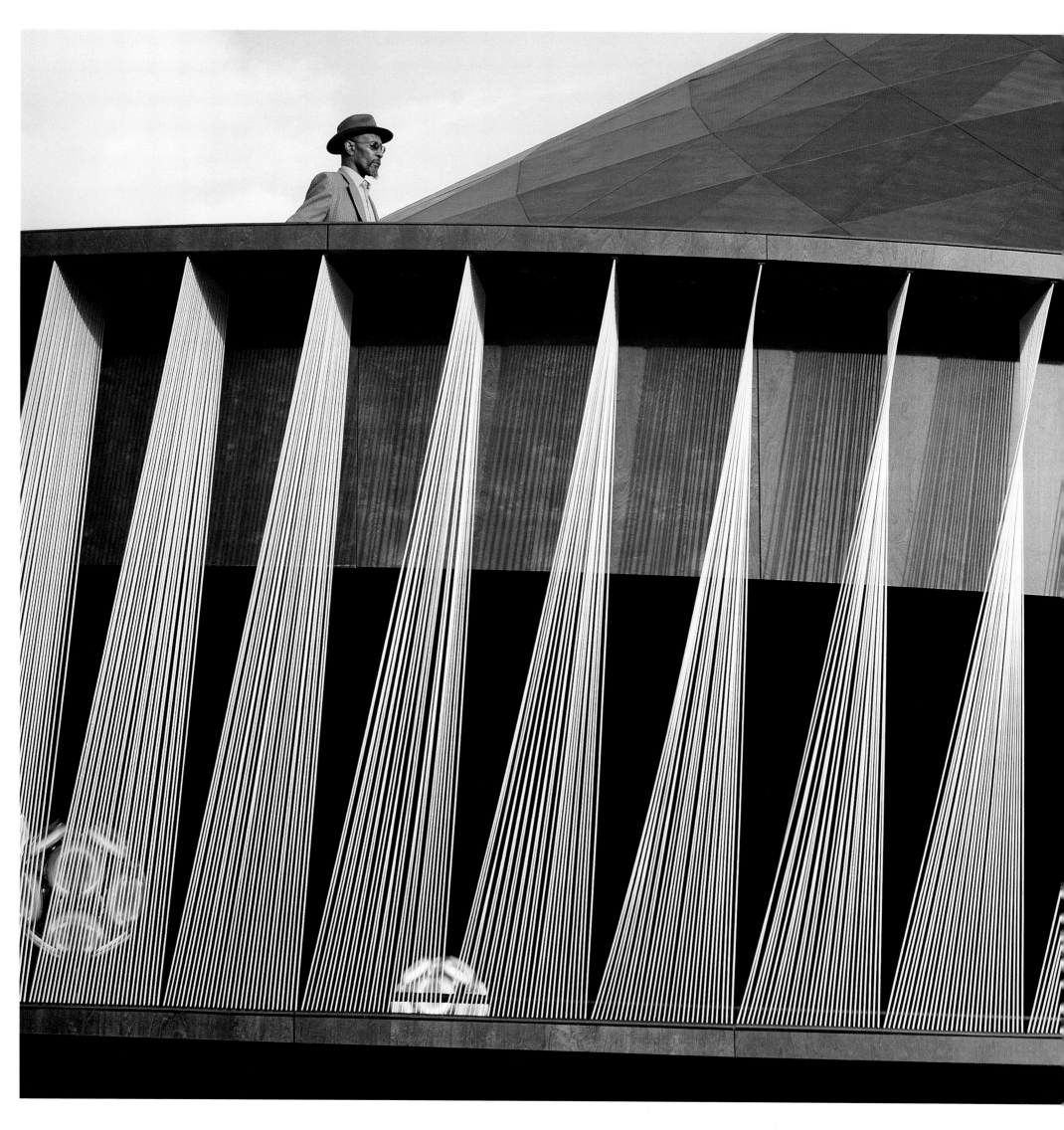

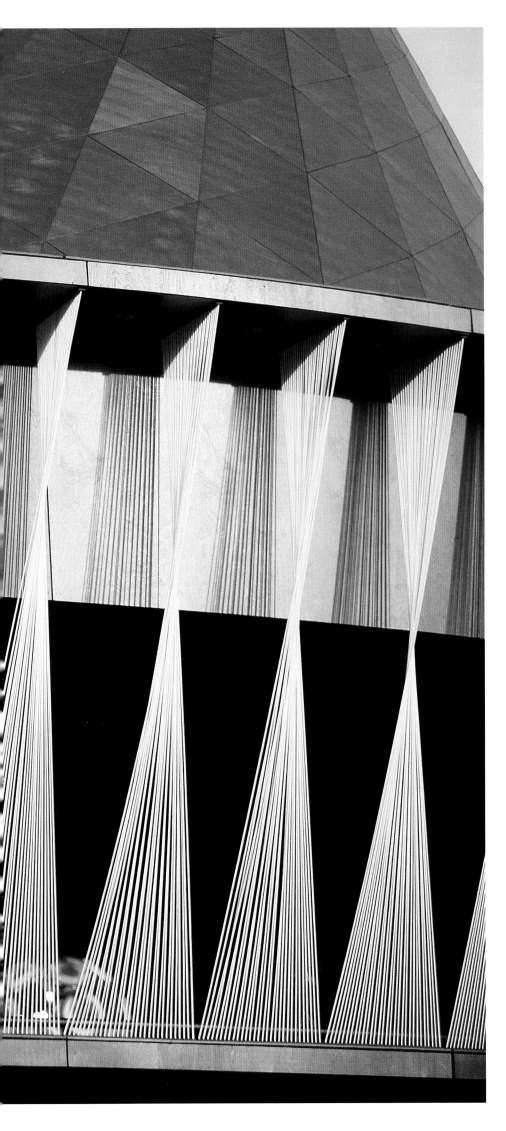

A broad spiraling ramp makes two complete turns around the single-level pavilion, allowing visitors to climb the outside of the structure all the way to the top.

Eine breite, spiralförmige Rampe umrundet den einstöckigen Pavillon zweimal vollständig und erlaubt den Besuchern, außen bis zur Spitze des Baus hinaufzulaufen.

Une large rampe en spirale exécutait deux tours complets autour du pavillon à niveau unique afin de permettre aux visiteurs d'escalader par l'extérieur la structure jusqu'à son sommet.

Views of the pavilion's spiraling ramp and of its generous column-free interior volume. The design was likened by the Serpentine to "a spinning top."

Ansichten der spiralförmigen Rampe und des großzügigen, stützenfreien Innenraums. Die Serpentine verglich den Entwurf mit einem „Kreisel".

Vues de la rampe en spirale du pavillon et de son généreux volume intérieur sans colonne. Le projet a été comparé par l'équipe de la Serpentine à une toupie.

The inclination of the ramp and of the cone-like shape of the pavilion itself give an impression of movement, which is heightened by the visitors who are walking either up or down the surface of the building.

Die Neigung der Rampe sowie die Trichterform des Pavillons selbst vermitteln den Eindruck von Dynamik, was durch die Besucher verstärkt wird, die am Bauwerk hinauf- und hinablaufen.

L'inclinaison de la rampe et la forme conique du pavillon donnaient une impression de mouvement, renforcée par les déplacements incessants des visiteurs sur ou sous le bâtiment.

As is always the case, the Serpentine Summer Pavilion, located in the midst of Kensington Gardens, attracts a large number of passersby who may not always be familiar with the latest trends in contemporary art and architecture.

Wie auch sonst lockte der Sommerpavillon der Serpentine – mitten in den Kensington Gardens gelegen – Passanten in großer Zahl an, die jedoch nicht unbedingt mit den neuesten Entwicklungen der zeitgenössischen Kunst und Architektur vertraut sind.

Comme souvent, le pavillon d'été de la Serpentine, situé au milieu des jardins de Kensington attire un grand nombre de passants qui ne sont pas toujours des familiers des dernières tendances de l'art et de l'architecture contemporains.

"This timberclad structure resembles a spinning top and brings a dramatic vertical dimension to the traditional single-level pavilion."
SERPENTINE GALLERY

Though its form is playful, the pavilion also has a kind of mystery generated by its dark surfaces and unusual forms. Here visitors climb the outside ramp after nightfall.

Trotz seiner spielerischen Form hat der Pavillon durch seine dunklen Oberflächen und ungewöhnliche Formgebung auch etwas Geheimnisvolles. Hier laufen Besucher nach Einbruch der Dunkelheit die Außenrampe hinauf.

De forme ludique, le pavillon ne projetait pas moins une sorte d'atmosphère mystérieuse générée par ses habillages sombres et ses formes étranges. Ici, des visiteurs empruntent la rampe extérieure après la tombée de la nuit.

The performance and audience spaces within the pavilion seem to converge on those speaking in a movement that is something like the spiral rise of the exterior ramp. The broad window band along the outside of the building allows those on the exterior to see activity inside.

Die Bühnen- und Zuschauerbereiche im Innern des Pavillons scheinen in einer kreisenden Bewegung, die an die spiralförmige Führung der Außenrampe erinnert, auf den Redner zuzulaufen. Das breite, außen um den Bau verlaufende Fensterband bietet von außen einen Blick auf das, was im Pavillon passiert.

Les espaces de spectacle et de réunion du pavillon semblent ici converger vers les intervenants dans un mouvement comparable à la montée extérieure de la rampe en spirale. La grande ouverture en bandeau permet aux passants de voir ce qui se déroule à l'intérieur.

The flexible interior space has dark wood cladding livened by round red cushions, ball-shaped seats, and elevated globular lighting fixtures. The window band brings natural light into this space and, of course, signals activity at night when the building glows from within.

Der flexibel nutzbare Innenraum ist mit dunklem Holz vertäfelt und wird durch rote Sitzbälle und Kugelleuchten auf Stativen aufgelockert. Das Fensterband lässt Tageslicht in den Raum und signalisiert abends Aktivität, wenn der Bau von innen leuchtet.

L'espace intérieur souple était habillé de bois de couleur sombre, égayée par des coussins rouges, des sièges en forme de boule et des luminaires globulaires suspendus. La baie en bandeau laissait pénétrer l'éclairage naturel et signalait les activités qui s'y déroulaient la nuit lorsque le bâtiment était éclairé de l'intérieur.

PLANS, DRAWINGS AND MODELS

Architectural Design Olafur Eliasson/Kjetil Thorsen
Design Team Andreas Eggertsen, Snøhetta, Architect
Ricardo Gomes, Studio Olafur Eliasson, Project Architect
Pre-Design Consultation Arup/Daniel Bosia/
Martin Manning

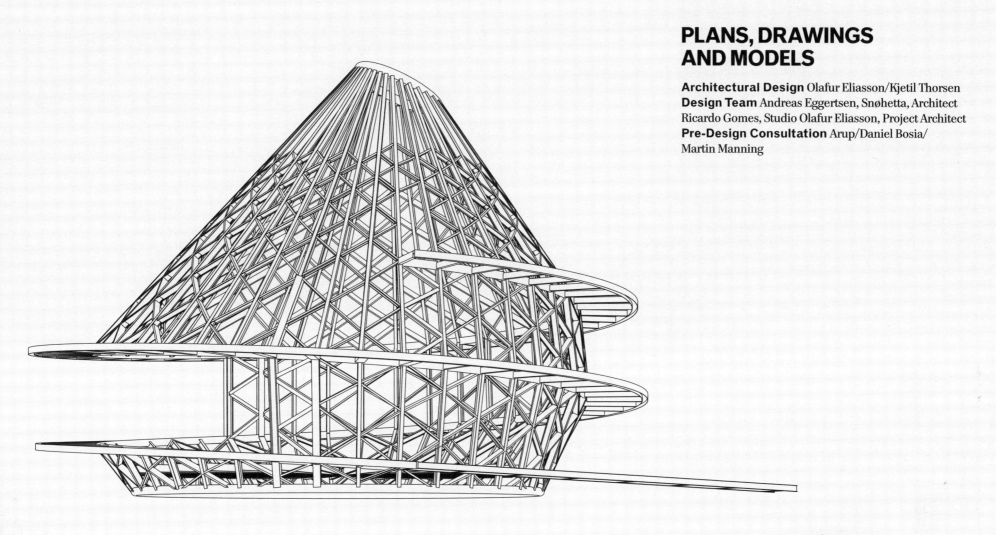

Structural drawings show the
ribbing of the pavilion.

Konstruktionszeichnungen zeigen
die Rippenstruktur des Pavillons.

Ces dessins de la structure montrent
la charpente du pavillon.

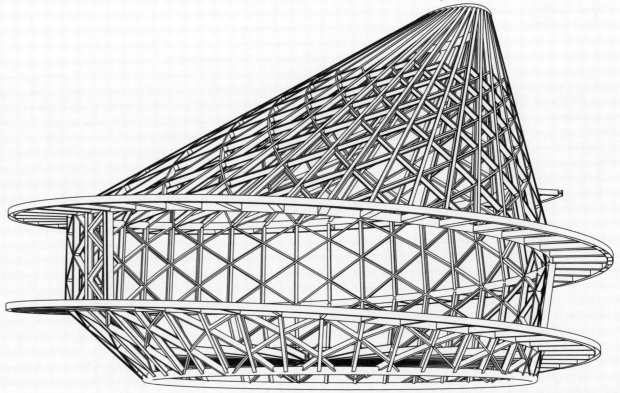

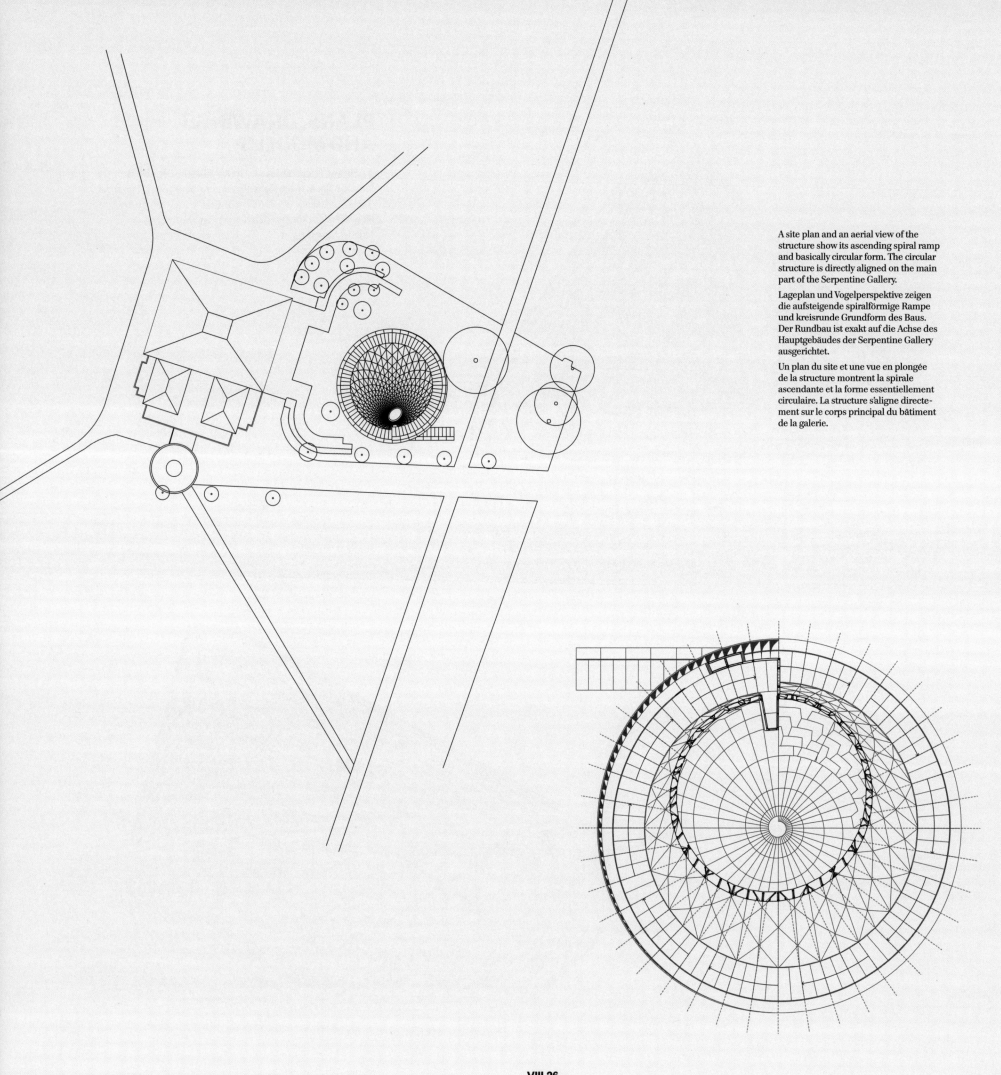

A site plan and an aerial view of the
structure show its ascending spiral ramp
and basically circular form. The circular
structure is directly aligned on the main
part of the Serpentine Gallery.

Lageplan und Vogelperspektive zeigen
die aufsteigende spiralförmige Rampe
und kreisrunde Grundform des Baus.
Der Rundbau ist exakt auf die Achse des
Hauptgebäudes der Serpentine Gallery
ausgerichtet.

Un plan du site et une vue en plongée
de la structure montrent la spirale
ascendante et la forme essentiellement
circulaire. La structure s'aligne directement sur le corps principal du bâtiment
de la galerie.

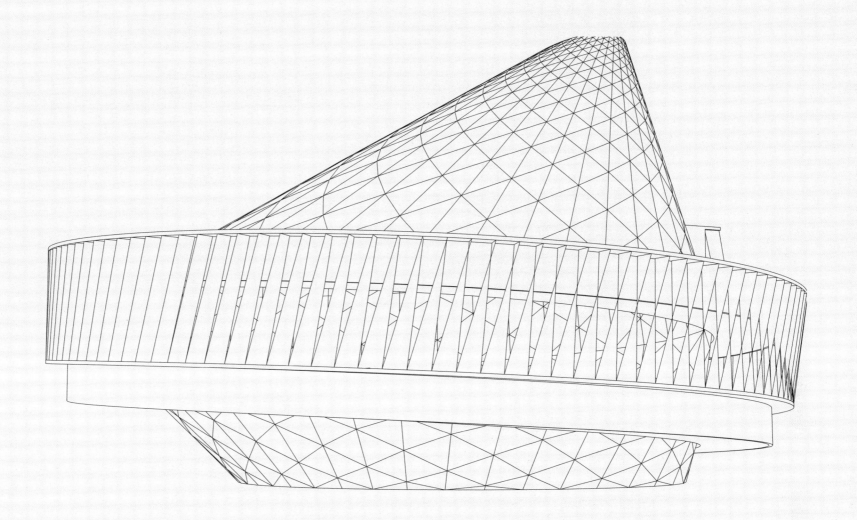

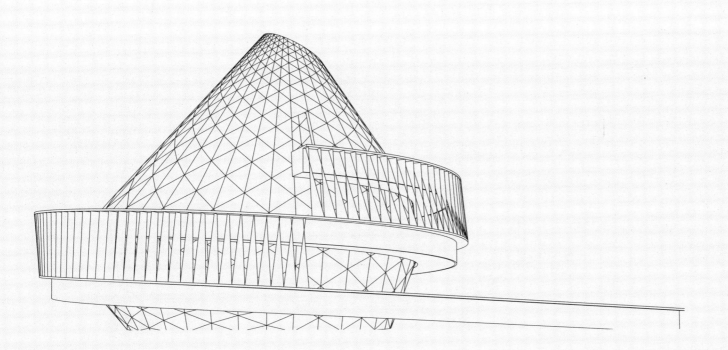

The structure is asymmetrical in elevation, as seen in these drawings. It is this "leaning" appearance together with the spiral ramp that lead observers to compare the structure to a spinning top.

Im Aufriss wirkt die Konstruktion asymmetrisch, wie diese Zeichnungen belegen. Die vermeintliche „Schieflage" ebenso wie die spiralförmige Rampe wecken beim Betrachter Assoziationen an einen Kreisel.

En élévation, la structure est de forme pyramidale, comme le montrent ces dessins. C'est cet aspect incliné et la rampe en spirale qui ont pu la faire comparer à une toupie.

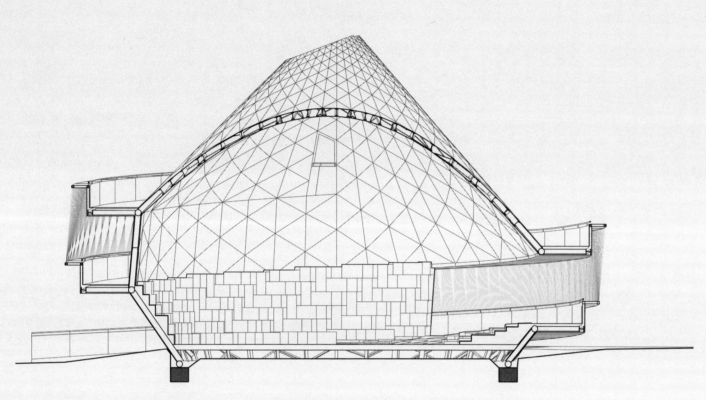

Two elevations make the ascending path of the exterior spiral ramp visible. Again, the structure is highly regular (circular) in plan and irregular (asymmetrical) as seen from the exterior.

Zwei Aufrisse zeigen den ansteigenden Verlauf der spiralförmigen Außenrampe. Auch hier fällt auf, wie ausgesprochen regelmäßig (kreisrund) die Konstruktion im Grundriss ist, während sie von außen unregelmäßig (asymmetrisch) wirkt.

Les deux élévations (à droite) matérialisent le cheminement ascensionnel sur la rampe en spirale. La structure est régulière (circulaire) en plan et irrégulière (asymétrique) vue de l'extérieur.

Section drawings show the leaning, conical form of the building, creating a generous, high interior space intended for the numerous events organized by the Serpentine in the Summer Pavilions.

Querschnitte veranschaulichen die geneigte, konische Form des Bauwerks, durch die ein großzügiger hoher Innenraum entsteht, der für die zahlreichen, von der Serpentine in den Sommerpavillons organisierten Veranstaltungen konzipiert wurde.

Ces coupes montrent la forme conique inclinée du bâtiment, qui dégageait un généreux espace intérieur destiné aux nombreuses manifestations organisées par la galerie dans le pavillon d'été.

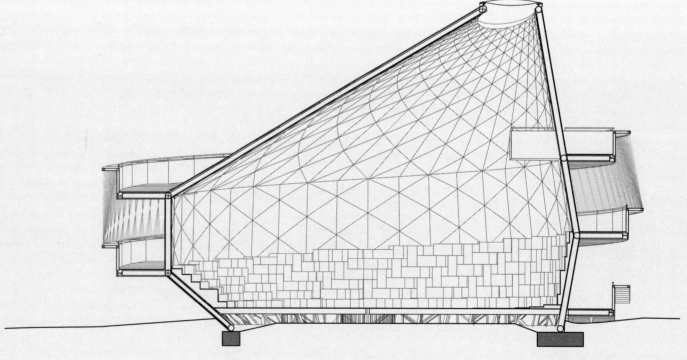

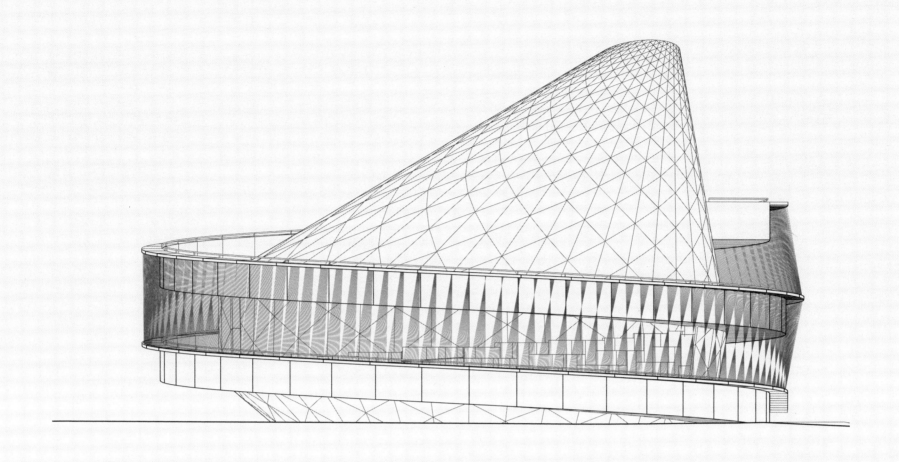

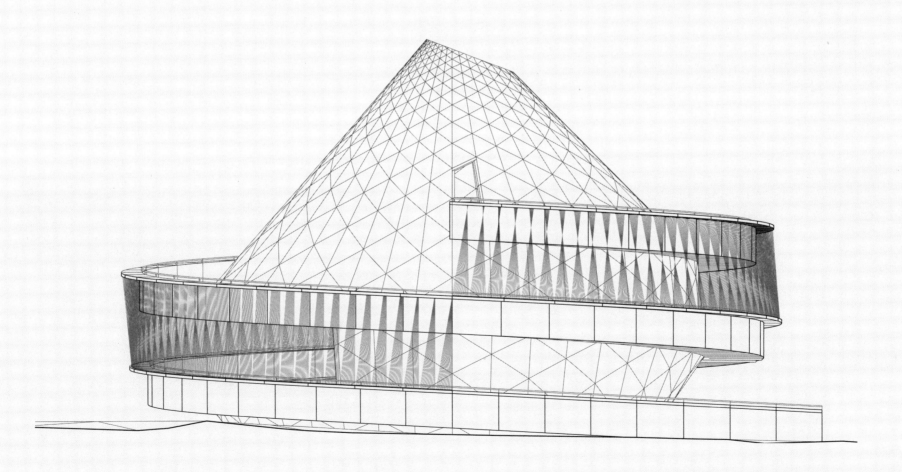

VIII.29

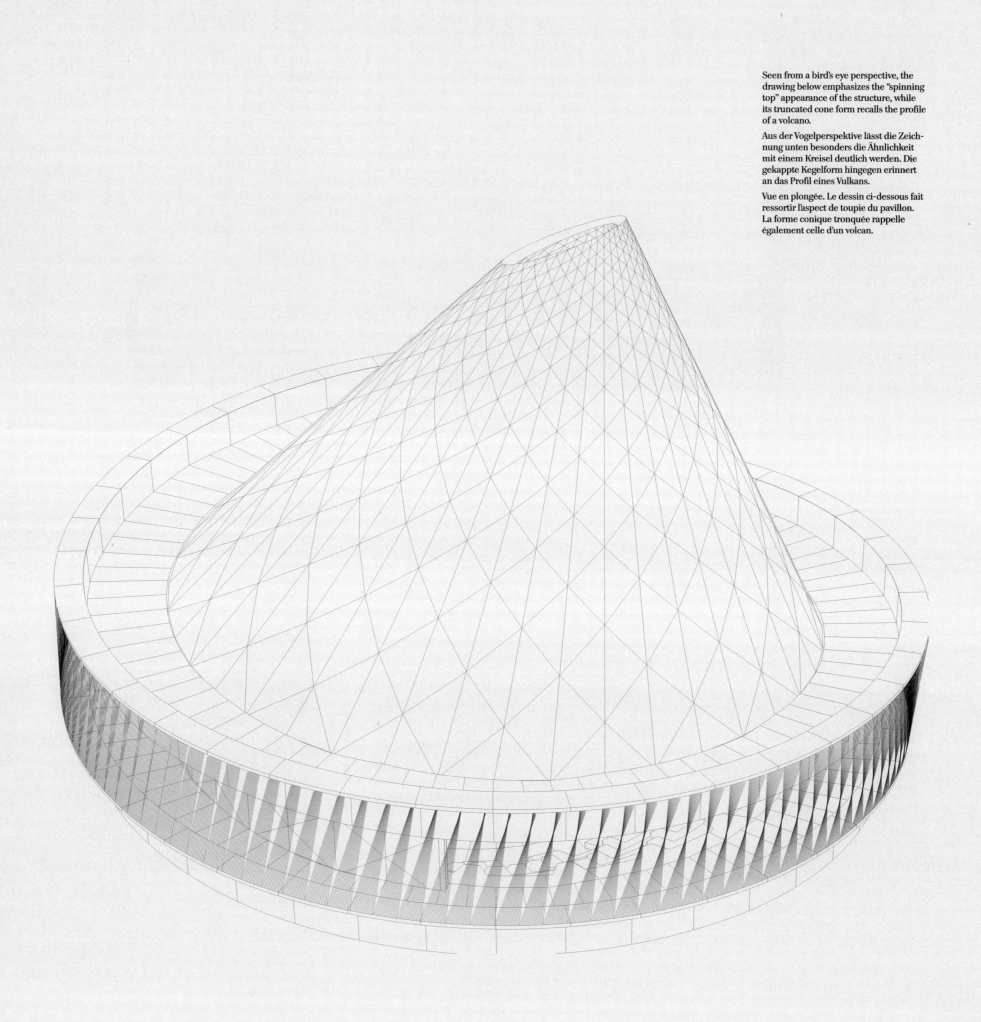

Seen from a bird's eye perspective, the drawing below emphasizes the "spinning top" appearance of the structure, while its truncated cone form recalls the profile of a volcano.

Aus der Vogelperspektive lässt die Zeichnung unten besonders die Ähnlichkeit mit einem Kreisel deutlich werden. Die gekappte Kegelform hingegen erinnert an das Profil eines Vulkans.

Vue en plongée. Le dessin ci-dessous fait ressortir l'aspect de toupie du pavillon. La forme conique tronquée rappelle également celle d'un volcan.

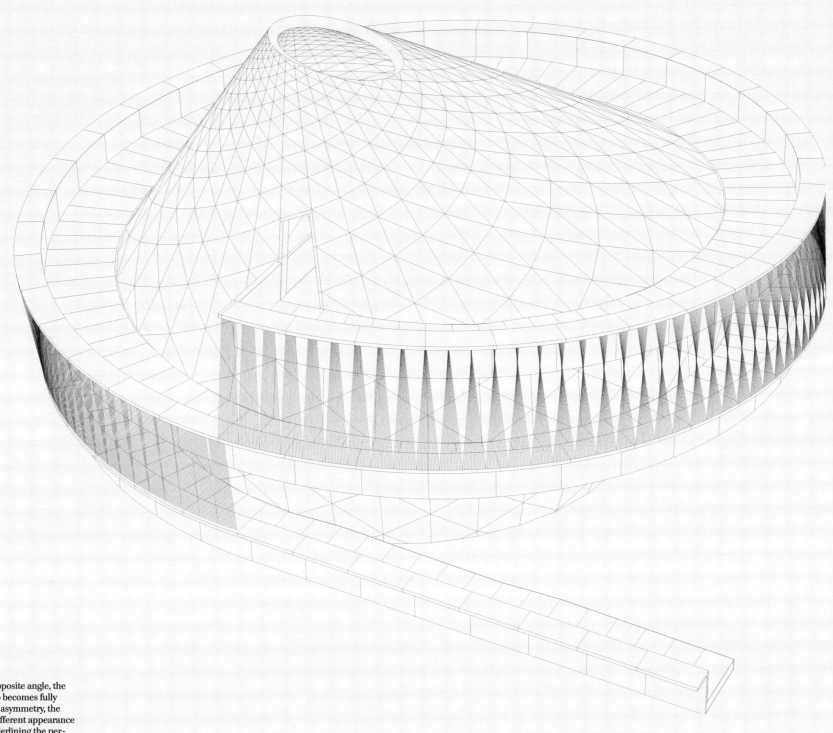

Perceived from the opposite angle, the spiraling access ramp becomes fully visible. Because of its asymmetry, the building takes on a different appearance from every angle, underlining the perceived impression of actual movement.

Aus der entgegengesetzten Perspektive ist die spiralförmige Zugangsrampe vollständig sichtbar. Aufgrund seiner asymmetrischen Form wirkt der Bau aus jedem Blickwinkel anders; der Eindruck tatsächlicher Bewegung wird verstärkt.

Vue sous l'angle opposé, la rampe d'accès en spirale devient pleinement visible. Du fait de son asymétrie, le pavillon change d'aspect selon le point de vue de l'observateur, ce qui renforce l'impression de mouvement.

FRANK O. GEHRY

2008

FRANK O. GEHRY

2008 **FRANK O. GEHRY**

Gehry Partners, LLP
12541 Beatrice Street
Los Angeles, CA 90066
USA

Tel: +1 310 482 3000
Fax: +1 310 482 3006

Born in Toronto, Canada, in 1929, Frank Gehry studied at the University of Southern California, Los Angeles (1949–51) and at Harvard (1956–57). He has been the Principal of Frank O. Gehry and Associates, Inc., Los Angeles, since 1962. His early work in Santa Monica and Venice (California) included the redesign of his own suburban-type house, the construction of a number of other small residences (Norton Residence, Venice, 1983), as well as restaurants and offices. Larger houses such as the Schnabel Residence (Brentwood, 1989) followed. Frank O. Gehry's career took a decidedly foreign emphasis with his Festival Disney building (Marne-la-Vallée, France, 1989–92) and the Guggenheim Museum (Bilbao, Spain, 1991–97), which is felt by many to be one of the most significant buildings of the late 20th century. He has completed the DG Bank Headquarters on Pariser Platz in Berlin (Germany, 2000); the Fisher Center for the Performing Arts at Bard College (Annandale-on-Hudson, New York, USA, 2002); and his first major building in Los Angeles, the Walt Disney Concert Hall in 2003. More recent work includes Maggie's Center (Dundee, Scotland, 1999–2003); the Jay Pritzker Pavilion in Millennium Park in Chicago (2004); the Hotel at the Marqués de Riscal winery (Elciego, Spain, 2003–06); an extension of the Art Gallery of Ontario (Toronto, 2005–08); and his first New York building, the InterActiveCorp Headquarters on West 19th Street in Manhattan (2003–07). He is currently working on the Louis Vuitton Foundation for Creation in the Bois de Boulogne in Paris, and the Dwight D. Eisenhower Memorial in Washington, D.C. Frank Gehry received the 1989 Pritzker Prize.

Frank Gehry wurde 1929 in Toronto in Kanada geboren und studierte an der University of Southern California, Los Angeles (1949–51) sowie in Harvard (1956 bis 1957). Seit 1962 ist Gehry Direktor von Frank O. Gehry and Associates, Inc., in Los Angeles. Zu seinem Frühwerk in Santa Monica und Venice (Kalifornien) zählen der Umbau seines eigenen, für einen Vorort typischen Wohnhauses und der Bau mehrerer weiterer kleiner Wohnbauten (Norton Residence, Venice, 1983) sowie Restaurants und Büros. Größere Wohnbauten wie die Schnabel Residence (Brentwood, 1989) folgten. Frank O. Gehrys Laufbahn verlagerte sich stark auf das Ausland mit seinem Bau für Festival Disney (Marne-la-Vallée, Frankreich, 1989–92) und dem Guggenheim Museum Bilbao (Spanien, 1991–97), das vielen als eines der bedeutendsten Bauwerke des späten 20. Jahrhunderts gilt. Gehry baute die DG-Bank-Zentrale am Pariser Platz in Berlin (2000), das Fisher Center for Performing Arts am Bard College (Annandale-on-Hudson, New York, 2002) und seinen ersten Großbau in Los Angeles, die Walt Disney Concert Hall (2003). Zu den jüngeren Arbeiten zählen Maggie's Center (Dundee, Schottland, 1999–2003), der Jay-Pritzker-Pavillon im Millennium Park in Chicago (2004), das Hotel am Weingut Marqués de Riscal (Elciego, Spanien, 2003–06), die Erweiterung der Art Gallery of Ontario (Toronto, 2005–08) und sein erster Bau in New York, die Zentrale von InterActiveCorp an der West 19th Street in Manhattan (2003–07). Zurzeit arbeitet er an der Fondation Louis Vuitton pour la Création in Paris sowie dem Dwight D. Eisenhower Memorial in Washington, D.C. 1989 erhielt Frank Gehry den Pritzker-Preis.

Né à Toronto en 1929, Frank Gehry étudie à l'université de Californie du Sud à Los Angeles (1949–51), puis à Harvard (1956–57). Depuis 1962, il dirige l'agence Frank O. Gehry and Associates, Inc. à Los Angeles. Parmi ses premiers projets à Santa Monica et Venice (Californie) figurent la transformation de sa propre maison de banlieue et la construction de quelques petites résidences (résidence Norton, Venice, 1983), ainsi que des restaurants et des bureaux. Ont suivi des maisons plus vastes comme la résidence Schnabel (Brentwood, 1989). La carrière de Gehry a pris un tour résolument international avec l'immeuble de Festival Disney (Marne-la-Vallée, France, 1989–92); le musée Guggenheim (Bilbao, Espagne, 1991–97), considéré par beaucoup comme l'un des bâtiments les plus exemplaires de la fin du XXᵉ siècle. Parmi ses autres grands chantiers figurent le siège de la DG Bank sur la Pariser Platz (Berlin, 2000); le Fisher Center for the Performing Arts à Bard College (Annandale-on-Hudson, New York, 2002); le Walt Disney Concert Hall (Los Angeles, 2003). Ses réalisations plus récentes incluent le Maggie's Center (Dunde, Écosse, 1999–2003); le Jay Pritzker Pavillion dans le Millenium Park à Chicago (2004); l'hôtel du chai Marqués de Riscal (Elciego, Espagne, 2003–06); l'extension de la Art Gallery of Ontario (Toronto, 2005–08) et son premier immeuble à New York, siège d'InteractiveCorp, West 19th Street à Manhattan (2003–07). Il travaille actuellement sur le projet de la Fondation Louis Vuitton pour la création dans le Bois de Boulogne à Paris, et le Dwight D. Eisenhower Memorial à Washington. Frank Gehry a reçu le prix Pritzker en 1989.

The 2008 Serpentine Summer Pavilion was a timber structure "which act[ed] as an urban street connecting the park with the permanent gallery building." Glass canopies hanging inside the structure provided shade and protected visitors from rain. It was intended as a place for live performances with a capacity of about 275 spectators. Gehry explains: "The interplay between the exoskeleton of timber planks and the multiple glazed roof surfaces invokes imagery of striped park tent structures and catapults, capturing the visual energy of a place created from the juxtaposition of random elements." In a sense, the temporary nature and apparently random juxtaposition of its elements bring to mind the early work of Frank Gehry, before he called on sophisticated computer technology and cladding materials such as titanium. In fact, the use of wood in this pavilion has echoes that concern his childhood and his first experiences of architecture. "It's a wood aesthetic," he stated in an interview with Julia Peyton-Jones and Hans Ulrich Obrist in 2008. "It comes from being Canadian, perhaps, because living in very cold climates like Ontario, where it can snow for 10 months of the year, there is a feeling of the heart and the warmth of wood. And you see it in Finland; you see it in Alvar Aalto's work. Aalto resonated with me from the very beginning. I became aware of his work when I went to his lecture in November 1946 at the University of Toronto." The relationship of the project to music, and even specifically to the opening performance, was clearly in the mind of the architect when he designed the pavilion. The noted British composer and pianist Thomas Adès launched the Gallery's annual summer events program, Park Nights, on 19 July 2008, with a unique performance in the pavilion. Gehry explained that "the idea of a concert platform in the Serpentine Pavilion gave me the reason for the way it grew. Once that was settled in my mind and we dealt with that as a primary issue, then I also realized that it could work for a lot more things, such as lectures and all the other events in the program. I did pick classical music as the priority, knowing that once you developed something with that priority then it would easily have multiple uses for all the other things, because they were much less difficult to accomplish. The classical music element was the most difficult thing to achieve with this kind of structure. It was important to me that once Thomas Adès had agreed to perform I didn't put him in a place that wasn't going to function." The 2008 Serpentine Summer Pavilion was sold and has now been installed at the Chateau La Coste near Aix-en-Provence, France, where it is due to be used for musical events, and where Frank Gehry is due to realize another structure in the near future.

Der Serpentine-Sommerpavillon 2008 war eine Holzkonstruktion, die „als öffentliche Straße funktionierte und den Park und das ständige Galeriegebäude miteinander verband". Im Bau hängende Glasbaldachine spendeten Schatten und schützten die Besucher vor Regen. Hier sollten Liveveranstaltungen für bis zu 275 Zuschauer stattfinden können. Gehry führt aus: „Das Zusammenspiel von Außenskelett aus Holzbindern und der Vielzahl gläserner Dachsegmente erinnert an gestreifte Gartenzelte oder auch an Katapulte und fängt die visuelle Energie eines Ortes ein, der aus den Gegensätzen willkürlicher Elemente geboren wurde." In gewisser Weise knüpfen die temporäre Form und die scheinbar zufällige Kombination gegensätzlicher Elemente an Gehrys Frühwerk an, an Zeiten, bevor er sich aufwendigen Computerprogrammen und Verblendmaterialien wie Titan zuwandte. Tatsächlich schwingt im Einsatz von Holz bei diesem Pavillon etwas mit, das mit seiner Kindheit und seinen ersten Erfahrungen mit Architektur zu tun hat. „Es ist eine Holzästhetik", erklärte er in einem Interview mit Julia Peyton-Jones und Hans Ulrich Obrist 2008. „Es hat vielleicht damit zu tun, dass ich Kanadier bin, denn wenn man in sehr kalten Klimazonen wie Ontario lebt, wo es zehn Monate im Jahr schneien kann, steht Holz für Wärme. Und das sieht man auch in Finnland, im Werk von Alvar Aalto. Aalto hat mich von Anfang an angesprochen. Ich wurde auf sein Werk aufmerksam, als ich im November 1946 eine Vorlesung von ihm an der Universität Toronto besuchte." Der Bezug seines Projekts zur Musik, insbesondere zum Eröffnungskonzert, beschäftigte den Architekten offensichtlich, als er den Pavillon entwarf. Der bekannte britische Komponist und Pianist Thomas Adès sollte das jährliche Sommerprogramm *Park Nights* am 19. Juli 2008 mit einer Sonderaufführung im Pavillon eröffnen. Gehry erklärte: „Die Idee einer Bühne für Konzerte im Serpentine-Pavillon gab den Anstoß für die weitere Entwicklung. Sobald mir das klar war und wir dieses Anliegen als Priorität behandelten, erkannte ich, dass er sich auch für viele andere Dinge eignen könnte, etwa Vorträge und sämtliche übrigen Veranstaltungen des Programms. Ich entschied mich für klassische Musik als oberste Priorität, denn ich wusste, dass der Pavillon dann auch für eine Vielzahl anderer Zwecke nutzbar wäre, die viel leichter realisierbar sind. Eine solche Konstruktion für klassische Musik zu bauen, ist am schwierigsten. Sobald Thomas Adès seinen Auftritt zugesagt hatte, war es mir wichtig, ihm einen Raum zu bieten, der funktionieren würde." Der Sommerpavillon 2008 wurde verkauft und steht nun am Chateau La Coste bei Aix-en-Provence, wo er für Konzerte genutzt werden soll. Dort wird Frank Gehry bald noch einen weiteren Bau realisieren.

Le Pavillon d'été 2008 de la Serpentine était une structure en bois « qui fonctionne comme une rue reliant le parc au bâtiment permanent de la galerie ». Des auvents de verre suspendus à l'intérieur fournissaient de l'ombre et protégeaient les visiteurs de la pluie. Le lieu était conçu pour accueillir 275 spectateurs à l'occasion des manifestations. Selon Gehry : « Le jeu entre l'exosquelette des planches de bois et les multiples plans vitrés de la couverture évoquent des tentes de réception en toile rayée et des catapultes, captant l'énergie visuelle d'un lieu créé à partir de la juxtaposition de ses éléments aléatoires. » En un sens, la nature temporaire et cette juxtaposition aléatoire rappellent les premières réalisations de Frank Gehry, avant qu'il ne fasse appel à des technologies informatiques sophistiquées et à des matériaux de parement tels le titane. En fait, l'utilisation du bois trouve des échos dans son enfance et ses premières expériences de l'architecture. « C'est une esthétique du bois », a-t-il précisé dans un entretien avec Julia Peyton-Jones et Hans Ulrich Obrist en 2008. « Elle vient peut-être du fait que je suis Canadien, car lorsque vous vivez dans un climat très froid comme celui de l'Ontario, où il peut neiger pendant dix mois, vous appréciez la chaleur du bois. Vous le voyez en Finlande, et dans l'œuvre d'Alvar Aalto. Aalto m'a interpellé dès le début. J'ai pris conscience de son travail lors d'une de ses conférences en 1946 à l'université de Toronto. » La relation de ce projet avec la musique, spécifiquement avec le concert d'ouverture, faisait réellement partie des préoccupations de l'architecte lorsqu'il conçut les plans du pavillon. Le 19 juillet 2008, le célèbre compositeur et pianiste britannique Thomas Adès ouvrit le programme des manifestations de l'été, les « Park Nights », avec une performance unique donnée dans le pavillon. Gehry expliqua que « l'idée d'un podium de concert dans le pavillon de la Serpentine a déterminé la façon dont il s'est développé. Une fois cette contrainte intégrée, nous l'avons traitée comme un enjeu essentiel et j'ai compris que le dispositif pouvait fonctionner pour beaucoup plus d'événements prévus dans le programme. J'ai pris la musique comme une priorité, sachant qu'une fois que vous mettez au point votre projet selon celle-ci, il est plus facile de multiplier des utilisations de ce dispositif. L'élément de musique classique a été la chose la plus difficile à traiter dans ce type de structure. Il était important pour moi qu'une fois que Thomas Adès avait donné son accord pour jouer, je ne le mette pas dans un cadre qui ne fonctionne pas. » Vendu, le Pavillon 2008 est maintenant installé au château La Coste, près d'Aix-en-Provence en France où il sera utilisé pour des manifestations musicales et où Frank Gehry devrait réaliser un autre projet dans un futur proche.

The first built project in England by Frank Gehry, this pavilion was made with four steel columns, timber planks, and a large number of overlapping glass panes.

Dieser Pavillon war Frank Gehrys erstes realisiertes Bauwerk in England und wurde aus vier Stahlstützen, Holzbohlen und einander überlappenden Glassegmenten errichtet.

Premier projet de Frank Gehry réalisé au Royaume-Uni, ce pavillon se composait de quatre colonnes d'acier, de planches et d'une multitude de panneaux de verre en chevauchement.

"The Pavilion is designed as a wooden timber structure that acts as an urban street running from the park to the existing Gallery."

FRANK GEHRY

Seen from the angle of the main axis of the Serpentine Gallery, the Gehry Pavilion takes on the air of a triumphal, asymmetric arch. In reality, the structure, more than previous ones, serves as an amphitheatre.

Aus der Hauptachse der Serpentine Gallery wirkt der Gehry-Pavillon wie ein asymmetrischer Triumphbogen. Tatsächlich funktioniert der Bau mehr noch als seine Vorgänger wie ein Amphitheater.

Vu dans l'axe principal de la Serpentine Gallery, le pavillon Gehry prenait une allure d'arc de triomphe asymétrique. En réalité, plus que les précédents pavillons, il faisait office d'amphithéâtre.

Inspired, according to the Serpentine, by the catapults designed by Leonardo da Vinci as well as by America's summer beach huts, the pavilion projects an image of suspended lightness that the architect's work does not always seek to achieve.

Der Pavillon, laut Serpentine ebenso von Katapultentwürfen Leonardo da Vincis wie von amerikanischen Strandhäuschen inspiriert, vermittelt eine Leichtigkeit, die für das übrige Werk des Architekten nicht immer typisch ist.

Inspiré – selon la galerie – des catapultes dessinées par Leonard de Vinci et des cabanes d'été des plages américaines, le pavillon projetait une image de légèreté en suspension atypique des recherches de l'architecte.

Depending on the angle from which it is seen, the structure sometimes looks like a jumble of wood and glass. Indeed, it changes completely in appearance depending on the position of the viewer.

Je nach Blickwinkel wirkt die Konstruktion mitunter wie ein Gewirr aus Holz und Glas. Tatsächlich verändert sich der Eindruck je nach Standpunkt des Betrachters grundlegend.

Selon l'angle de vue, le pavillon faisait parfois penser à un enchevêtrement de bois et de verre. Il changeait entièrement d'apparence selon la position du spectateur.

More than almost any other Serpentine Summer Pavilion, Gehry's work frames and presents the gallery building. The powerful balanced wood beams of the structure contrast completely with the much more traditional, older building.

Mehr noch als fast alle übrigen Sommerpavillons der Serpentine rahmt und präsentiert Gehrys Entwurf das Galeriegebäude. Die eindrucksvoll austarierten Holzträger der Konstruktion bilden einen extremen Gegensatz zum traditionelleren Altbau.

Plus que n'importe quel autre pavillon d'été de la Serpentine, le projet de Gehry cadrait et mettait en valeur le bâtiment ancien. La puissance formelle de ses poutres de bois en équilibre contrastait fortement avec le bâtiment ancien traditionnel.

The partially covered, open space beneath the dramatically angled glass and wood canopy allows a full and free program to take place on the lawn in front of the Serpentine.

Der teils überdachte, offene Bereich unter dem dramatisch schrägen Überbau aus Glas und Holz ermöglicht es, ein großes und offen gehaltenes Programm auf dem Rasen vor der Serpentine zu veranstalten.

L'espace ouvert, en partie protégé par de spectaculaires auvents de bois et de verre, permettait le déroulement normal des activités devant la galerie.

Despite its apparently free and expressive forms, the pavilion creates an excellent space for concerts and conferences directly in front of the Gallery. High and open, the structure is less enclosed and protective than many of its predecessors.

Trotz der offensichtlich freien und expressiven Formen war der Pavillon ein hervorragender Veranstaltungort für Konzerte und Konferenzen direkt vor der Galerie. Die hohe, offene Konstruktion war weniger geschlossen und Schutz bietend als viele Vorgängerbauten.

Malgré ses formes expressives et apparemment libres, le pavillon constituait un excellent espace pour donner des concerts et des conférences devant la galerie. De bonne hauteur, cette structure ouverte était moins fermée que celle de beaucoup de pavillons antérieurs.

Breaking up the roof and ceiling of the pavilion into an orchestration of fractured planes, the architect has gone even further with the walls of the structure, which have all but disappeared. The work is sculptural and yet usable, while also forming an archway.

Der Architekt teilte das Dach und die Decke des Pavillons in eine orchestrierte Anordnung fragmetierter Flächen auf und ging bei den Wänden der Konstruktion, die hier fast gänzlich verschwunden sind, sogar noch weiter. Der Entwurf ist skulptural und dennoch nutzerfreundlich und bildet zugleich einen Bogengang.

Rompant la continuité de la toiture – ou du plafond – du pavillon dans une orchestration de plans fracturés, l'architecte a poussé encore plus loin cette démarche sur les murs pratiquement éliminés. La composition sculpturale est néanmoins fonctionnelle puisqu'elle forme une sorte d'arche de protection.

Silkscreened patterns mark glass barriers while an exploded grid hangs between earth and sky—a tour de force in formal, artistic terms, and a joyous celebration of the ambitious summer program of the Serpentine.

Während Glasbrüstungen mit Siebdruckmustern versehen sind, schwebt das explodierte Grundraster zwischen Himmel und Erde – formal und künstlerisch eine Tour de Force und eine fröhliche Hommage an das ambitionierte Sommerprogramm der Serpentine.

Des motifs sérigraphiés signalaient les garde-corps en verre tandis que la trame semblait suspendue entre terre et ciel, tour de force artistique formel et célébration joyeuse de l'ambitieux programme d'été de la galerie.

The suspended planes forming the roof of the pavilion hang high above the performance and seating space. The result is an unprecedented openness that might well be at the limits of being able to protect the audience from a passing shower.

Die abgehängten Segmente des Pavillondachs schweben hoch über dem Bühnen- und Zuschauerbereich. So entsteht eine beispiellose Offenheit, die an ihre Grenzen stoßen könnte, wenn sie das Publikum vor einem Schauer schützen müsste.

Les plans suspendus qui formaient la toiture du pavillon étaient accrochés bien au-dessus des sièges et de la scène. Il en résultait une ouverture sans précédent, peut-être à la limite de la capacité du dispositif à protéger le public des averses.

Lit essentially from below after nightfall, the pavilion affirms its sculptural nature even more than during the day.

Der nach Einbruch der Dunkelheit vor allem von unten beleuchtete Pavillon wirkt nachts noch skulpturaler als tagsüber.

Principalement éclairé par le bas pendant la nuit, le pavillon affirmait alors encore davantage sa nature sculpturale qu'en journée.

With its visible heavy wooden beams hanging in the air at precarious angles, the pavilion is the complete opposite of the anchored brick structure of the Serpentine. As befits a temporary pavilion, the design exemplifies the famous definition of architecture as frozen music.

Der Pavillon mit seinen bedenklich schief in der Luft hängenden, schweren Holzträgern ist die vollendete Antithese zum fest verankerten Backsteinbau der Serpentine. Wie es sich für einen temporären Pavillon gehört, ist er ein Sinnbild der berühmten Definition von Architektur als erstarrter Musik.

Avec ses poutres de bois massives suspendues selon des angles critiques, le pavillon venait en opposition complète à la structure de briques ancrée de la galerie. Pavillon temporaire, ce projet est une belle mise en œuvre de la fameuse définition de l'architecture comme « musique figée ».

PLANS, DRAWINGS AND MODELS

Architectural Design Frank Gehry, Gehry Partners LLP
Design Team Gehry Partners LLP/Terry Bell, Project Partner
Anand Devarajan, Project Architect/Sam Gehry, Project Designer
Structural Engineering Arup/Cecil Balmond/
David Glover/Ed Clark

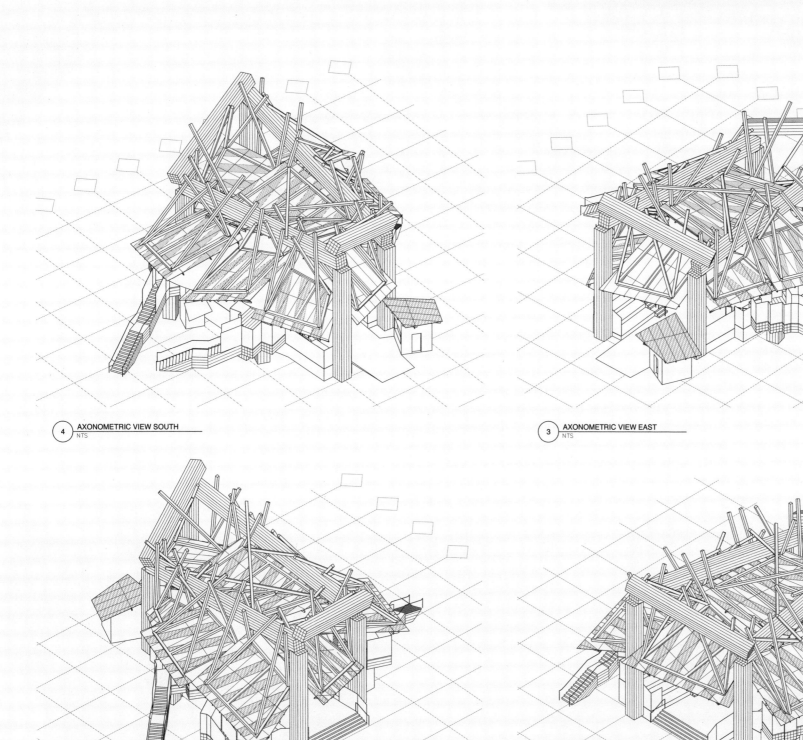

4 AXONOMETRIC VIEW SOUTH
NTS

3 AXONOMETRIC VIEW EAST
NTS

2 AXONOMETRIC VIEW NORTH
NTS

1 AXONOMETRIC VIEW WEST
NTS

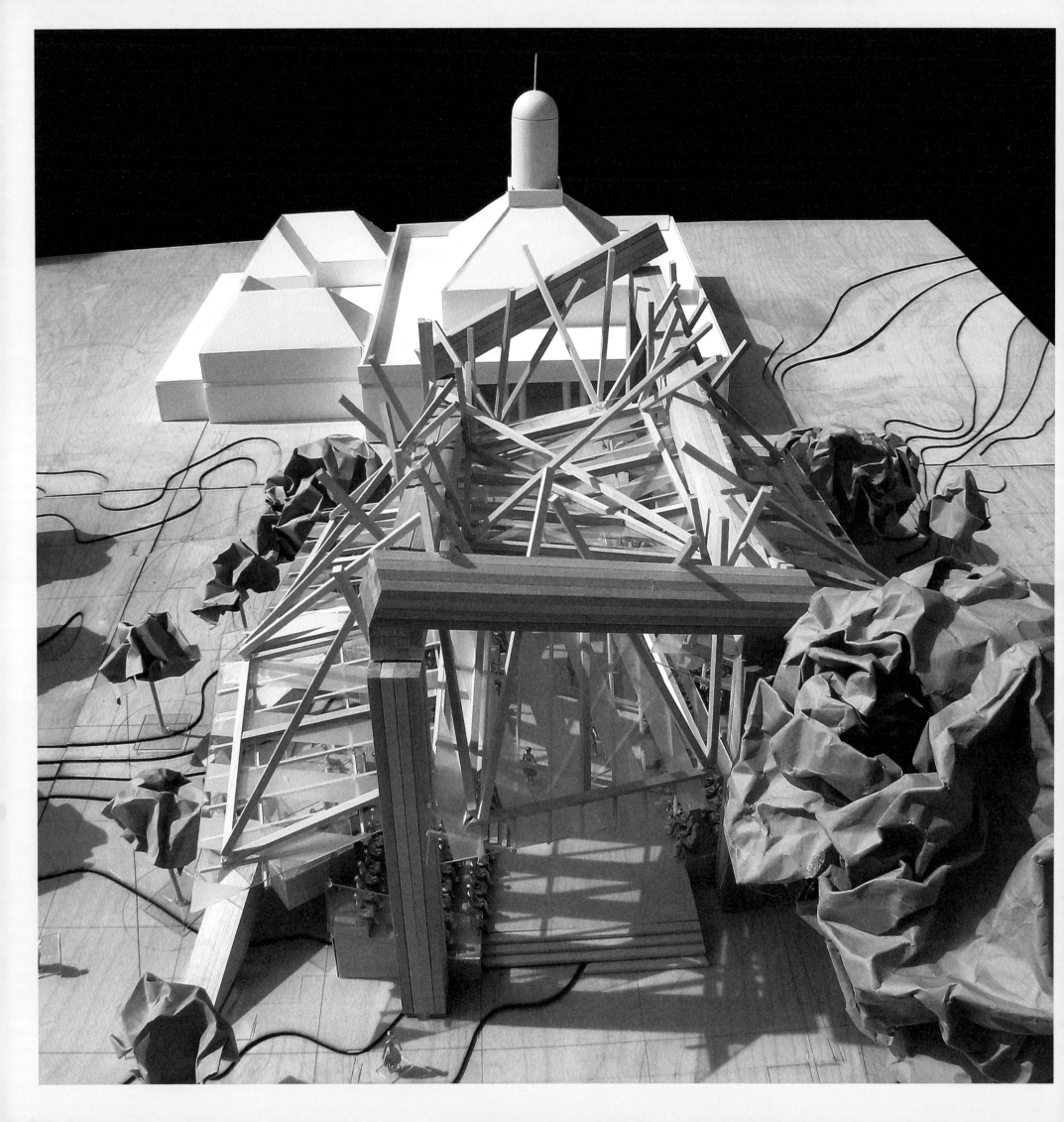

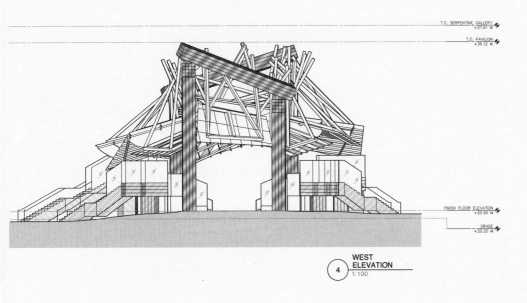

WEST
ELEVATION
4   1:100

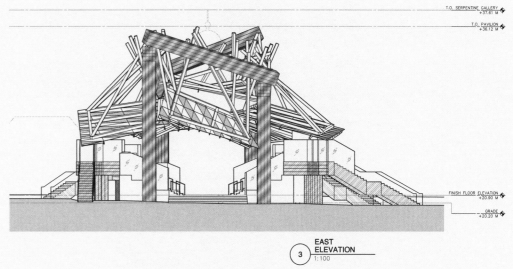

EAST
ELEVATION
3   1:100

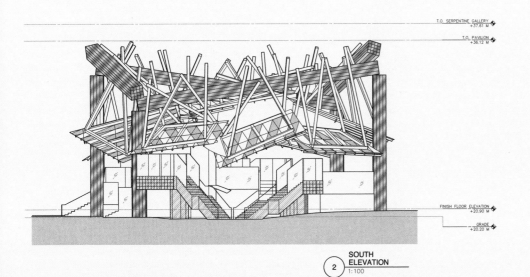

SOUTH
ELEVATION
2   1:100

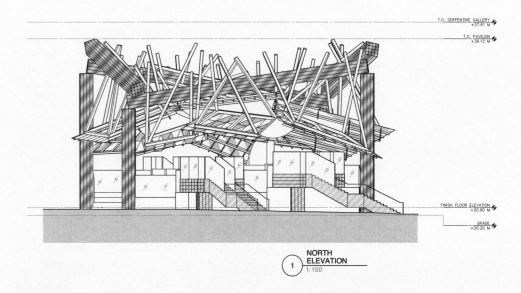

NORTH
ELEVATION
1   1:100

Elevations of the pavilion from various angles give an impression of a complex accumulation of wooden or glass elements, while the model on the left page comes closer to the actual lightness of the realization.

Aufrisse des Pavillons aus verschiedenen Blickwinkeln geben einen Eindruck von der Komplexität der sich überschneidenen Holz- und Glassegmente. Das Modell (links) kommt der tatsächlichen Umsetzung in ihrer Leichtigkeit näher.

Ces élévations du pavillon vu sous divers angles donnent l'impression d'une accumulation complexe d'éléments de bois et verre. La maquette de la page de gauche est plus proche de l'impression de légèreté que donnait le projet réalisé.

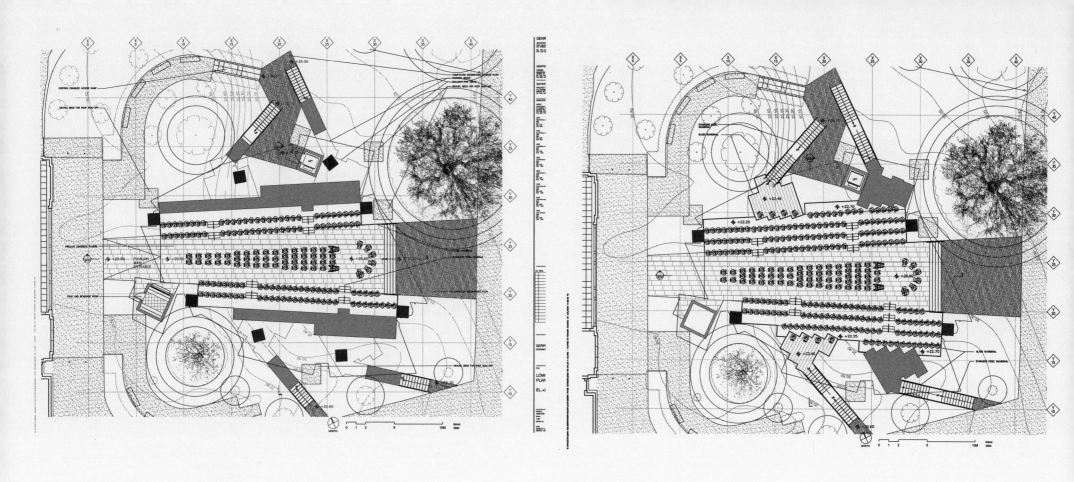

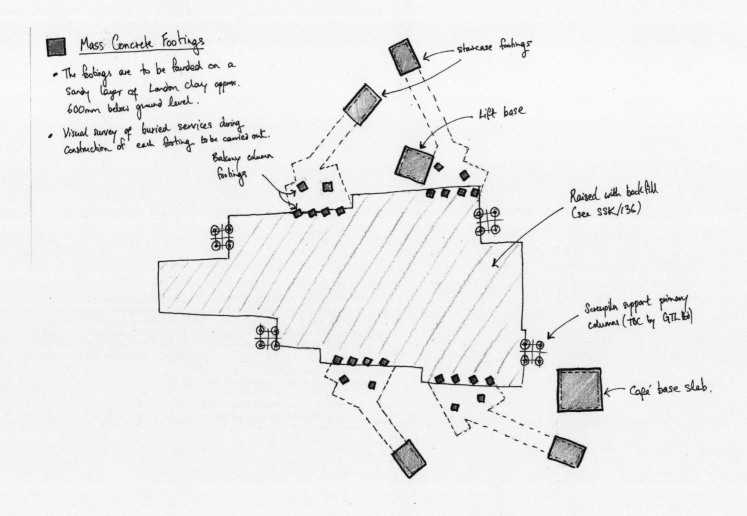

Mass Concrete Footings

- The footings are to be founded on a sandy layer of London clay approx. 600mm below ground level.
- Visual survey of buried services during construction of each footing to be carried out.

staircase footings

Lift base

Balcony column footings

Raised with back fill (see SSK/136)

Screwpiles support primary columns (TBC by GTL ltd)

Café base slab.

Plans show the slightly skewed angle of the main elements of the pavilion, forming the bleachers and leaning toward the central volume of the gallery. Left, a drawing shows the placement of the concrete footing that allows the structure to stand.

Grundrisse zeigen die leicht schiefwinklige Anordnung der Hauptelemente des Pavillons, die die Tribüne bilden und zum Hauptbaukörper der Galerie orientiert sind. Links eine Zeichnung mit der Platzierung der Betonfundamente, mit deren Hilfe die Konstruktion steht.

Ces plans montrent l'implantation légèrement en biais des principaux éléments constitutifs du pavillon qui forment les gradins, orientés vers le volume central de la galerie. À gauche, un dessin indique l'implantation des ancrages en béton qui permettent à la structure de tenir.

Seen from above, a model shows the relative size of the permanent and temporary structures, contrasting rectangular solidity with sculptural freedom.

Die Ansicht eines Modells von oben veranschaulicht die relativen Größenverhältnisse der permanenten und temporären Bauten zueinander. Hier trifft rechtwinklige Beständigkeit auf skulpturale Freiheit.

Vue de dessus, une maquette montre les dimensions relatives des bâtiments permanent et temporaire et le contraste entre la massivité orthogonale de la galerie et la liberté sculpturale du pavillon.

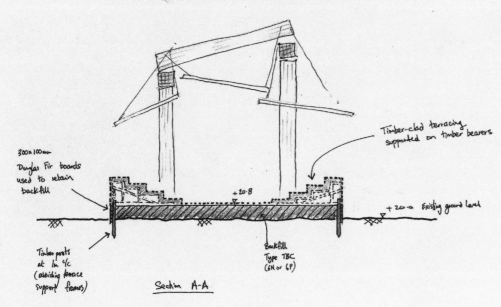

300x100mm
Douglas Fir boards
used to retain
backfill

Timber-clad terracing
supported on timber bearers

+ 20·8

+ 20·0 Existing ground level

Timber posts
at 1m c/c (abutting terrace
support frames)

Backfill
Type TBC
(6N or 6P)

Section A-A

The model seen from various angles offering an obvious difference of approach as opposed to the more boxlike shape of the gallery. Left, an engineer's drawing showing the catapultlike form of the design.

Das Modell aus verschiedenen Perspektiven: Hier zeigt sich der allzu deutliche konzeptuelle Unterschied zur eher kastenförmigen Gestalt der Galerie. Eine Bauzeichnung (links) veranschaulicht die katapultartige Form des Entwurfs.

Vue sous divers angles, la maquette souligne la différence entre la liberté d'approche du pavillon et l'aspect de bloc géométrique de la galerie. À gauche, dessin technique illustrant la forme en « catapulte » du projet.

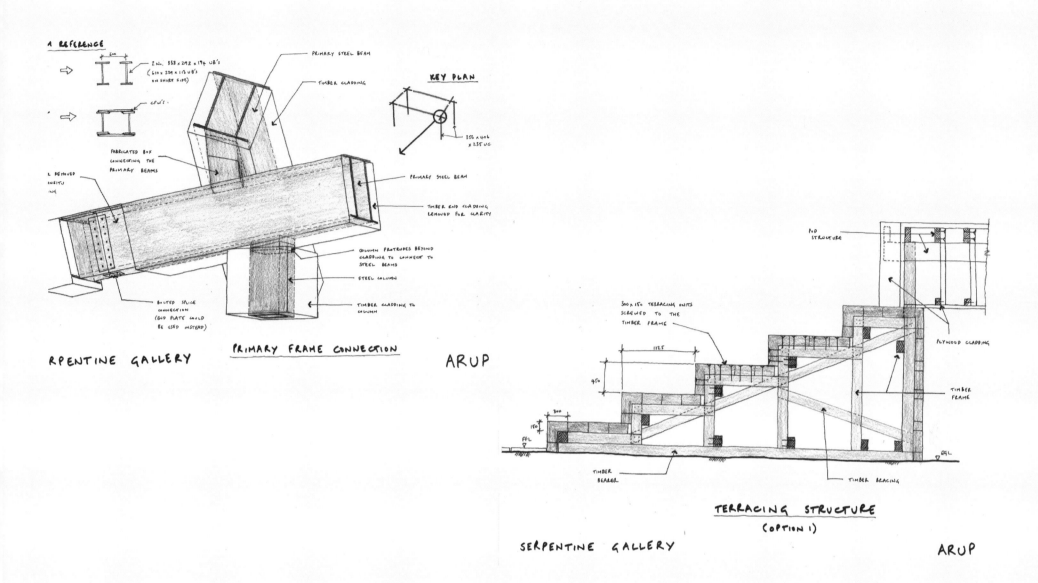

A REFERENCE

2 No. 838 x 292 x 174 UB's
(610 x 234 x 18 UB's on short side)

CFU's

PRIMARY STEEL BEAM

TIMBER CLADDING

KEY PLAN

356 x 406 x 235 UC

FABRICATED BOX CONNECTING THE PRIMARY BEAMS

L REMOVED INSITU ING

PRIMARY STEEL BEAM

TIMBER END CLADDING REMOVED FOR CLARITY

COLUMN PROTRUDES BEYOND CLADDING TO CONNECT TO STEEL BEAMS

STEEL COLUMN

TIMBER CLADDING TO COLUMN

BOLTED SPLICE CONNECTION (END PLATE COULD BE USED INSTEAD)

RPENTINE GALLERY

PRIMARY FRAME CONNECTION

ARUP

POD STRUCTURE

300 x 150 TERRACING UNITS SCREWED TO THE TIMBER FRAME

1125

PLYWOOD CLADDING

450

TIMBER FRAME

300

150

FFL

FGL

TIMBER BEARER

TIMBER BRACING

TERRACING STRUCTURE
(OPTION 1)

SERPENTINE GALLERY

ARUP

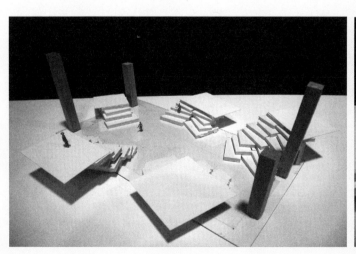

Drawings from the engineers (Arup) show the careful attention to detail required to give a free and light appearance to the final structure. Below, a model shows the main supports of the building.

Zeichnungen der Bauingenieure (Arup) belegen die sorgsame Ausarbeitung kleinster Details, die erforderlich war, um dem fertigen Bau seine freie und leichte Anmutung zu geben. Ein Modell (unten) zeigt die Hauptstützen der Konstruktion.

Les dessins techniques (Arup) montrent le souci poussé du détail afin de donner un aspect de légèreté et de liberté au projet final. En dessous, une maquette montrant les quatre supports principaux.

SANAA

2009
SANAA
(Kazuyo Sejima & Ryue Nishizawa)

2009 SANAA

SANAA/Kazuyo Sejima + Ryue Nishizawa
7-A Shinagawa-Soko
2-2-35 Higashi-Shinagawa
Shinagawa-ku
Tokyo 140
Japan

Tel: +81 33 450 1754
Fax: +81 33 45 0757
E-mail: sanaa@sanaa.co.jp
Web: www.sanaa.co.jp

Born in Ibaraki Prefecture, Japan, in 1956, Kazuyo Sejima received her M.Arch degree from the Japan Women's University in 1981 and went on to work in the office of Toyo Ito the same year. She established Kazuyo Sejima and Associates in Tokyo in 1987. Ryue Nishizawa was born in Tokyo in 1966, and graduated from the National University (Yokohama, 1990). He began working with Sejima the same year, and the pair created the new firm Kazuyo Sejima + Ryue Nishizawa / SANAA in 1995. From the outset, the built work of Kazuyo Sejima was widely publicized and admired. Her Saishunkan Seiyaku Women's Dormitory (Kumamoto, 1990–91) and her Pachinko Parlors in Ibaraki Prefecture (1992–95) were unexpected and somehow nearly evanescent in their forms. The work of SANAA includes the 21st Century Museum of Contemporary Art (Kanazawa, Ishikawa, 2002–04), whose rectangular galleries are placed within a circular glass perimeter; and abroad for the first time, the Glass Pavilion of the Toledo Museum of Art (Ohio, USA, 2003–06) and a theater and cultural center in Almere (Die Kunstlinie, the Netherlands, 2007). In terms of media exposure, they reached still higher with the New Museum of Contemporary Art, located on the Bowery in New York (USA, 2007), and the vast open spaces of the Rolex Learning Center at the EPFL in Lausanne (Switzerland, 2009). Current work of SANAA includes the new building of the Louvre in Lens (France, 2009–12). SANAA / Kazuyo Sejima + Ryue Nishizawa was awarded the 2010 Pritzker Prize.

Die 1956 in der Präfektur Ibaraki geborene Kazuyo Sejima erlangte 1981 ihren M.Arch an der Japanischen Frauenuniversität und begann noch im selben Jahr, für Toyo Ito zu arbeiten. 1987 gründete sie in Tokio ihr Büro Kazuyo Sejima and Associates. Ryue Nishizawa wurde 1966 in Tokio geboren, schloss sein Studium 1990 an der Nationaluniversität in Yokohama ab und begann, mit Sejima zu arbeiten. Gemeinsam gründeten sie 1995 das neue Büro Kazuyo Sejima + Ryue Nishizawa/SANAA. Von Anfang an wurden die gebauten Projekte von Kazuyo Sejima weithin publiziert. Ihr Frauenwohnheim Saishunkan Seiyaku (Kumamoto, 1990–91) und ihre Pachinko Parlors in der Präfektur Ibaraki (1992–95) waren formal überraschend und geradezu flüchtig. Zum Werk von SANAA zählen das Museum für Kunst des 21. Jahrhunderts (Kanazawa, Ishikawa, 2002–04), dessen rechteckige Ausstellungsräume in eine gläserne Rundform eingefügt sind, sowie, erstmalig im Ausland, der Glaspavillon am Toledo Museum of Art (Ohio, USA, 2003 bis 2006) und ein Theater und Kulturzentrum in Almere (De Kunstlinie, Niederlande, 2007). Noch bekannter wurde das Team durch das New Museum of Contemporary Art an der Bowery in New York (2007) und die weitläufigen, offenen Räume des Rolex Learning Center an der EPFL in Lausanne (Schweiz, 2009). SANAA baut derzeit unter anderem einen Neubau für den Louvre in Lens (Frankreich, 2009–12). 2010 wurden SANAA/Kazuyo Sejima + Ryue Nishizawa mit dem Pritzker-Preis ausgezeichnet.

Née dans la préfecture d'Ibaraki en 1956, Kazuyo Sejima obtient son diplôme M. Arch. de l'Université féminine du Japon en 1981, et est engagée par Toyo Ito la même année. Elle crée l'agence Kazuyo Sejima and Associates à Tokyo en 1987. Ryue Nishizawa, né à Tokyo en 1966, est diplômé de l'Université nationale de Yokohama (1990). Il a commencé à travailler avec Sejima la même année, avant de fonder ensemble Kazuyo Sejima + Ryue Nishizawa/SANAA en 1995. Dès le départ, les réalisations de Kazuyo Sejima ont été beaucoup publiées et admirées. Son foyer pour jeunes filles Saishunkan Seiyaku (Kumamoto, 1990–91) et ses salles de jeux Pachinko (Ibaraki, 1992–93) témoignaient d'un style entièrement nouveau exprimé dans des formes presque évanescentes. Parmi les références de SANAA figurent le Musée d'art contemporain du XXIe siècle (Kanazawa, Ishikawa, 2002–04) dont les galeries rectangulaires sont comprises dans un bâtiment circulaire en verre et, à l'étranger pour la première fois, le pavillon de verre du Musée d'art de Toledo (Ohio, 2003–06) ainsi qu'un théâtre et centre culturel à Almere (Die Kunstlinie, Pays-Bas, 2004–07). En termes médiatiques, ils connu un succès plus grand encore avec le New Museum of Contemporary Art (Bowery, New York, 2005–07) et les vastes espaces ouverts du Rolex Learning Center à l'EPFL de Lausanne (Suisse, 2009). Parmi leurs travaux actuels figurent le Louvre à Lens (France, 2009–12). SANAA/ Kazuyo Sejima + Ryue Nishizawa ont reçu le prix Pritzker 2010.

This pavilion was essentially a continuous 26-millimeter-thick aluminum roof supported by random 50-millimeter-diameter steel columns. The freely curving lines of the roof, occupying the space without blocking it, can only be described as completely innovative and quintessentially contemporary, as befits a pavilion created for the contemporary art galleries of the Serpentine. An event space, a café, a music area, and a rest space were placed beneath this graceful canopy. Although there are some curved acrylic partitions, the work of SANAA is as close to being truly evanescent in every sense of the word as possible. In this sense it is perfectly related to other work by these gifted designers that challenges the limits of perception, inviting visitors to enter a kind of floating world where appearances can change in the blink of an eye or a slight movement of the visitor. The architects stated in 2009: "The Pavilion is a simple floating aluminum roof. It is not designed as an object so much as a field space that provides a different experience within the continuity of the park. The extent of the roof is such that it wraps around trees and itself acts as another canopy. Its height varies from point to point and one leaf sweeps down very low, becoming a table. This part of the roof also shelters interior spaces from wind and driving rain. Other parts of the roof rise up and flow into the sky. Both sides are reflective, showing the sky above and the park below." One interesting impact of the pavilion was to create an unexpected continuity between the park space and the actual gallery building, reflected at every turn, from above or below. Indeed, with the variations in the height of the mirrored canopy, visitors could look down on parts of the surface, not only up. Kazuyo Sejima commented on one relatively little known aspect of the Summer Pavilion commissions—the fact that part of their cost is met by the sale and reuse of the structure. "If it was really temporary," she stated, "it would have been easier. Since it will then have a permanent home, it was more difficult—it needs a permanent building solution that can be taken apart. Somehow, however, we can take more liberties with the design of a pavilion." In the same interview with Julia Peyton-Jones and Hans Ulrich Obrist, Ryue Nishizawa spoke of the evolution of the design: "We wanted to create a roof that drifts through the park, and the shape is determined primarily by the existing trees. When we first decided to make an undulating roof the option on the table was very big, extending into the park toward the Round Pond. It became smaller as the design process developed. At first it was more like a stream in the landscape."

Der Pavillon besteht im Grunde aus einem durchgängigen, 26 mm starken Aluminiumdach, das auf unregelmäßig platzierten, 50 mm starken Stahlstützen ruht. Die freie, geschwungene Linienführung des Dachs nimmt den Raum ein, ohne ihn zu verstellen, und lässt sich nur als absolut innovativ und zeitgemäß beschreiben, passend für einen Pavillon, der für eine Galerie für zeitgenössische Kunst entworfen wurde. Unter dem zierlichen Dach gab es einen Veranstaltungsbereich, ein Café, einen Konzertbereich und Ruhezonen. Trotz der vereinzelten geschwungenen Trennwände aus Acrylglas war dieses Projekt in jeder Hinsicht geradezu flüchtig. Das verbindet den Pavillon mit anderen Arbeiten von SANAA, die die Grenzen der Wahrnehmung verschieben und Besucher in eine Art fließende Welt einladen, in der sich der Eindruck schon mit einer kleinen Bewegung verändern kann. Die Architekten erklärten 2009: „Der Pavillon ist ein einfaches, fließendes Aluminiumdach. Es wurde nicht als Objekt entworfen, sondern vielmehr als Spannungsfeld, das innerhalb des Kontinuums des Parks ein eigenes Erlebnis bietet. Das Dach breitet sich aus, windet sich um die Bäume herum und wird zu einem zweiten Laubdach. Seine Höhe variiert, ein ‚Blatt' senkt sich so tief hinab, dass es zum Tisch wird. Dieser Teil des Dachs schützt die Innenbereiche vor Wind und Regen. Andere Abschnitte des Dachs schwingen sich in die Höhe, in den Himmel. " Ein interessanter Effekt des Pavillons war, dass er eine Kontinuität zwischen dem Parkraum und dem Galeriegebäude schuf, die an jeder Ecke, von oben und unten gespiegelt wurden. Durch die Höhenunterschiede des reflektierenden Dachs konnten die Besucher auf einige Abschnitte herunterblicken. Kazuyo Sejima äußerte sich zu einem wenig bekannten Aspekt der Sommerpavillon-Aufträge, der Tatsache, dass ein Teil der Kosten durch den Verkauf und die Weiternutzung der Bauten bestritten wird. „Wäre er wirklich temporär", erklärte sie, „wäre es einfacher gewesen. Weil er aber einen dauerhaften Standort haben wird, brauchten wir eine permanente bauliche Lösung, die abgebaut werden kann. Trotzdem gewährt der Entwurf eines Pavillons größere Freiheiten." Über die Entwicklung des Entwurfs berichtete Ryue Nishizawa: „Wir wollten ein Dach gestalten, das durch den Park zu schweben scheint; seine Form wurde primär vom Baumbestand bestimmt. Als wir beschlossen hatten, ein geschwungenes Dach zu bauen, brachten wir zunächst eine viel größere Option auf dem Tisch, eine Ausdehnung in den Park hinein, bis hin zum Round Pond. Im Lauf des Entwurfsprozesses wurde alles kleiner. Anfangs war der Pavillon eher ein Fluss in der Landschaft."

Ce pavillon se composait d'une couverture d'aluminium de 26 millimètres d'épaisseur soutenue par des colonnes d'acier de 50 millimètres de diamètre disposées de façon apparemment aléatoire. Les lignes courbes libres de cette couverture étaient totalement novatrices et contemporaines, comme il se doit pour un pavillon créé pour la galerie d'art de la Serpentine. Un espace pour événements et concerts, un café et une zone de repos trouvaient place sous cet auvent gracieux. Malgré quelques cloisonnements incurvés en acrylique, l'œuvre de SANAA apparaissait évanescente. Elle rappelait l'esprit de certaines réalisations d'architectes talentueux qui remettent en cause les limites de la perception et invitent le visiteur dans un monde en suspension, où les apparences changent suite à un simple déplacement. En 2009, ils déclaraient : « Le pavillon est un simple toit d'aluminium flottant. Il n'est pas tant conçu comme un objet que comme un champ d'espace offrant une expérience différente dans la continuité du parc. La projection de ce toit s'enroule autour des arbres et compose elle-même une autre forme de canopée. Sa hauteur varie d'un point à un autre et une partie s'abaisse même jusqu'à se transformer en table. Cette partie du toit protège également divers espaces intérieurs du vent et de la pluie. D'autres parties s'élèvent et se fondent avec le ciel. Les deux faces sont réfléchissantes et montrent le ciel au-dessus et le parc en dessous. » Un des effets intéressants de ce pavillon est de créer une continuité inattendue entre l'espace du parc et celui du bâtiment de la galerie, qui se reflètent sans cesse. Grâce aux variations de hauteur de l'auvent poli comme un miroir, les visiteurs peuvent également voir le dessus. Kazuyo Sejima parle aussi d'un aspect assez peu remarqué de la commande des Pavillons d'été : une partie de leur coût est compensée par leur vente à l'issue de la saison. « Si le pavillon avait été réellement temporaire », a-t-elle expliqué, « les choses auraient été plus faciles ; puisqu'il devait être installé ailleurs de façon permanente, il fallait trouver une solution constructive permanente et démontable. Mais nous disposons néanmoins de plus de liberté que pour la conception d'un pavillon permanent. » Dans le même entretien avec Julia Peyton-Jones et Hans Ulrich Obrist, Ryue Nishizawa a parlé de l'évolution de ce projet : « Nous voulions créer un toit qui se glisse dans le parc. Sa forme est d'abord déterminée par la présence des arbres. Lorsque nous nous sommes décidés pour un toit ondulé, nous pensions à quelque chose de très grand, allant jusqu'au bassin rond. Le projet s'est rétréci au fur et à mesure de son développement. Au départ, il avait été davantage pensé comme un ruisseau dans le paysage. »

The SANAA Pavilion reaches for the most extreme lightness that can be imagined in architecture. A series of very thin posts support a freely curving mirrored roof, which reverses and reflects the green environment as well as visitors.

Der Pavillon von SANAA strebt nach der größtmöglichen in der Architektur vorstellbaren Leichtigkeit. Besonders schlanke Stützen tragen ein geschwungenes, spiegelndes Dach, das sowohl das umgebende Grün als auch die Besucher reflektiert und auf den Kopf stellt.

Le pavillon SANAA voulait parvenir à la plus extrême légèreté imaginable en architecture. Une succession de poteaux très fins soutenant un toit curviligne fluide, poli comme un miroir, reflétait et inversait la verdure environnante et les visiteurs.

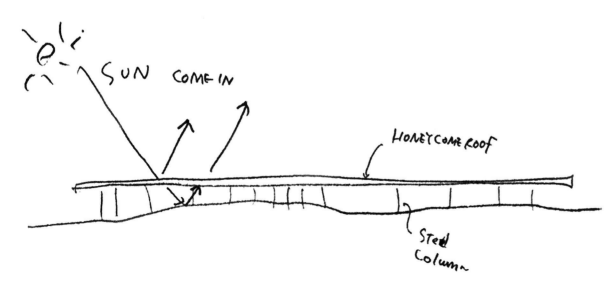

SUN COME IN

HONEYCOMB ROOF

STEEL COLUMN

A flat, floating sheet of reflective aluminum appears not to contrast with the environment, but to absorb it while offering some shelter from the elements.

Das flache, geradezu schwebende, spiegelnde Aluminiumblech wirkt weniger wie ein Kontrast zu seinem Umfeld, sondern scheint es vielmehr in sich aufzunehmen. Zugleich bietet es Schutz vor den Elementen.

Un plan d'aluminium suspendu et réfléchissant absorbe son environnement plutôt qu'il ne contraste avec lui, tout en offrant un abri du soleil et de la pluie.

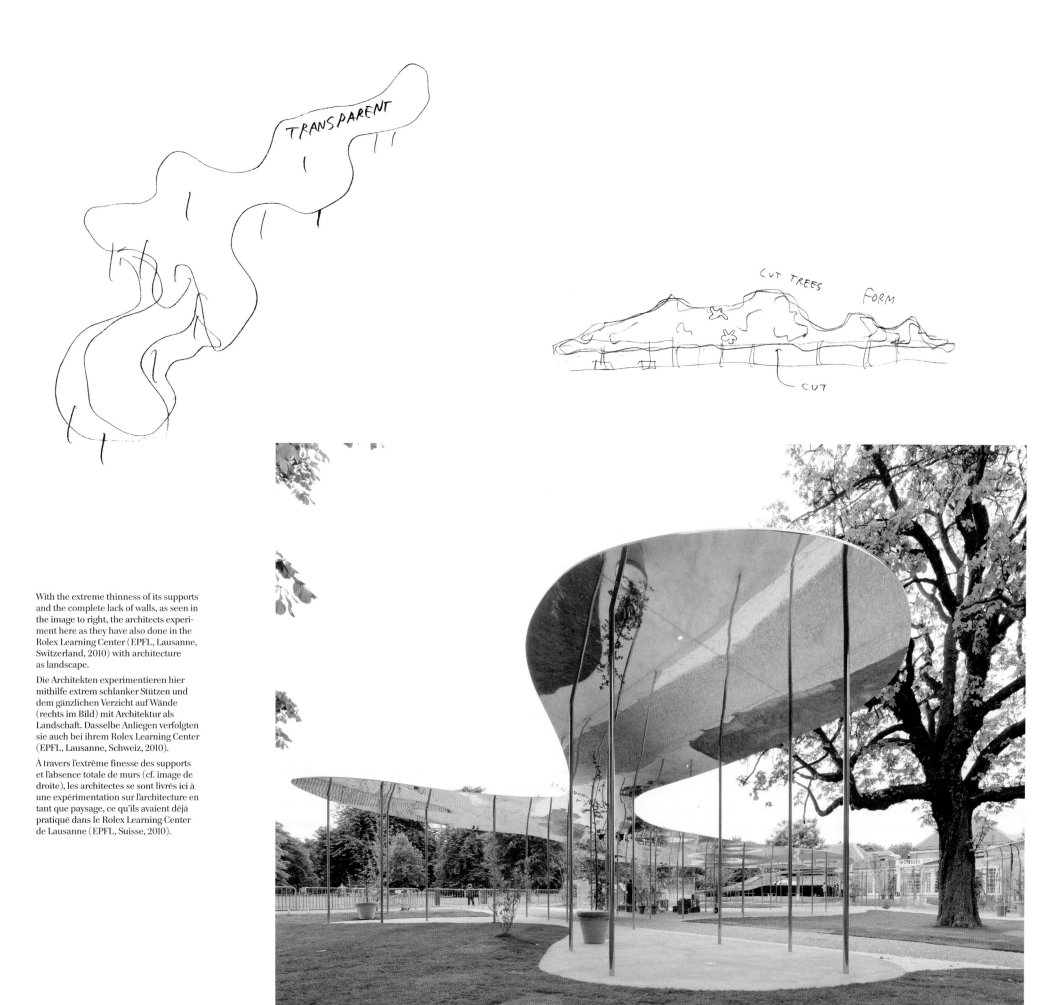

TRANSPARENT

CUT TREES   FORM

CUT

With the extreme thinness of its supports and the complete lack of walls, as seen in the image to right, the architects experiment here as they have also done in the Rolex Learning Center (EPFL, Lausanne, Switzerland, 2010) with architecture as landscape.

Die Architekten experimentieren hier mithilfe extrem schlanker Stützen und dem gänzlichen Verzicht auf Wände (rechts im Bild) mit Architektur als Landschaft. Dasselbe Anliegen verfolgten sie auch bei ihrem Rolex Learning Center (EPFL, Lausanne, Schweiz, 2010).

À travers l'extrême finesse des supports et l'absence totale de murs (cf. image de droite), les architectes se sont livrés ici à une expérimentation sur l'architecture en tant que paysage, ce qu'ils avaient déjà pratiqué dans le Rolex Learning Center de Lausanne (EPFL, Suisse, 2010).

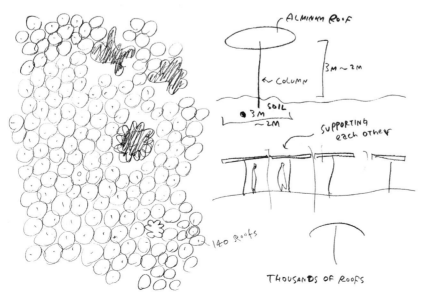

Flowing across the lawn of the Serpentine, the pavilion leads to and reflects the gallery building, while offering the required space for the summer events program.

Der Pavillon scheint über den Rasen der Serpentine zu fließen. Während er zur Galerie hinführt und diese reflektiert, bietet er zugleich den erforderlichen Platz für das sommerliche Veranstaltungsprogramm.

Coulée d'aluminium sur la pelouse, le pavillon conduit à la galerie qu'il reflète tout en offrant l'espace nécessaire au programme de manifestations estivales de la Serpentine.

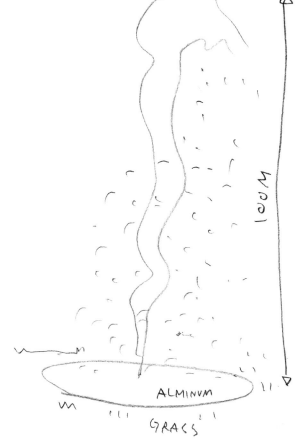

The metal surface of the pavilion "roof" varies in height, offering its equally mirrored topside to the view of visitors. Reflections and lightness form a "floating world" that is suspended between the earth and the sky.

Die Höhe des Metall-„Dachs" variiert und zeigt den Besuchern auch die ebenfalls reflektierende Oberseite. Aus Spiegelungen und Leichtigkeit entsteht eine „fließende Welt", die zwischen Himmel und Erde zu hängen scheint.

La hauteur variable du plan métallique du « toit » du pavillon offrait aux visiteurs la vision de sa face supérieure, également en aluminium poli. Ces reflets et cette légèreté créaient un effet de « monde suspendu » entre terre et ciel.

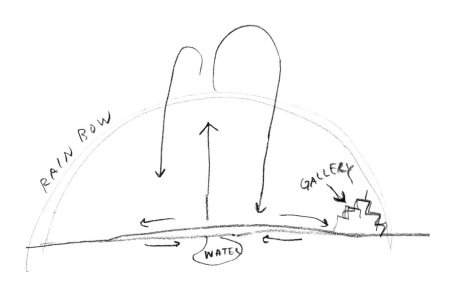

"The Pavilion is floating aluminum, drifting freely between the trees like smoke."
SANAA

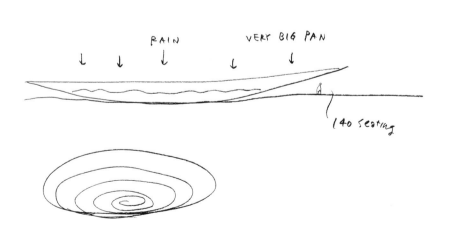

VERY BIG PAN OPTION

In a much more ethereal mode than the Frank Gehry Pavilion, the work of SANAA also tends toward a purely sculptural expression. Like Gehry, however, the Japanese architects have not forgotten that sheltering events is one of the "architectural" requirements that they face.

Der SANAA-Entwurf ist, ebenso wie der Pavillon von Frank Gehry, eher skulptural – wenn auch wesentlich ätherischer. Wie Gehry, so haben auch die Japaner nicht vergessen, dass es eine der „architektonischen" Anforderungen war, Veranstaltungen Schutz vor der Witterung zu bieten.

Sur un mode beaucoup plus éthéré que celui du pavillon Frank Gehry, l'œuvre de SANAA tend également vers une expression purement sculpturale. Comme Gehry, les architectes japonais n'ont cependant pas oublié qu'abriter les manifestations prévues faisait partie de leurs contraintes « architecturales ».

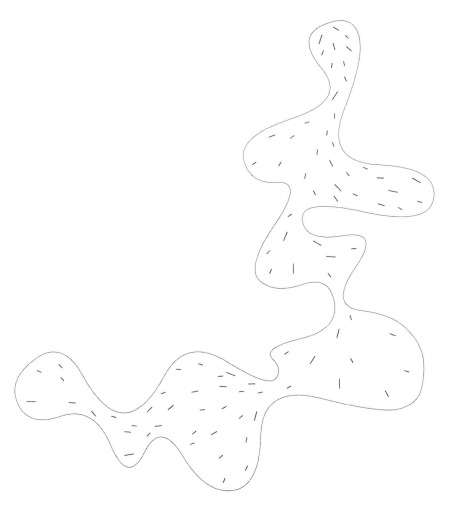

Where the roof surface approaches the earth, children and others take delight in seeing their own suspended and reversed images.

Wo sich das Dach zur Erde neigt, haben Kinder und andere Besucher Spaß daran, ihr eigenes schwebendes und auf dem Kopf stehendes Spiegelbild zu betrachten.

Des enfants, mais aussi des adultes, s'amusent à regarder leur image suspendue et inversée à l'endroit où le plan du toit se rapproche du sol.

Whether a single visitor or an entire audience takes their place in the pavilion, the reflective roof surfaces offer unexpected, deformed reflections that make the usual essential ideas of up and down, or inside and out, completely relative.

Ob nun einzelne oder viele Besucher im Pavillon Platz nehmen, zeigt das spiegelnde Dach überraschende, verzerrte Reflexionen, die übliche Vorstellungen von „oben und unten" sowie „innen und außen" vollkommen relativieren.

Si un seul visiteur ou un groupe prenait place dans le pavillon, la surface réfléchissante du toit provoquait des reflets déformés surprenants qui relativisaient entièrement les notions de haut et de bas, d'intérieur et d'extérieur.

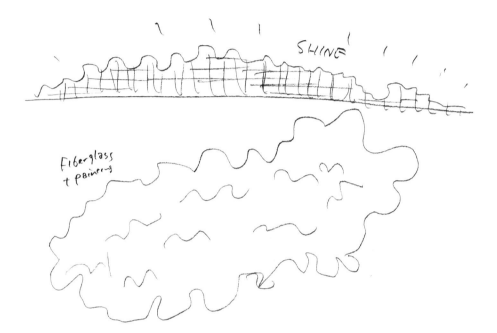

SHINE

Fiberglass + painting

From certain angles the pavilion roof resembles a curving pond hanging in the air. The architects bring in an element of humor and irony by placing potted plants in their artificial environment despite its location in the midst of a park.

Aus bestimmten Blickwinkeln wirkt das Dach wie ein geschwungener, schwebender Teich. Mit den Kübelpflanzen – die sie trotz der Lage des Pavillons inmitten eines Parks in diesem künstlichen Umfeld platzierten – brachten die Architekten ein humoristisches, ironisches Element ein.

Sous certains angles, le toit du pavillon évoque un bassin suspendu dans les airs. Les architectes avaient ajouté une touche d'humour, ou d'ironie, en répartissant des plantes en pot dans cet environnement artificiel malgré son implantation au milieu d'un parc.

PLANS, DRAWINGS
AND MODELS

Architectural Design Kazuyo Sejima & Ryue Nishizawa, SANAA
Design Team SANAA/Sam Chermayeff/Lucy Styles
Structural Engineering Arup/Cecil Balmond/David Glover/Ed Clark
Project & Construction Management Mace/Steve Pycroft

Drawings almost as light as the resulting architecture explore such issues as the angles of view from beneath the floating aluminum roof, looking toward the Serpentine.

Zeichnungen, die fast so leicht wirken wie die realisierte Architektur, beschäftigen sich mit Aspekten wie den Blickwinkeln, die sich unterhalb des schwebenden Aluminiumdachs zur Serpentine hin ergeben.

Ces dessins, d'un trait aussi léger que l'architecture qui en résulte, explorent divers problèmes, comme les angles de vue sous le plan d'aluminium flottant lorsque l'on regarde vers la Serpentine Gallery.

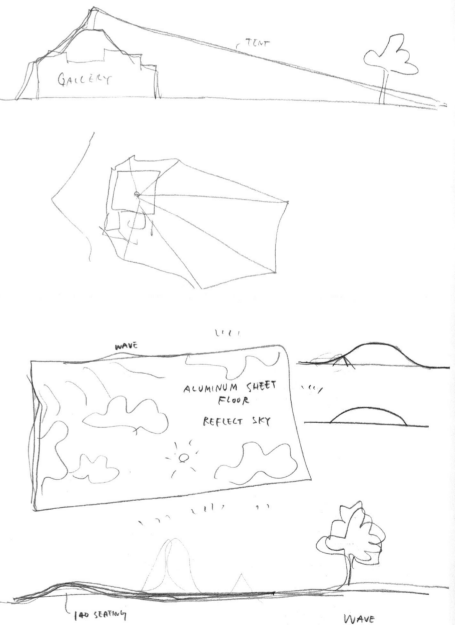

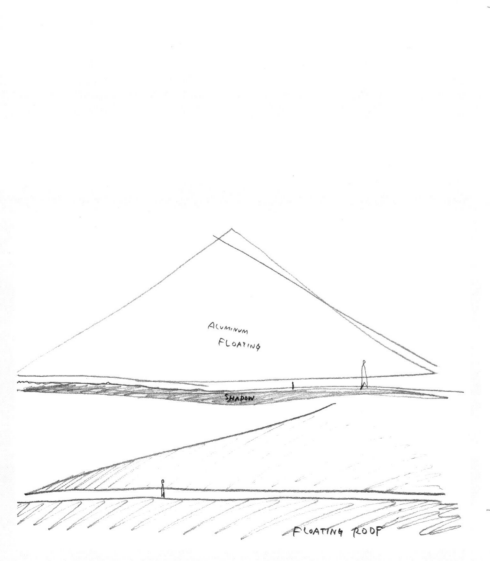

Fragile models and evanescent references, such as clouds or mirrored helium balloons, express sources of inspiration and the means of employing them.

Zarte Modelle und flüchtige Referenzen, wie Wolken oder verspiegelte Heliumballons, sind ein Hinweis auf unterschiedliche Inspirationsquellen und Mittel, diese nutzbar zu machen.

De fragiles maquettes et des références évanescentes comme des nuages ou des ballons métalliques gonflés à l'hélium, ont servi de source d'inspiration aussi bien formelle que technique.

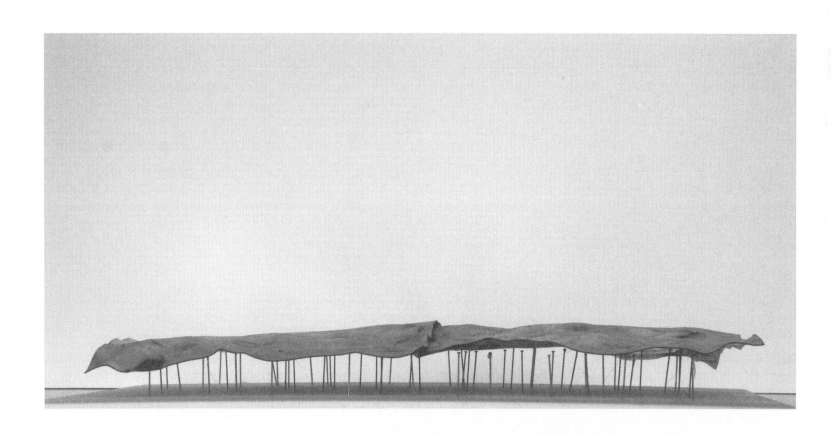

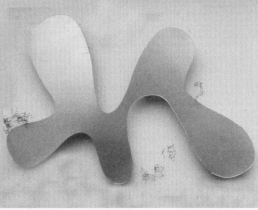
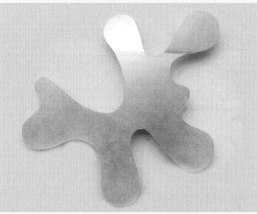
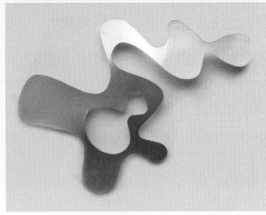

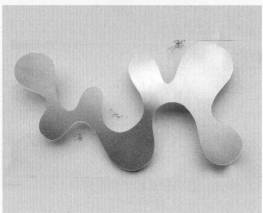

A model shows the structure as it fits between existing trees. Below, elevations of the structure also show its relation to the trees and identify the aluminum sandwich roof and the extremely thin stainless-steel support columns.

Ein Modell zeigt, wie sich die Konstruktion in den Baumbestand einfügt. Aufrisse des Entwurfs (unten) verdeutlichen das Verhältnis zu den Bäumen und zeigen das Aluminium-Sandwichdach sowie die extrem schlanken Stahlstützen.

Une maquette montre la structure qui se glisse entre les arbres. Ci-dessous, élévations de la structure montrant également sa relation avec les arbres et précisant la nature de la toiture à panneaux sandwich en aluminium et des colonnes extrêmement fines.

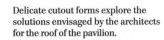

Delicate cutout forms explore the solutions envisaged by the architects for the roof of the pavilion.

Fragile, ausgeschnittene Formen dienen dazu, die von den Architekten gewünschten Effekte für das Pavillondach näher zu untersuchen.

Ces délicates formes découpées sont des explorations des solutions envisagées par les architectes pour la toiture du pavillon.

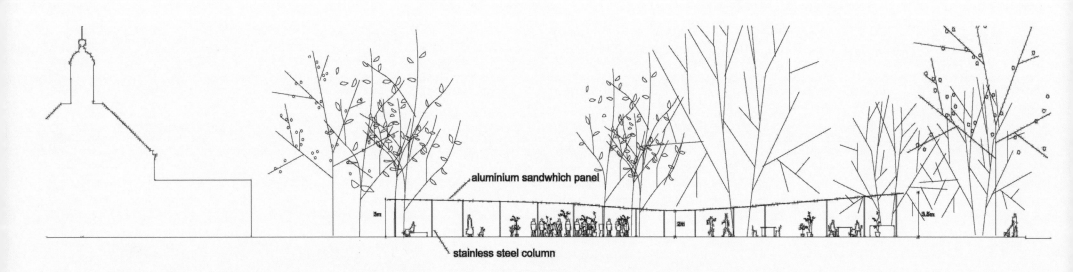

aluminium sandwhich panel

stainless steel column

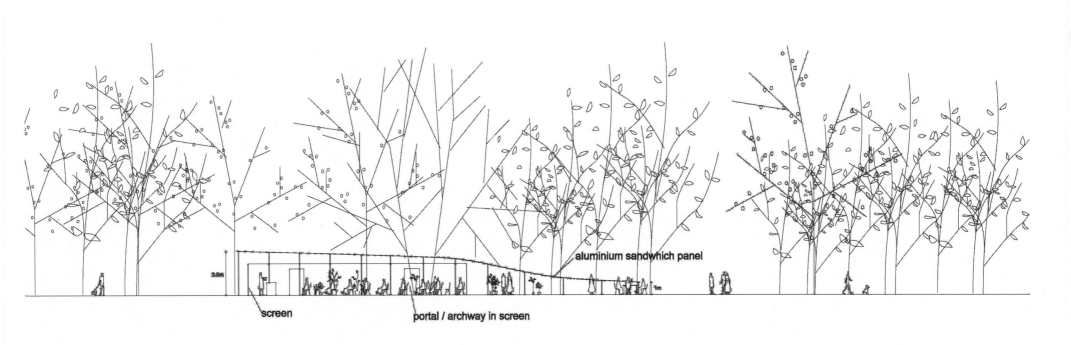

aluminium sandwhich panel

3.5m

1m

screen

portal / archway in screen

A model seen against the background of site photos examines issues of scale and the placement of furnishings.

Ein vor Aufnahmen des Geländes platziertes Modell erlaubt, Größenverhältnisse sowie die Anordnung von Mobiliar zu beurteilen.

Une maquette devant des fonds photographiques du site précise les enjeux d'échelle et d'implantation du mobilier.

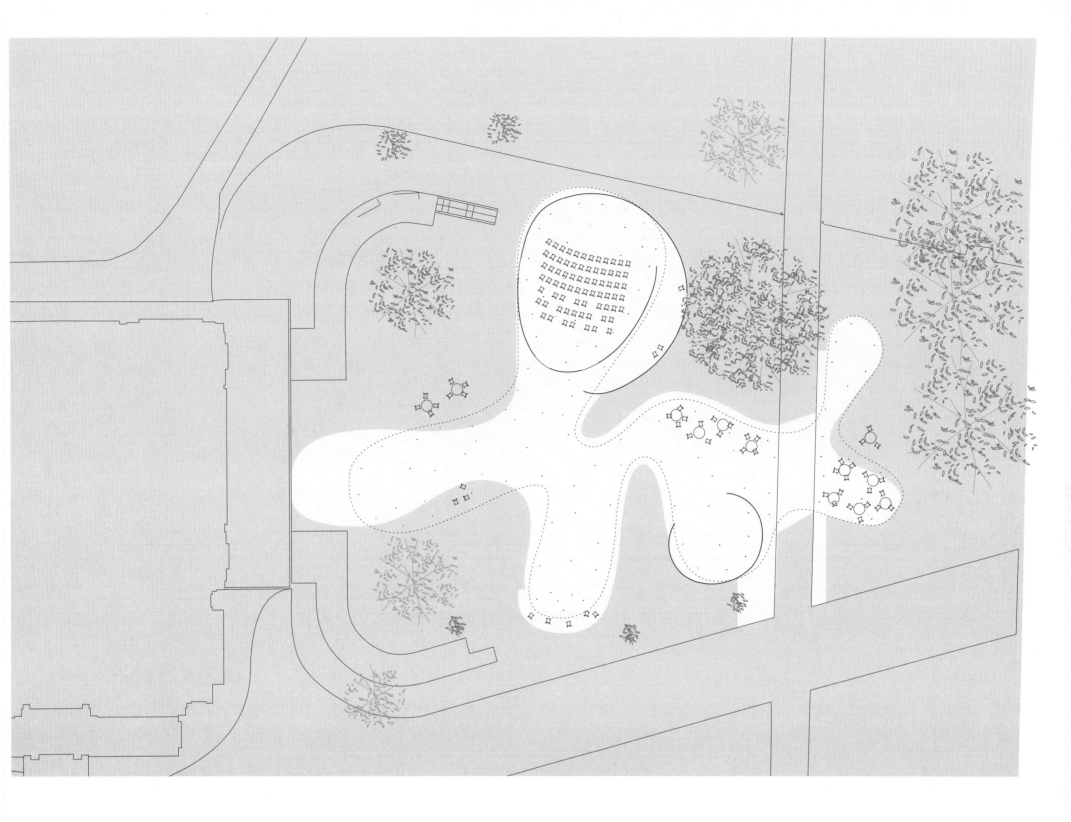

A site plan shows the overall form of the
pavilion with a location for concerts or
gatherings seen at the top center.

**Ein Lageplan zeigt die gesamte Pavil-
lonanlage und den für Konzerte und
Veranstaltungen vorgesehenen Platz
(oben Mitte).**

Un plan du site montre la forme
d'ensemble du pavillon et l'emplacement
prévu pour les concerts ou les réunions,
au centre en haut.

JEAN NOUVEL

2010
JEAN NOUVEL

By selecting such an intense red for his pavilion, Jean Nouvel truly makes color an integral part of the design, a fact that he playfully emphasizes by writing the word "GREEN" on a window seen in this image.

Indem Nouvel sich für ein so intensives Rot entschied, ließ er die Farbe zu einem integralen Bestandteil seines Pavillonentwurfs werden. Diese Tatsache unterstreicht er spielerisch durch den Schriftzug „GREEN" auf der Glasfläche im Bild.

En choisissant un rouge d'une telle intensité, Jean Nouvel a fait de la couleur une partie intégrante de son projet, ce que renforçait de manière ludique le mot « GREEN » (vert) inscrit sur une baie.

Retractable fabric awnings dip down to the ground at the rear (Serpentine) side of the pavilion, with the leaning wall visible right on the image above. Sitting in the park, the structure might bring to mind the follies in the Parc de la Villette in Paris, by Bernard Tschumi.

Ausfahrbare textile Markisen auf der Rückseite des Pavillons (zur Serpentine hin) reichen bis zum Boden. Rechts oben im Bild die schräge Wand. Sitzt man im Park, erinnert die Konstruktion an die Follies von Bernard Tschumi im Pariser Parc de la Villette.

Des auvents en tissu rétractables plon-geaient jusqu'au sol à l'arrière du pavillon, côté de la galerie, cadrés à droite par le mur incliné (ci-dessus). La structure de Nouvel pouvait rappeler les Folies de Bernard Tschumi pour le parc de la Villette à Paris.

The word "GREEN," actually written in transparent letters, is colored by the park environment. Here glass surfaces reflect a fractured and reddened image of the Serpentine Gallery.

Das als transparenter Schriftzug erscheinende Wort „GREEN" (grün) wirkt erst durch die Parkumgebung farbig. Auf den Glasflächen zeichnet sich ein fragmentiertes und rot getöntes Bild der Serpentine Gallery ab.

Le mot GREEN (vert) en réserve transparente sur les panneaux rouges était coloré par l'environnement du parc. Ici, les parois de verre reflètent une image fracturée et teintée de la galerie.

In the café space, the omnipresence of red changes the perception of color, tinting everything but the openings that allow a refreshing hint of green to enter the field of view.

Im Cafébereich beeinflusst das allgegenwärtige Rot die Farbwahrnehmung. Alles erscheint getönt, nur durch die Öffnungen dringt frisches Grün in den Blick.

Dans le café, l'omniprésence du rouge changeait la perception des couleurs, à l'exception des ouvertures qui offraient au regard une touche de vert rafraichissante.

A tilted, freestanding 12-meter-high wall marks one end of the pavilion, where it is most convenient to accede to the Serpentine building, hardly visible in these images because Nouvel has not sought to frame it.

Eine schräge, freistehende, 12 m hohe Wand markiert das eine Ende des Pavillons. An dieser Stelle ist das Gebäude der Serpentine am leichtesten zugänglich. Auf den Bildern ist es jedoch kaum zu sehen, da Nouvel sich dagegen entschied, den Altbau zu rahmen.

Un grand plan incliné autoporteur de douze mètres de haut marquait une extrémité du pavillon, à proximité de l'accès le plus direct à la galerie, à peine visible dans ces images car Nouvel n'avait pas cherché à obtenir des perspectives particulières sur le bâtiment ancien.

With its operable awnings and pivoting glass surfaces, the pavilion offers a maximum amount of flexibility and provides both for enclosure and for areas that are open to the park in good weather. The auditorium space accommodates the *Serpentine Gallery Park Nights* no matter what the summer weather.

Dank ausfahrbarer Markisen und drehbaren Glasflächen bietet der Pavillon ein Maximum an Flexibilität und neben den umbauten Flächen auch Bereiche, die bei gutem Wetter zum Park hin offen sind. Das Auditorium bietet, unabhängig von sommerlichem Wetter, Platz für die *Park Nights* der Serpentine Gallery.

Doté d'auvents mobiles et de plans de verre pivotants, le pavillon offrait le maximum de souplesse et proposait aussi bien des zones fermées que d'autres ouvertes sur le parc par beau temps. L'espace de l'auditorium pouvait recevoir les *Park Nights* de la Serpentine Gallery, quelles que soient les conditions météorologiques.

High red windows have single, transparent words like "SKY" written on them, leading the visitor's gaze up to the only points above ground that are not colored, like the "the iconic British images of traditional telephone boxes, post boxes, and London buses," as the Serpentine puts it.

Hohe rote Fenster sind mit einzelnen Begriffen wie „SKY" (Himmel) transparent beschriftet. Sie lenken den Blick der Besucher nach oben, hin zu den einzigen Punkten über dem Boden, die nicht farbig gestaltet sind. Die Serpentine zieht den Vergleich zu „britischen Wahrzeichen, wie den alten Telefonzellen, Briefkästen und Londoner Bussen".

De grandes baies rouges étaient marquées de mots transparents comme *Sky* (ciel) qui incitaient le visiteur à regarder vers les seuls éléments qui n'étaient pas à la couleur « des images iconiques britanniques des cabines téléphoniques, des boîtes à lettres et des bus londoniens », comme le notait la galerie.

Playing on the strong contrast between the green of the park and his own bright red, Nouvel orchestrates entrances and exits, voids and transparency that alternate with solid forms and, here, glass that reflects the whole.

Nouvel spielt mit dem starken Kontrast der grünen Parkumgebung mit dem von ihm gewählten leuchtenden Rot. Er inszeniert Ein- und Ausgänge sowie Zwischenräume und Transparenz im Wechsel mit massiven Elementen. Hier spiegelt Glas das Ganze.

Jouant du puissant contraste entre le vert du parc et son rouge éclatant, Nouvel a orchestré des entrées et des sorties, des vides et des transparences en alternance avec des pleins, et du verre qui reflète ici le tout.

"The entire design is rendered in a vivid red that, in a play of opposites, contrasts with the green of its park setting."

SERPENTINE GALLERY

Seen from the park, with its awnings and shades open, a red hammock in the grass, the pavilion is inviting and playful, just as the architect, sometimes better known for his frequent use of black, had intended.

Vom Park aus gesehen wirkt der Pavillon mit seinen geöffneten Markisen und Sonnenblenden sowie einer roten Hängematte auf dem Rasen einladend und spielerisch. Genau dies hatte der Architekt beabsichtigt, der oftmals eher für seinen häufigen Einsatz von Schwarz bekannt ist.

Vu du parc, avec ses auvents et ses volets déployés et son hamac rouge suspendu, le pavillon ludique paraissait accueillant, comme l'avait voulu son architecte, plus généralement connu pour son fréquent recours à la couleur noire.

Although the land of Kensington Gardens is relatively flat, Jean Nouvel's 2010 Serpentine Summer Pavilion stood out from its green background by virtue of its 12-meter-high sloping wall but, above all, because of its unremitting red color. "Red," says Jean Nouvel, "is the heat of summer. It is the complementary color of green. Red is alive, piercing. Red is provocative, forbidden, visible. Red is English like a red rose, like objects in London that one has to see: a double-decker bus, an old telephone booth, transitional places where one has to go." The pavilion is bold and geometric, but then, too, with its retractable awnings and generous seating spaces, bars, red ping-pong tables, and hammocks, it is playful and inviting. Aside from the more informal daily visits of tourists, the structure was, of course, also intended for the Gallery's program of public talks and events, Park Nights. Some commentators noted that the structure might recall Bernard Tschumi's Follies at the Parc de la Villette in Paris, but Nouvel used softer materials than Tschumi did—red plastic or vast expanses of cloth. The Follies were, of course, also intended to be "permanent" structures. "His pavilion is another step into something new. A series of theatrical red planes, bars, and canopies, it stands somewhere between a hip Ibiza nightclub and Soviet constructivist agit-prop," wrote Edwin Heathcote in the *Financial Times* (9 July 2010). While some of Nouvel's predecessors in the Summer Pavilion series made a real point of framing the Gallery's more permanent building, the Frenchman almost seemed to veil it, seeking to exist in a different continuum, though his sloping wall bowed away from the entrance path to the gallery. Although Nouvel's red certainly differentiates the structure from its environment, he spoke of its presence in more modest terms than one might expect. "I would like the Serpentine Summer Pavilion to meet with the habits of Londoners in Hyde Park, not to perturb them, to simply invite them to enjoy a complementary experience that is by no means obligatory. It would be good if their curiosity were to be slightly aroused, and the desire to discover holiday feelings could spread out naturally, beginning with everyday conversations." Again, somehow obviating the structure's radical red difference from its environment, he says: "The reason the Pavilion exists is to invite in the summer and the sun, and to play with them."

Obwohl das Gelände der Kensington Gardens recht flach ist, hob sich Jean Nouvels Serpentine-Sommer-pavillon 2010 von seinem grünen Hintergrund ab – dank seiner 12 m hohen schiefen Wand, vor allem aber wegen seiner kompromisslosen roten Farbe. „Rot", so Jean Nouvel, „ist die Hitze des Sommers. Es ist die Komplementärfarbe zu Grün. Rot ist lebendig, durchdringend. Rot ist provokativ, verboten, offen-sichtlich. Rot ist englisch wie eine rote Rose, wie Lon-doner Sehenswürdigkeiten: ein Doppeldeckerbus, eine alte Telefonzelle, Plätze, zu denen man muss." Der Pavillon ist kühn und geometrisch, mit seinen ausfahrbaren Markisen, großzügigen Sitzbereichen, Bars, roten Tischtennisplatten und Hängematten je-doch auch spielerisch und einladend. Neben den eher beiläufigen Tagesbesuchen der Touristen war der Bau natürlich auch für die *Park Nights* gedacht, das Programm der Galerie mit öffentlichen Vorträgen und Veranstaltungen. Manche Kommentatoren erin-nerte der Bau an die Follies von Bernard Tschumi im Pariser Parc de la Villette, doch Nouvel nutzte weiche-re Materialien als Tschumi – roten Kunststoff und große Flächen aus Stoff. Außerdem waren die Follies natürlich auch als „dauerhafte" Strukturen angelegt. „Sein Pavillon ist ein weiterer Schritt hin zu etwas Neuem. Mit vielen dramatischen roten Ebenen, Bars und Markisen ist er irgendwo zwischen einem hip-pen Club in Ibiza und sowjetischem Agitprop anzu-siedeln", schrieb Edwin Heathcote in der *Financial Times* (9. Juli 2010). Während manche frühere Som-merpavillons die Galerie ganz dezidiert rahmten, schien der Franzose sie fast zu verstellen, schien in einem anderen Kontinuum existieren zu wollen – auch wenn seine schiefe Wand sich vom Zugangsweg zur Galerie neigte. Obwohl Nouvels Rot den Bau frag-los von seinem Umfeld abhob, äußerte er sich sehr zurückhaltend: „Ich möchte den Gewohnheiten der Londoner in den Kensington Gardens mit dem Ser-pentine-Pavillon entgegenkommen und sie nicht stören, sondern sie einfach einladen, ein alternatives, offenes Angebot zu nutzen. Ich möchte ihre Neugier etwas wecken, damit sich die Sehnsucht nach Ur-laubsgefühlen wie von selbst schon in alltäglichen Gesprächen verbreitet." Ohne noch einmal auf die radikale Andersartigkeit des roten Baus einzugehen, sagt er: „Den Pavillon gibt es, um den Sommer und die Sonne einzuladen und mit ihnen zu spielen."

Bien que le sol des jardins de Kensington soit plutôt plat, le Pavillon 2010 de Jean Nouvel se détache avec force de son cadre de verdure de ses 12 mètres de haut de mur incliné, par sa couleur rouge sans concession. « Le rouge, dit Jean Nouvel, c'est la cha-leur de l'été. C'est la couleur complémentaire du vert. Rouge c'est vif, c'est-à-dire vivant, perçant. Rouge c'est provocant, interdit, voyant. Rouge c'est anglais, comme une rose rouge, comme les objets londoniens que l'on doit repérer : un bus à étage ou une vieille ca-bine téléphonique, comme ces lieux transitoires vers lesquels on doit aller. » Le pavillon arbore une géo-métrie audacieuse, mais à travers ses auvents rétrac-tables et ses généreux espaces pour s'asseoir, ses bars, ses tables de ping-pong rouges et ses hamacs, il est ludique et accueillant. En dehors des visites tou-ristiques en journée, il était bien sûr adapté au pro-gramme d'été de la galerie, les « Park Nights ». Cer-tains auront aussi noté qu'il pouvait rappeler les Folies de Bernard Tschumi au parc de la Villette à Paris, mais Nouvel a utilisé des matériaux plus doux, comme du plastique rouge ou de grandes quantités de toile. Les Folies étaient, elles, permanentes. « Son pavillon est un autre pas vers quelque chose de nou-veau. Succession de plans rouges théâtraux, de pou-tres et d'auvents, il se positionne quelque part entre un night-club hip d'Ibiza et l'agit-prop », écrit Edwin Heathcote dans le *Financial Times* du 9 juillet 2010. Si certains prédécesseurs de Nouvel du programme des Pavillons d'été avaient voulu cadrer le bâtiment de la galerie, lui semble presque le masquer, cherchant son existence dans un continuum différent, même si le grand mur s'inclinait vers l'allée d'entrée de la gale-rie. Bien que le rouge de Nouvel singularise cette structure dans son environnement, il en parle en ter-mes modestes : « J'aimerais que le Pavillon d'été de la Serpentine rencontre les habitudes des Londoniens d'Hyde Park, qu'il ne les perturbe pas, que simple-ment il les sollicite, qu'il s'offre comme une expé-rience complémentaire, non obligatoire. Ce serait bien si la curiosité un peu aiguisée et le désir de la découverte de sensations estivales se répandaient naturellement à partir des conversations de tous les jours. » Gommant encore la radicale hétérogénéité chromatique du pavillon dans son cadre, il ajoute : « La raison d'être du pavillon est d'accueillir l'été, et le soleil, pour mieux jouer avec lui. »

Jean Nouvel designed his all-red pavilion, the 11th commission in the Gallery's annual series, for the Serpentine's 40th anniversary. Despite its apparent solidity, the structure has large areas of polycarbonate and fabric.

Jean Nouvel entwarf den ganz in Rot ge-haltenen Bau als elften Auftrag der jährli-chen Pavillonreihe, zum 40. Jubiläum der Galerie. Die Konstruktion besteht trotz ihrer vermeintlichen Massivität zu weiten Teilen aus Polycarbonat und Textil.

Jean Nouvel a conçu ce pavillon entièrement rouge, le onzième de ce programme annuel, pour le quarantième anniversaire de la Serpentine Gallery.

2010 JEAN NOUVEL

Ateliers Jean Nouvel
10 Cité d'Angoulème
75011 Paris
France

Tel: +33 1 49 23 83 83
Fax: +33 1 43 14 81 10
E-mail: info@jeannouvel.fr
Web: www.jeannouvel.com

Jean Nouvel was born in 1945 in Fumel, France. He studied in Bordeaux and then at the École des Beaux-Arts (Paris, 1964–72). From 1967 to 1970, he was an assistant of the noted architects Claude Parent and Paul Virilio. He created his first office with François Seigneur in Paris in 1970. Jean Nouvel received the RIBA Gold Medal in 2001 and the Pritzker Prize in 2008. His first widely noticed project was the Institut du Monde Arabe (Paris, France, 1981–87, with Architecture Studio). Other works include the Lyon Opera House (Lyon, France, 1986–93) and the Vinci Conference Center (Tours, France, 1989–93). His Fondation Cartier (Paris, France, 1991–94) made him one of the most noted French architects. His major completed projects since 2000 are the Music and Conference Center (Lucerne, Switzerland, 1998–2000); the Agbar Tower (Barcelona, Spain, 2001–03); an extension of the Reina Sofia Museum (Madrid, Spain, 1999–2005); the Quai Branly Museum (Paris, France, 2001–06); the Guthrie Theater (Minneapolis, USA, 2006); the Danish Radio Concert House (Copenhagen, Denmark, 2003–09); and an office tower in Doha (Qatar, 2010). Current work includes the City Hall in Montpellier (France, 2008–11); a hotel in Barcelona (Spain, –2011); the new Philharmonic Hall in Paris (France, –2012); the Louvre Abu Dhabi (UAE, 2009–13); the Tour de Verre in New York (New York, USA); and the National Museum of Qatar (Doha, Qatar). Furthermore, Jean Nouvel is the architect-manager of all the projects for the Ile Seguin in Boulogne-Billancourt (Paris, France, 2012–2023).

Jean Nouvel, geboren 1945 in Fumel in Frankreich, studierte in Bordeaux und an der Pariser École des Beaux-Arts (1964–72). Von 1967 bis 1970 war er Assistent bei den Architekten Claude Parent und Paul Virilio. 1970 gründete er sein erstes Büro in Paris mit François Seigneur. 2001 wurde er mit der RIBA-Goldmedaille ausgezeichnet, den Pritzker-Preis erhielt er 2008. Sein erstes weithin bekanntes Projekt ist das Institut du Monde Arabe (Paris, 1981–87, mit Architecture Studio). Weitere Projekte sind die Oper in Lyon (1986–93) und das Konferenzzentrum Vinci (Tours, 1989–93), alle in Frankreich. Seine Fondation Cartier (Paris, 1991–94) machte ihn zu einem der bekanntesten Architekten Frankreichs. Seine bedeutendsten realisierten Projekte seit 2000 sind das Kultur- und Kongresszentrum Luzern (Schweiz, 1998–2000), der Torre Agbar (Barcelona, Spanien, 2001–03), die Erweiterung der Reina Sofia (Madrid, Spanien, 1999 bis 2005), das Museum am Quai Branly (Paris, 2001–06), das Guthrie-Theater (Minneapolis, USA, 2006), das Konzerthaus für den Dänischen Rundfunk (Kopenhagen, Dänemark, 2003–09) sowie ein Bürohochhaus in Doha (Katar, 2010). Aktuelle Projekte sind das Rathaus in Montpellier (Frankreich, 2008–11), ein Hotel in Barcelona (Spanien, bis 2011), die neue Philharmonie in Paris (bis 2012), der Louvre Abu Dhabi (VAE, 2009–13), der Tour de Verre in New York (USA) und das Nationalmuseum von Katar (Doha, Katar). Darüber hinaus ist Jean Nouvel Architekt und Manager für sämtliche Projekte auf der Île Seguin, Boulogne-Billancourt (Paris, 2012–2023).

Né en 1945 à Fumel, Jean Nouvel étudie à l'École des beaux-arts de Bordeaux puis à celle de Paris (1964–72). De 1964 à 1970, il est l'assistant de Claude Parent et de Paul Virilio. En 1970, il crée une première agence avec François Seigneur à Paris. Son premier projet largement salué par la presse est l'Institut du monde arabe (Paris, 1981–87) en collaboration avec Architecture Studio. Parmi ses autres réalisations : l'Opéra de Lyon (1986–93) et le Centre de congrès Vinci à Tours (1989–93). Sa Fondation Cartier (Paris, 1991–95) a fait de lui l'un des plus célèbres architectes français. Parmi ses principaux projets depuis 2000 : le Centre de congrès et de musique de Lucerne (Suisse, 1992–99) ; la tour Agbar (Barcelone, Espagne, 2001–03) ; l'extension du musée Reina Sofia (Madrid, 1999–2005) ; le musée du quai Branly (Paris (2001–06) ; le Guthrie Theater (Minneapolis, Minnesota, 2006) ; la salle de concert de la radio danoise (Copenhague, 2003–09) et une tour de bureaux à Doha (Qatar, 2010). Il travaille actuellement à l'Hôtel de Ville de Montpellier (France, 2008–11) ; à un hôtel à Barcelone (Espagne, –2011) ; à la nouvelle salle philharmonique à Paris (–2012) ; au Louvre Abou Dhabi (EAU, 2009–13) ; à la Tour de Verre à New York et au Musée national du Qatar à Doha. Par ailleurs, Jean Nouvel est l'architecte en chef de tous les projets de l'île Seguin à Boulogne-Billancourt (Paris, France, 2012–2023). Il a reçu la médaille d'or du RIBA en 2001 et le prix Pritzker en 2008.

PLANS, DRAWINGS AND MODELS

Architectural Design Jean Nouvel
Design Team Gaston Tolila, Project Partner, Ateliers Jean Nouvel
Ute Rinnebach, Project Manager, Ateliers Jean Nouvel
Structural Engineering Arup/Cecil Balmond/David Glover/Ed Clark
Construction Management Mace/Stephen Pycroft

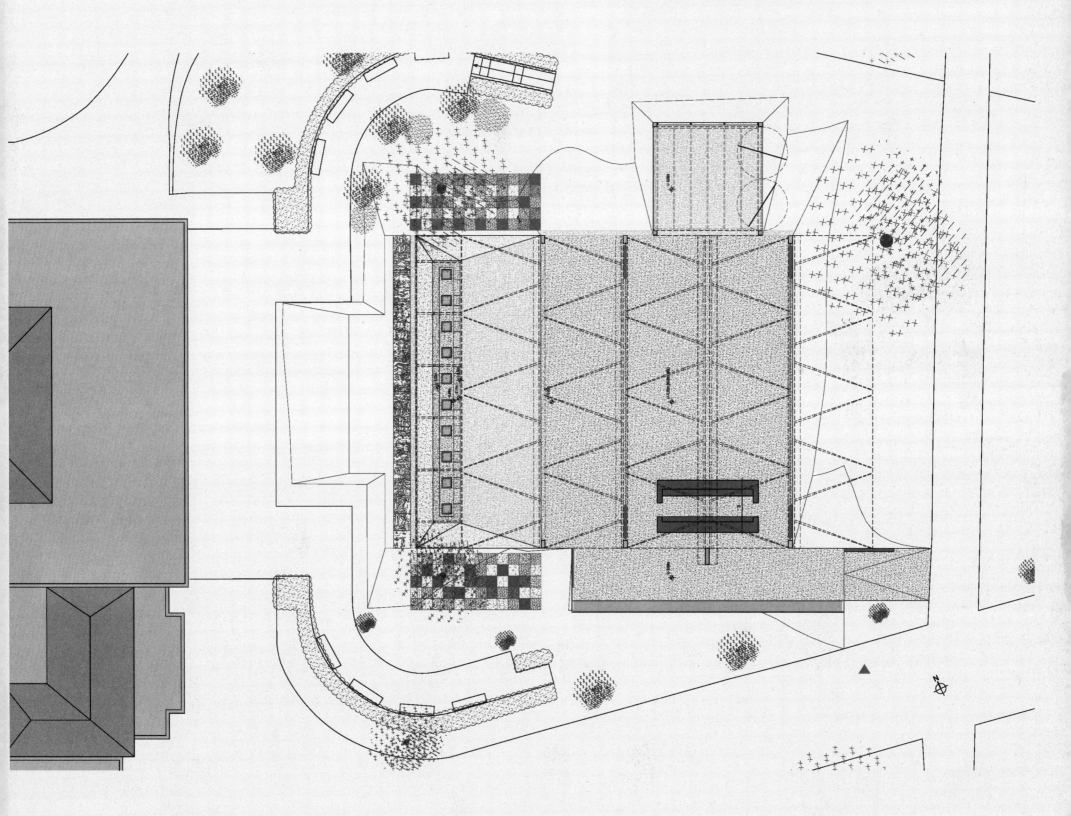

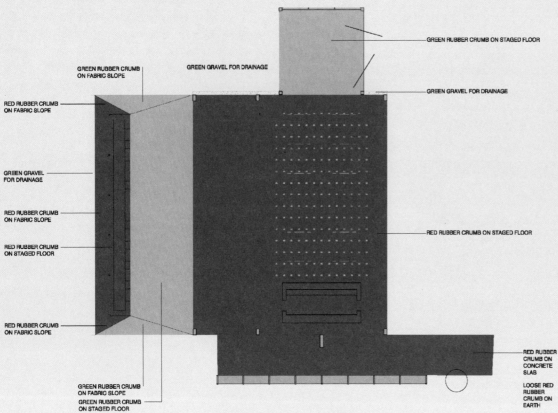

GREEN RUBBER CRUMB ON STAGED FLOOR

GREEN RUBBER CRUMB
ON FABRIC SLOPE

GREEN GRAVEL FOR DRAINAGE

GREEN GRAVEL FOR DRAINAGE

RED RUBBER CRUMB
ON FABRIC SLOPE

GREEN GRAVEL
FOR DRAINAGE

RED RUBBER CRUMB
ON FABRIC SLOPE

RED RUBBER CRUMB
ON STAGED FLOOR

RED RUBBER CRUMB ON STAGED FLOOR

RED RUBBER CRUMB
ON FABRIC SLOPE

RED RUBBER
CRUMB ON
CONCRETE
SLAB

LOOSE RED
RUBBER
CRUMB ON
EARTH

GREEN RUBBER CRUMB
ON FABRIC SLOPE

GREEN RUBBER CRUMB
ON STAGED FLOOR

Seen in plan, above, and in an elevation
drawing vis-à-vis the Serpentine Gallery,
the building is firmly rectilinear and
looks much more substantial and solid
than it actually is because of its many
openings and fabric surfaces.

Auf einem Grundriss (oben) und einem
Aufriss wirkt der Bau gegenüber der
Serpentine Gallery streng rechtwinklig
und wesentlich massiger und massiver,
als er es dank der zahlreichen Öffnungen
und textilen Flächen tatsächlich ist.

Vu en plan (toit) et élévation le situant
vis-à-vis de la Serpentine Gallery, le
bâtiment rigoureusement rectiligne
semble ici beaucoup plus substantiel et
fermé que dans la réalité où il multiplie
les ouvertures et les plans en tissu.

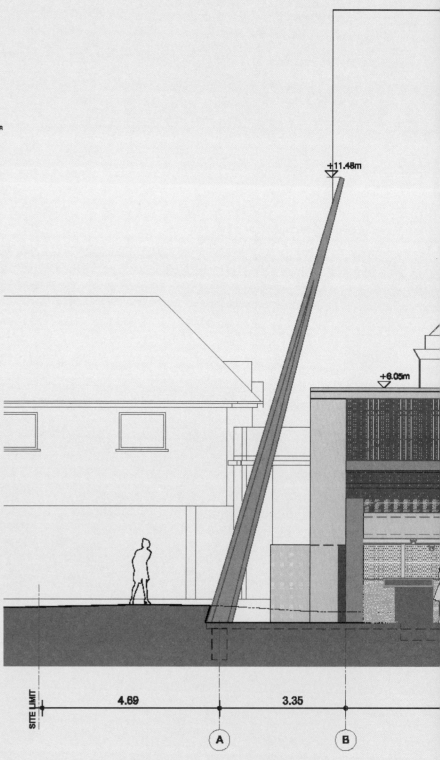

+11.48m

+6.05m

SITE LIMIT

4.89

3.35

A

B

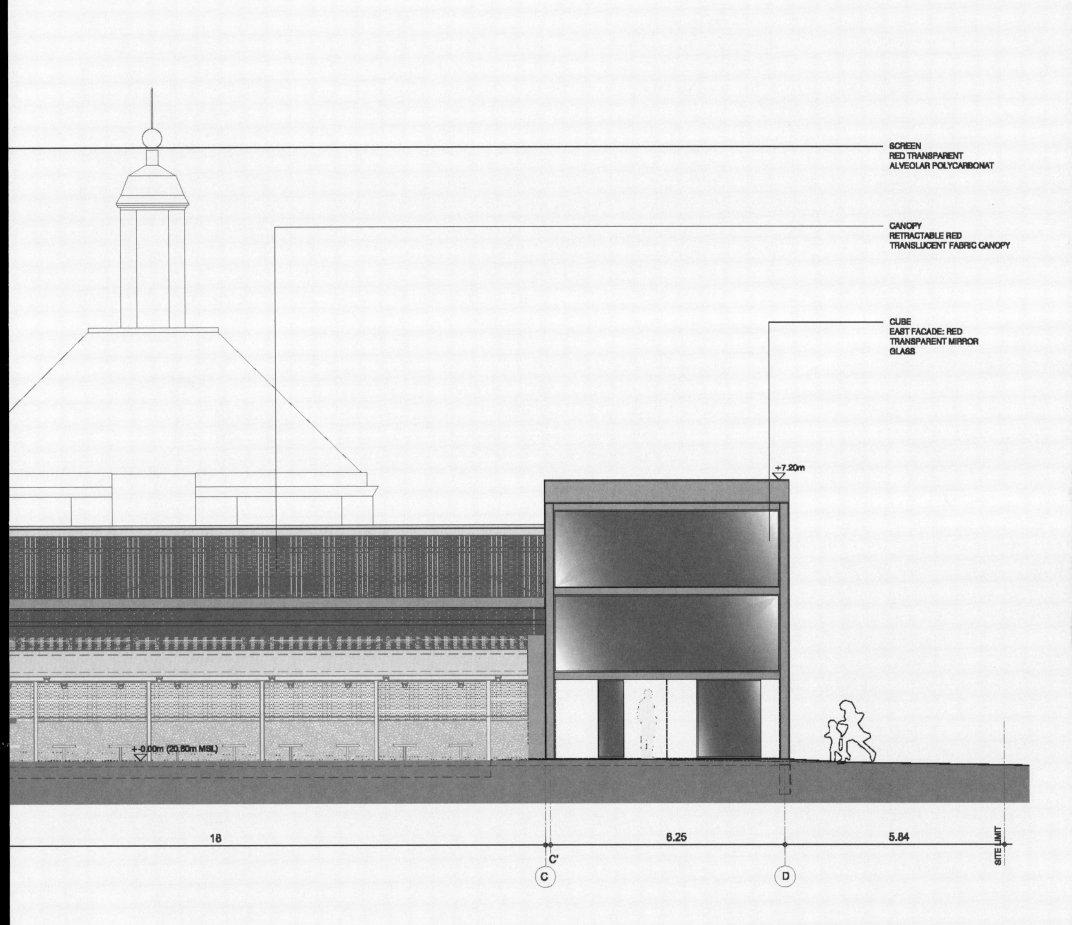

SCREEN
RED TRANSPARENT
ALVEOLAR POLYCARBONAT

CANOPY
RETRACTABLE RED
TRANSLUCENT FABRIC CANOPY

CUBE
EAST FACADE: RED
TRANSPARENT MIRROR
GLASS

+7.20m

+-0.00m (20.60m MSL)

18   6.25   5.84   SITE LIMIT

C'   D

C

XI.27

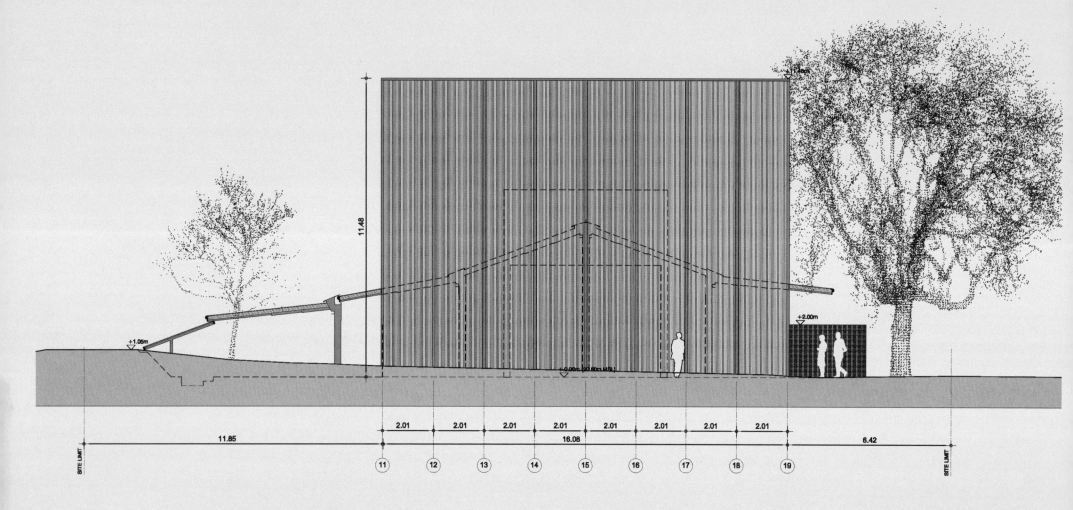

+1.05m

11,48

+2.00m

SITE LIMIT

11.85

2.01 2.01 2.01 2.01 2.01 2.01 2.01 2.01

16.08

6.42

SITE LIMIT

⑪ ⑫ ⑬ ⑭ ⑮ ⑯ ⑰ ⑱ ⑲

Seen in north and south elevations, the
building is seen with such indications
as "Red transparent glass with colorless
transparent text and green transparent
line." A screen is made of "red transparent
alveolar polycarbonate."

Nord- und Südaufrisse zeigen den Bau
mit Hinweisen wie „rotes Klarglas mit
farblosem transparentem Text und
grüner transparenter Linie". Eine Trenn-
wand besteht aus „transparenten roten
Polycarbonatstegplatten".

Élévations nord et sud accompagnées
d'indications comme « verre rouge
transparent avec texte transparent sans
couleur et ligne verte transparente », ou,
pour un écran : « polycarbonate alvéolaire rouge transparent ».

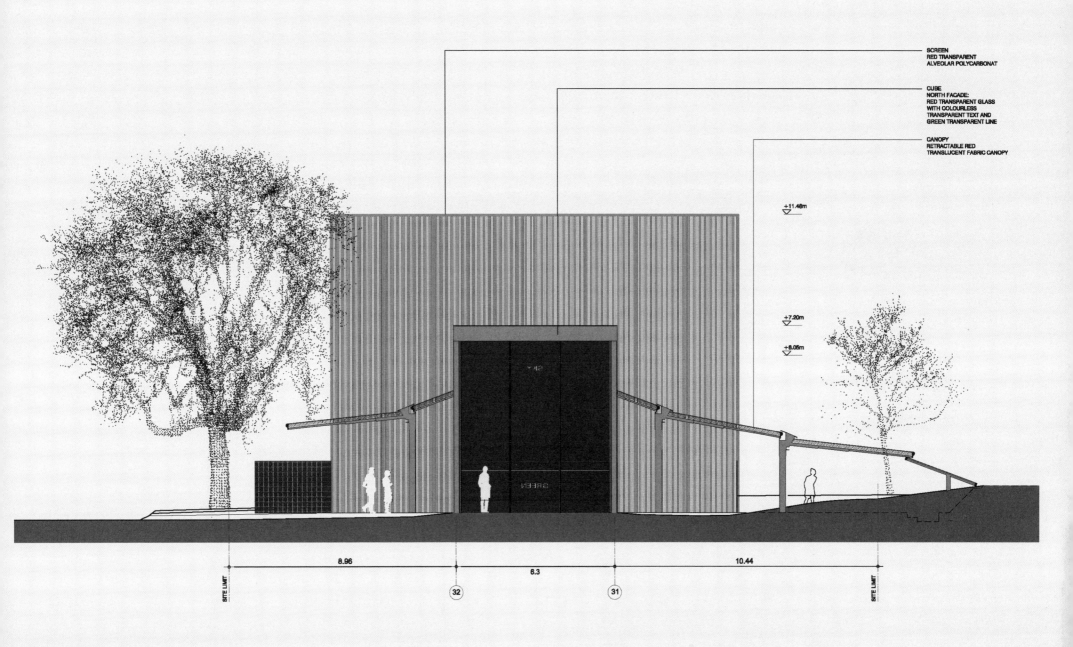

SCREEN
RED TRANSPARENT
ALVEOLAR POLYCARBONAT

CUBE
NORTH FACADE:
RED TRANSPARENT GLASS
WITH COLOURLESS
TRANSPARENT TEXT AND
GREEN TRANSPARENT LINE

CANOPY
RETRACTABLE RED
TRANSLUCENT FABRIC CANOPY

+11.48m

+7.20m

+6.06m

8.96

6.3

10.44

SITE LIMIT

32

31

SITE LIMIT

Seen from the east and west in elevation, the tallest feature of the building is its slanting 11.48-meter-high wall, clad in alveolar polycarbonate sheeting. As the drawings show, the structure is not centered on the gallery.

Aufrisse von Ost und West zeigen das höchste Element des Baus, die schräge, 11,48 m hohe Wand, die mit Polycarbonatstegplatten verblendet ist. Wie die Zeichnungen erkennen lassen, ist die Achse des Bauwerks nicht mittig auf die Galerie ausgerichtet.

Vue des élévations est et ouest. L'élément le plus haut du projet est le mur incliné de 11,48 mètres de haut, habillé de polycarbonate alvéolaire. Comme le montre ce dessin, le pavillon n'est pas centré sur l'axe de la galerie.

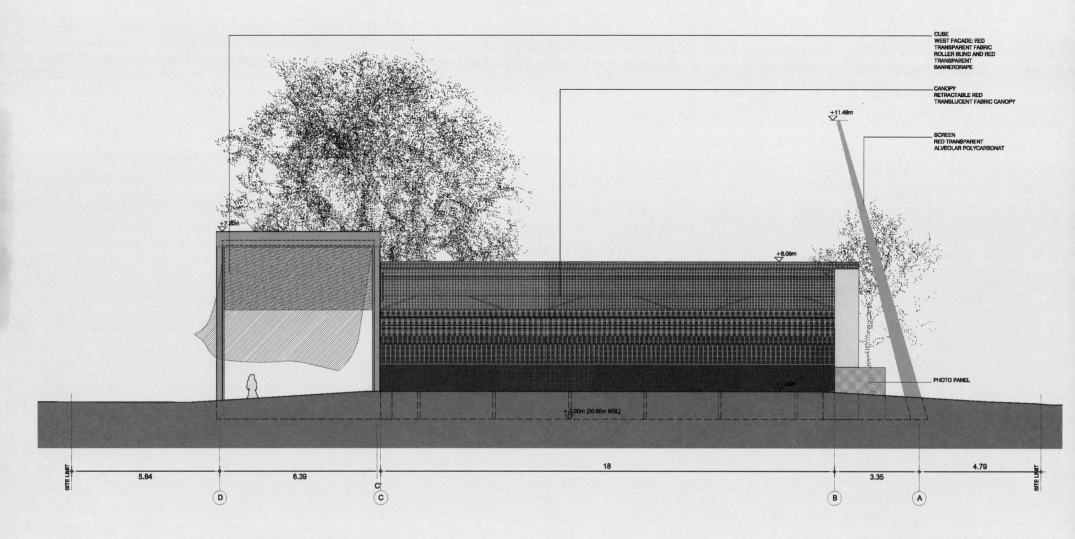

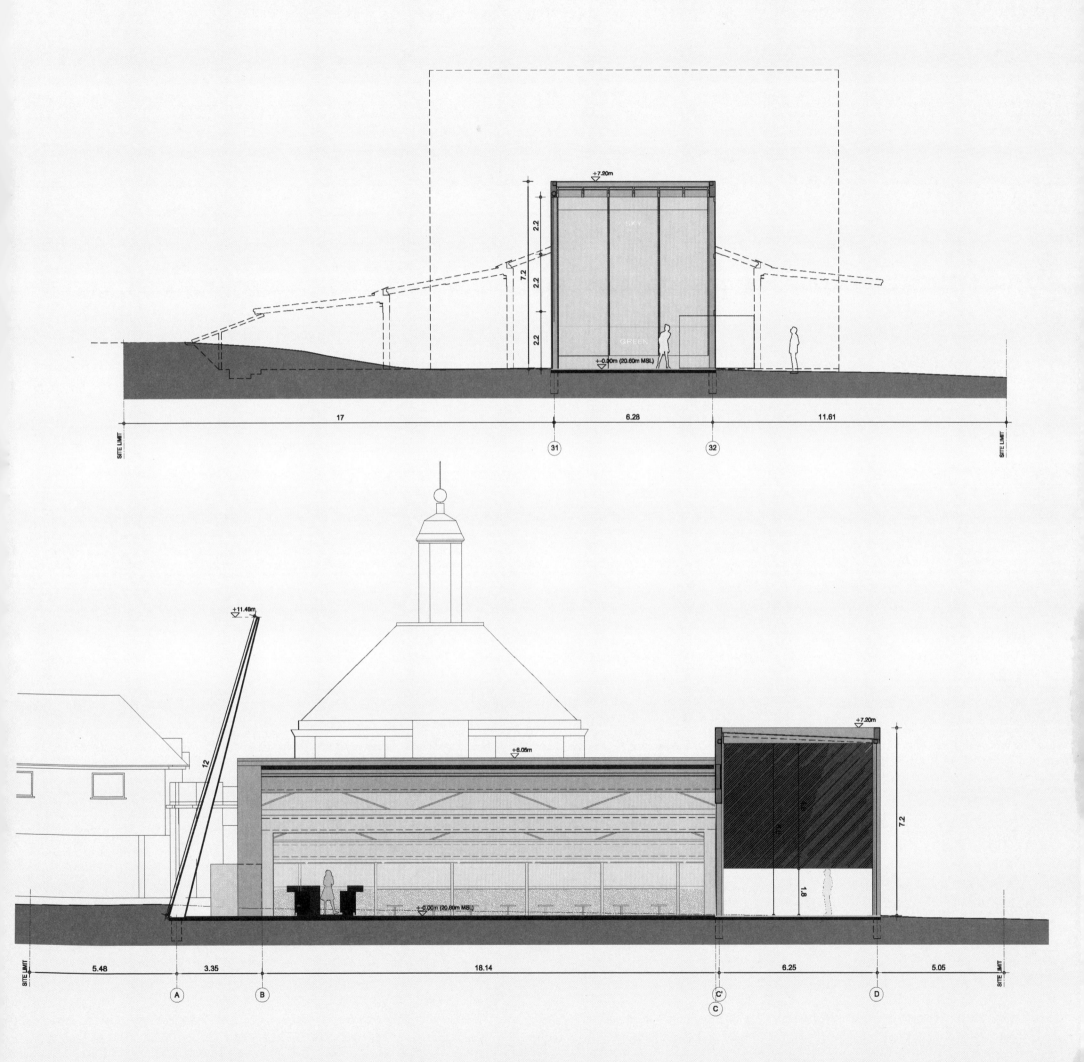

XI.31